Mechanics

29
Manuscript and
Letter Form
ms

30
Underlining
for Italics
ital

31
Spelling
sp

32
Hyphenation
and
Syllabication
-

33
The
Apostrophe
'

34
Capital
Letters
cap

35
Abbreviations
ab

36
Numbers
num

Diction and Style

37
Standard
English and
Style
d

38
Wordiness
w

39
Repetition
rep

40
Vagueness
vag

41
Connotation
con

42
Figurative
Language
fig

43
Flowery
Language
f l

44
Clear and
Logical
Thinking
log

45
Writing Good
Paragraphs
¶

46
Writing Good
Themes

47
Writing about
Literature

48
Writing the
Research
Paper

Glossary
of Usage
and Terms
g

P9-AEW-482

725

Practical English Handbook

Practical English Handbook

Fifth Edition

Floyd C. Watkins
Emory University

William B. Dillingham
Emory University

Edwin T. Martin
late of Emory University

Houghton Mifflin Company
Boston   Dallas   Geneva, Ill.
Hopewell, N.J.   Palo Alto   London

Printed in the U.S.A.

Library of Congress Catalog Card Number: 77-75888

Student's Edition ISBN: 0-395-25825-1

Instructor's Edition ISBN: 0-395-25824-3

Acknowledgment is made to the following sources of reprinted materials, alphabetically listed by author.

From Edward Abbey, *Desert Solitaire* (New York: Simon & Schuster, 1970).

From Henry Adams, *The Education of Henry Adams* (New York: Modern Library, 1931).

From William O. Aydelotte, "The Detective Story as a Historical Source," *Yale Review,* 1949. Reprinted by permission of The Yale Review, copyright Yale University.

From James Baldwin, "Everybody's Perfect Novel," *Notes of a Native Son* (New York: Dial Press, 1955).

Adapted from p. 1 in *Titans of the Seas* by James H. Belote and William M. Belote. Copyright © 1975 by James H. Belote and William M. Belote. By permission of Harper & Row, Publishers, Inc.

From J. Bronowski, "The Real Responsibilities of the Scientist," *Bulletin of the Atomic Scientists,* January 1956.

From Carlos Clarens, *An Illustrated History of the Horror Films* (New York: G. P. Putnam's Sons, 1967).

From Alexander DeConde, *Half Bitter, Half Sweet: An Excursion into Italian-American History* (New York: Charles Scribner's Sons, 1972). Adapted for the exercise by permission of the publishers.

From Philip Durham and Everett L. Jones, *The Frontier in American Literature,* copyright © 1969 by Western Publishing Co., Odyssey Press, reprinted by permission of The Bobbs-Merrill Company, Inc.

From William Faulkner, "Fate or Fear," *Atlantic Monthly,* August 1953.

From James K. Feibleman, *The Stages of Human Life: A Biography of Entire Man* (Atlantic Highlands, N.J.: Humanities Press, 1976).

From Charles A. Fenton, *The Apprenticeship of Ernest Hemingway* (New York: Farrar, Straus & Giroux, 1954).

From *It Pays to Increase Your Word Power* by Peter Funk, used with permission of Funk and Wagnalls Publishing Company, publishers. Copyright © 1969 by Peter Funk.

From Paul Goodman, "Freedom and Learning: The Need for Choice," *Saturday Review,* May 18, 1968.

From Ira J. Gordon, *Human Development: From Birth to Adolescence,* 2nd ed. (New York: Harper & Row, 1969).

From Gilbert Highet, *The Art of Teaching* (New York: Alfred A. Knopf, 1950). Copyright 1950 by Gilbert Highet. Reprinted with permission.

From Ivan Illich, "The Alternative to Schooling," *Saturday Review,* June 19, 1971.

From Martin Jezer, "Quo Peanuts?" *The Funnies: An American Idiom* (The Free Press of Glencoe, 1963).

From Susanne K. Langer, "The Cultural Importance of Art," *Philosophical Sketches* (Baltimore, Md.: Johns Hopkins Press, 1962).

From Mary McCarthy, "America the Beautiful," *New Directions* 10 (1957).

From Malcolm X, "The Black Revolution," *Malcolm X Speaks,* ed. George Breitman (New York: Grove Press, 1966).

From Edmund S. Morgan, "George Washington: The Aloof American," *The Meaning of Independence* (Charlottesville, Va.: University Press of Virginia, 1976). Reprinted with permission.

From Robert Moses, "Are Cities Dead?" *Atlantic Monthly,* January 1962.

From Lewis Mumford, *Faith for Living* (New York: Harcourt Brace Jovanovich).

Reprinted by permission from *Newswriting and Reporting* by James M. Neal and Suzanne S. Brown © 1976 by Iowa State University Press, Ames, Iowa.

From Elizabeth Nitchie, *Mary Shelley: Author of "Frankenstein"* (New Brunswick, N.J.: Rutgers University Press, 1953).

From Sean O'Faolain, *The Short Story* (Greenwich, Conn.: Devin-Adair).

From Jacqueline St. John, "Women's Legislative Issues Today and Tomorrow," *Vital Speeches of the Day,* June 15, 1972. Reprinted with permission.

From Harry J. Skornia, "Ratings and Mass Values," *Television and Society* (New York: McGraw-Hill, 1965).

Contents

Preface   xv
Writing and Revising   xvii

Sentence Errors and Grammar   1

1   **Sentence Fragment**   1
2   **Comma Splice and Fused Sentence**   3
3   **Verb Forms**   8
4   **Tense and Sequence of Tenses**   11
5   **Voice**   15
6   **Subjunctive Mood**   17
7   **Subject and Verb: Agreement**   17
    a   Compound subject with *and*   18
    b   Compound subject with *or*, *nor*, etc.   18
    c   Intervening phrases or clauses   19
    d   Collective nouns   19
    e   Nouns plural in form but singular in meaning   20
    f   Indefinite pronouns   20
    g   *None*, *some*, *part*, etc.   21

	h	*There, here* 22
	i	Agreement with subject, not subjective complement 22
	j	Relative pronouns 23
	k	Titles 23
8		**Pronouns: Agreement and Reference** 27
	a	Compound antecedent with *and* 27
	b	Compound antecedent with *or, nor*, etc. 27
	c	Collective noun as antecedent 28
	d	*Each, either,* etc. 28
	e	*Which, who, that* 29
	f	Vague antecedents 29
	g	Ambiguous antecedents 30
9		**Case** 34
	a	Subjects and subjective complements 34
	b	Object of a preposition 34
	c	Subject of an infinitive 35
	d	Appositives 35
	e	Pronouns after *than* or *as* 36
	f	Words preceding a gerund 36
	g	*Of* phrase for possession 37
	h	Possessive of personal and indefinite pronouns 37
	i	Interrogative and relative pronouns 37
10		**Adjectives and Adverbs** 41
	a	Forms of the comparative and superlative 42
	b	Comparative, two things; superlative, more than two 42
	c	After linking verbs *be, seem, become,* etc. 43
	d	After a verb and its object 43

Sentence Structure 45

11		**Excessive Coordination** 45
12		**Subordination** 47
	a	Subordination of minor thoughts 48
	b	Overlapping subordination 48

13 **Completeness** 51
   a   After *so, such, too*   51
   b   Omission of verbs and prepositions   52
   c   Omission of *that*   52

14 **Comparisons**   52

15 **Consistency**   56
   a   Shifts in tense   56
   b   Shifts in person   56
   c   Shifts in mood   57
   d   Shifts in voice   57
   e   Shifts of relative pronoun   57
   f   Shifts from indirect to direct discourse   58

16 **Position of Modifiers**   59
   a   Dangling   60
   b   Misplaced   62
   c   Squinting   62

17 **Separation of Elements**   64

18 **Parallelism**   65

19 **Variety**   68

Punctuation   77

20 **The Comma**   77
   a   Between two independent clauses   77
   b   In a series   78
   c   Between coordinate adjectives   80
   d   After long introductory phrases or clauses   82
   e   With nonrestrictive appositives, phrases, and clauses   84
   f   With sentence modifiers, conjunctive adverbs, and elements out of order   87
   g   With degrees, titles, dates, places, addresses   89
   h   For contrast or emphasis   89
   i   With mild interjections and *yes* or *no*   89
   j   With direct address and salutations   90
   k   With expressions like *he said, she remarked*   90

	l	With absolute phrases 90
	m	To prevent misreading or to mark an omission 90
21	**Unnecessary Commas** 97	
	a	Between subject and verb, verb and complement, or adjective or adverb and modifier 97
	b	Between two compound elements 98
	c	Between dependent clauses 98
	d	Before *than* or between *as . . . as, so . . . as, so . . . that* 98
	e	After *like, such as* 99
	f	With period, question mark, exclamation point, and dash 99
	g	With parentheses 99
	h	After short introductory modifiers and coordinating conjunctions 99
	i	With restrictive clauses, phrases, and appositives 100
	j	Between noncoordinate adjectives 100
22	**The Semicolon** 102	
	a	Between two independent clauses 102
	b	Between long or complex independent clauses 102
	c	Between items in a series 103
	d	Between noncoordinate elements 103
23	**The Colon** 105	
	a	Before elements introduced formally 105
	b	Between two independent clauses 106
	c	Before formal appositives 106
	d	In times, salutations, and bibliographical entries 106
	e	After a linking verb or a preposition 106
24	**The Dash** 107	
25	**Parentheses** 107	
26	**Brackets** 108	
27	**Quotation Marks** 108	
	a	Direct quotations and dialogue 108
	b	Quotation within a quotation 109
	c	Titles of short works 109
	d	Titles of themes 110
	e	For emphasis, slang, colloquialisms, and humor 110
	f	With other punctuation 110

28 **End Punctuation** 111
    a   Period at the end of a sentence 112
    b   Period after abbreviations 112
    c   Ellipsis dots for omissions 113
    d   Punctuation of titles 113
    e   Question mark at the end of a direct question 113
    f   Question mark within parentheses 114
    g   Exclamation point 114

Mechanics 120

29 **Manuscript and Letter Form** 120
30 **Underlining for Italics** 124
    a   Titles of books 124
    b   Names of ships and trains 125
    c   Foreign words 125
    d   Words used as words 125
    e   Emphasis 125
    f   Titles of themes 126
31 **Spelling** 126
32 **Hyphenation and Syllabication** 131
    a   Compound words 131
    b   Compound adjectives 132
    c   Compound numbers 132
    d   Breaking a word at the end of a line 132
33 **The Apostrophe** 133
34 **Capital Letters** 134
35 **Abbreviations** 137
36 **Numbers** 138

Diction and Style 140

37 **Standard English and Style** 140
    a   Slang 141
    b   Illiteracies and dialect 142
    c   Archaic words 143
    d   Improprieties 144

e   Idioms   145
f   Specialized vocabulary   146
g   Triteness   149
h   Exactness   149
i   Learning new words   151

38   **Wordiness**   156
39   **Repetition**   159
a   Redundancy   159
b   Unpleasant repetition   160
c   Repetition for emphasis or clarity   160
40   **Vagueness**   162
41   **Connotation**   165
42   **Figurative Language**   167
a   Figurative comparisons   167
b   Mixed, worn out, and inappropriate figures   168
43   **Flowery Language**   169

The Process of Composition   171

44   **Clear and Logical Thinking**   172
a   Accurate, verified data   172
b   Reliable authorities   173
c   Sweeping generalizations   173
d   Specific evidence   174
e   Sticking to the point   174
f   Conflicting evidence   175
g   Begging the question and circular reasoning   175
h   Omission of essential steps; unstated assumptions   175
i   Appeal to emotion   176
j   Cause and effect   177
k   Moderation   177
l   Adequate alternatives   177
45   **Writing Good Paragraphs**   182
a   Main idea in the topic sentence   182
b   Unity   184
c   Skimpiness   187

| | | d | Excessive length | 189 |

d   Excessive length   189
e   Adequate development   192
f   Appropriate development   194
g   Transitions   195

46   **Writing Good Themes**   202
a   Choosing a subject   202
b   Limiting the topic   202
c   Thesis statement   204
d   Appropriate and consistent tone   204
e   Organization   205
f   Adequate examples   208
g   Checklist of essentials   209

47   **Writing about Literature**   227
a   Precise subject   227
b   Exact title   228
c   Appropriate development   228
d   Excessive summary and paraphrase   230
e   Originality   231
f   Writing about yourself   231
g   Sufficient evidence   231
h   Organization by ideas   232
i   Moralizing   233
j   Acknowledgment of sources   233

48   **Writing the Research Paper**   242
a   Choosing and limiting a subject   242
b   Working bibliography   244
c   Primary and secondary materials   250
d   Taking notes   251
e   Outlining   260
f   Acknowledgment of sources   260
g   Documentation   262
     Model paper: "Frankenstein's Lonely Monster"   269

49   Glossary of Usage and Terms   297
Index   319

Preface

Since the *Practical English Handbook* was first published, it has undergone the test of hard usage by legions of students, many of whom have since become teachers themselves. The nature of *PEH* has not changed fundamentally during these many years. Its aim now is the same as it was originally: to help its users identify clearly and solve quickly their problems in writing. Its strength is still its practicality, which we define as the happy combination of thoroughness and simplicity.

Many of the changes that have been made in this Fifth Edition were undertaken with an eye toward even greater compactness and simplification. Trimming and rewording have often resulted in more directness of expression, in greater efficiency through economy. Innovating, updating, and expanding can be as important as refining and tightening, and numerous aspects of the Fifth Edition reflect this conviction. Several new sample student themes have been added which users of the book can mark themselves and evaluate as a different kind of exercise in learning to write better. Many new exercises of other kinds have also been included in answer to requests for enrichment. Readers will notice new sample papers of several kinds, including a new literary paper. New and more realistic vocabulary tests have taken the place of the older one. Each section of the book has been painstakingly examined for its effectiveness, and several—among them the sections on outlining and paragraphing—have been greatly refined and improved. And for those who wish supplementary exercises, the *Practical English Workbook* is now available.

With each new edition of *PEH* our debt to users of the book who have offered valuable suggestions becomes more pronounced. They have helped immensely in fitting the Fifth Edition to the real needs of today's students. We wish to thank all of them for their perceptiveness and their generosity. Most especially we thank the following for their reading of the manuscript and for their thoughtful and constructive criticism: Claudene Atkinson, Houston Community College; Larry Hartsfield, Southern Illinois University; Joyce Lipkis, Santa Monica College; and William H. Pixton, Troy State University.

F.C.W.
W.B.D.

Writing
and
Revising

Whether the instructor uses this book as a basis for class discussions and exercises or for student self-help, it can be of great use in correcting and revising papers. The model paper on the following pages illustrates two ways in which an instructor may mark a paper for revision. It also shows the student author's corrections. In the left margin are section and subsection numbers; in the right margin are abbreviations asking for the same set of corrections. The instructor may prefer to use section numbers, abbreviations, or a combination of both methods. Sometimes a comment will not quite fit into either category.

The numerical symbols are given on the chart inside the front cover. The abbreviations (with page numbers) are listed on the chart inside the back cover. With either method of marking, the student should study the relevant sections with their explanations, examples, and (if necessary) exercises and make the appropriate corrections and revisions. These may range from removing an unnecessary comma to reorganizing and rewriting a paragraph or an entire paper.

It is helpful to keep a chart of the numbers or abbreviations used for errors in order to see how the frequency of errors diminishes and how new kinds of errors occur in later themes. If the instructor writes an overall comment on a cover sheet, the student might keep those sheets together and in order; they will provide information about improvement, change, and ways to study and revise. Certainly the student or the instructor should keep all themes until the end of the term and study the changes in the writing.

In any corrected theme many of the problems mentioned in the sections throughout this book may confront the student almost simultaneously. At the very beginning of the course students should use the entire book, especially the index and the glossary of terms and common problems not covered in any single section.

Travel and Snob Appeal

Up through the last century only the well-to-do could afford the luxury of travel; therefore, traveling took on a kind of snob appeal. If people were financially able to take trips abroad or even long journeys to other parts of their own country, they usually did so because all the best families were doing it. Travel became a sign of affluence and culture. Wealthy young people took what used to be called the "grand tour," an extended trip over the European continent, in order to complete their education. A mark of the lower classes and the uneducated was lack of travel experience.

As the cost of traveling came within the financial range of more and more people, they began to overrun the favorite tourist cities of Europe. Americans seemed almost frantic to see as much of another part of the world as possible in a short period of time. The name of a modern motion picture satirically expressed this frenzied activity of Americans traveling on tight schedules: If It's Tuesday, This Must Be Belgium. So inexpensive did touring become that a book called Europe on Five Dollars a Day became a guide for countless travelers on limited budgets. Youths on motorcycles and even on bicycles began to turn up in foreign cities with empty pockets and with sleeping bags, eager to see the great places of history.

Aside from intellectual curiosity and the sheer fun of

1

31   going to <u>far away</u> *faraway* places, snob appeal is still one reason so ¶

many people travel. Many old prejudices have faded with time,

37e   but the <u>bias on</u> *bias against* the untraveled remains. The grand tour is not d

37d   now a <u>necessity</u> *necessary* part of every cultured person's formal education, d

but its prestige is hardly diminished as a social value. More

than ever, traveling is fashionable. Many of these travelers will

suffer through three weeks of food alien to their digestive sys-

tems, languages noncommunicative to their ears, and hotels uncom-

fortably strange to their accustomed way of living--all for the

purpose of saying that they, too, have been there.

Practical
English
Handbook

Sentence Errors and Grammar

1 Sentence fragment *frag*

Do not use meaningless or ineffective fragments.

A **fragment** is a part of a sentence written and punctuated as a complete sentence. It is harder to recognize in a group of several sentences than it is when it is written separately. It may be a dependent clause, a phrase, or any other word group which violates the accepted subject-verb sentence pattern. Fragments usually reflect incomplete or confused thinking.

FRAGMENT

That she had heard all the trite comments about the weather which she could endure in one day. (dependent noun clause)

COMPLETE SENTENCE

She had heard all the trite comments about the weather which she could endure in one day.

FRAGMENT

The poem which refers to fish that have one fin cut off to show that they are stocked by the government. (noun plus dependent clause)

COMPLETE SENTENCE

The poem refers to fish that have one fin cut off to show that they are stocked by the government.

FRAGMENT

Although some graduates are well schooled in all the forensic devices used by college debaters. (dependent adverbial clause)

COMPLETE SENTENCE

Some graduates are well schooled in all the forensic devices used by college debaters.

FRAGMENT

The dense forest humming with sounds of insects and teeming with animal life. (noun plus participial phrases)

COMPLETE SENTENCE

The dense forest hummed with sounds of insects and teemed with animal life.

FRAGMENT

The color of neon lights reflected in the rain, the greenery of parks amid concrete, the sparkling glass of new buildings. (nouns and phrases)

COMPLETE SENTENCE

A city offers much beauty: the color of neon lights reflected in the rain, the greenery of parks amid concrete, the sparkling glass of new buildings.

Fragments are often permissible in dialogue when the meaning is clear from the context.

> "See the geese."
> "Where?"
> "Flying north."

Sometimes fragments create special effects or emphasis.

> It is one of the loveliest of stories. *So much irony; so much humour; so kind and understanding; and wrapped up in the most delicate poetic mood.*
>
> SEAN O'FAOLAIN, *The Short Story*

This long fragment lacks subject and verb ("It has" or "It contains"), but the careful parallelism of the elements set off by semicolons indicates skill—not ignorance or carelessness.

---

2 Comma splice and fused sentence *co/ſus*

Use a semicolon or a comma and a coordinating conjunction (*and, but, or, nor, for, yet, so*) to join two independent clauses.

A **comma splice** or comma fault occurs when independent clauses have a comma but no coordinating conjunction between them. In a **fused sentence** or run-on sentence the independent clauses have neither punctuation nor coordinating conjunctions between them.

Comma splices and fused sentences fail to indicate the strong break between independent clauses. They may be corrected in four principal ways:

1. Use a *period* and write two sentences.
2. Use a *semicolon*.
3. Use a *comma* and a *coordinating conjunction*.
4. Make one of the clauses *dependent*.

See also **23**.

SPLICE
Human nature is seldom as simple as it appears, hasty judgments are therefore often wrong.

FUSED
Human nature is seldom as simple as it appears hasty judgments are therefore often wrong.

CORRECTIONS
1. Human nature is seldom as simple as it appears. Hasty judgments are therefore often wrong.
2. Human nature is seldom as simple as it appears; hasty judgments are therefore often wrong.
3. Human nature is seldom as simple as it appears, *and* hasty judgments are therefore often wrong.
4. Because human nature is seldom as simple as it appears, hasty judgments are often wrong.

Some solutions may be more appropriate than others. Here (4) seems preferable to (3) because *and* does not suggest the cause-effect relationship between human nature and hasty judgments.

When possible, subordinate one clause or reduce it to a phrase or even a single word. In (4) one of the independent clauses is made a dependent adverbial clause. The sentence might also be rewritten as follows:

CLAUSE
Human nature is *so* complex *that hasty judgments are often wrong.*
PHRASE
Hasty judgments often overlook *the complexities of human nature.*

Before conjunctive adverbs (*however, moreover, therefore, furthermore,* and so on), use a semicolon to join independent clauses.

The rare book had a torn flyleaf; therefore it was advertised at a reduced price.

▶ Exercise 1
Make the following fragments complete sentences by deleting one word, adding one word or a verb phrase, or changing one word.

1. The various colors and designs of academic regalia revealing the wearers' schools, degrees, and fields of learning.

2. That the time will come when the last bald eagle has flown high over the mountain tops looking for prey.

3. Rivers with poisonous chemicals from factories, garbage dumped by sportsmen and towns, and various other ugly products of civilization.

4. Because the most difficult educational situation occurs when the learner simply does not have the intelligence to understand the problem that must be solved.

5. There in the desert a mirage of cool water running over rocks.

▶ Exercise 2
Identify (with CS or F) and correct comma splices and fused sentences. Write C to the left of correct sentences.

1. Television sometimes offers worthwhile shows as well as trivia, it should not be condemned uncritically.

2. After twelve years of silence, the great composer finished two brilliant symphonies within six months.

3. Conflicts almost always exist within a family however, it is still the most enduring of social units.

4. One ancient culture practiced the art of carving masks another expressed itself creatively in weaving elaborate tapestries.

5. A famous rose enthusiast wrote that it is necessary to love roses in order to cultivate them successfully the grower must have roses in his heart if he is to have them in his garden.

▶ Exercise 3
Change the following fragments, comma splices, or fused sentences into correct sentences. Write C to the left of correct sentences.

1. Economy is a virtue up to a point, beyond that it may become a vice.

2. Destroyers uproot trees and move vast quantities of earth but do not replace the soil.

3. Young people have always created their own varieties of music. Growing older, they reject the music that comes after their youth.

4. Most women seem to know more about men's clothing than men themselves do at any rate they claim to know more.

5. Extreme nervousness sometimes makes a patient sullen and quiet. Then for no apparent reason arrogant and insulting.

6. New York's Washington Square has changed considerably since it was a haven for writers in the 1890's.

7. In a lonely village on the seacoast, where the primitive beauty of nature still survives.

8. The Depression in the 1930's caused much unhappiness in some families, others it brought closer together.

9. Earth may be the only planet which will support human life. If humanity is to prosper, therefore, the natural environment must be preserved.

10. An adventurer will sometimes participate in a pastime despite great danger, sky diving, for example, is perilous.

▶ Exercise 4
Follow the instructions for Exercise 3.

1. In some parts of the world marriages are still arranged by parents consequently practical matters take precedence over love.

2. After all, the students argued, any imbecile can punctuate, studying the mechanics of composition is a complete waste of time.

3. Most generous people are naive, they simply do not realize when they are being imposed upon.

4. Some say that nonconformity has become a fad. Nonconformity for its own sake.

5. Science and art are not incompatible, some learned scientists are also philosophers or poets.

6. The art of pleasing is a very necessary one to possess. But a very difficult one to acquire.

7. Kindness can hardly be reduced to rules good will and thoughtfulness will lead to congenial relationships with others.

8. "Do as you would be done by" is the surest method of pleasing.

9. Clothes inappropriate to a place or situation are absurd a mink coat on a beach in July might be comical.

10. If a trout fisherman tires of tangled lines and hooks caught in limbs of trees overhead. He may give up mountain-stream fishing for boats and the open spaces of lakes.

---

3 Verb forms *vb*
Use the correct form of the verb.

All verbs have three principal parts: the present infinitive, the past tense, and the past participle. Verbs are regular or irregular in their principal parts.

Regular verbs (*help, talk, nail, open, close*) form the past tense and the past participle by adding *-d* or *-ed* or sometimes *-t* (as in *burnt, dwelt*). Thus the principal parts of *to close* are *close, closed, closed;* those of *to talk* are *talk, talked, talked.*

Irregular verbs usually form the past tense and the past participle by changing an internal vowel: *drink, drank, drunk.* Consult a dictionary when in doubt; if only the infinitive form is given, the verb is regular. For an irregular verb like *think,* the dictionary also gives *thought* (the form of the past tense and the past participle) and *thinking* (the present participle). The principal parts are *think, thought, thought.* For a verb as irregular as *see,* the dictionary lists all three principal parts—*see, saw, seen*—and *seeing.* You should know the troublesome verbs that follow so well that you automatically use them correctly.

INFINITIVE	PAST TENSE	PAST PARTICIPLE
awake	awoke, awaked	awoke, awaked
be	was	been
begin	began	begun
bid (to offer as a price or to make a bid in playing cards)	bid	bid
bid (to command, order)	bade, bid	bidden, bid
blow	blew	blown
bring	brought	brought
build	built	built
burst	burst	burst
choose	chose	chosen
come	came	come
deal	dealt	dealt
dig	dug	dug
dive	dived, dove	dived
do	did	done
drag	dragged	dragged
draw	drew	drawn
drink	drank	drunk
drive	drove	driven
drown	drowned	drowned

INFINITIVE	PAST TENSE	PAST PARTICIPLE
fly	flew	flown
freeze	froze	frozen
give	gave	given
go	went	gone
grow	grew	grown
hang (to execute)	hanged	hanged
hang (to suspend)	hung	hung
know	knew	known
lead	led	led
lend	lent	lent
ring	rang	rung
run	ran	run
see	saw	seen
shine (to give light)	shone	shone
shine (to polish)	shined	shined
sing	sang	sung
sink	sank, sunk	sunk
sting	stung	stung
swim	swam	swum
swing	swung	swung
take	took	taken
teach	taught	taught
throw	threw	thrown
wear	wore	worn
write	wrote	written

In a few confusing pairs of verbs, it helps to remember that one is **transitive** (has voice, may take an object) and that the other is **intransitive** (does not have voice, does not take an object):

	PAST TENSE	PAST PARTICIPLE
TRANSITIVE		
lay (to place)	laid	laid
INTRANSITIVE		
lie (to recline)	lay	lain
TRANSITIVE		
set (to place in position)	set	set
INTRANSITIVE		
sit (to be seated)	sat	sat

	PAST TENSE	PAST PARTICIPLE
TRANSITIVE		
raise (to lift)	raised	raised
INTRANSITIVE		
rise (to get up)	rose	risen

NOTE The intransitive verbs *lie, sit,* and *rise* all have the root vowel *i* in the present tense form. The transitive verb *set* also has intransitive forms (a hen *sets;* concrete *sets;* the sun *sets*).

4 Tense and sequence of tenses *t/seq*

Use verbs to express distinctions in time. Avoid unnecessary shifts in tense.

For each of the three kinds of time—present, past, and future—verbs have different tense forms: simple, progressive, and perfect.[1]

	REGULAR	IRREGULAR
SIMPLE		
Present	I walk	I go
Past	I walked	I went
Future	I shall (will) walk	I shall (will) go
PROGRESSIVE		
Present	I am walking	I am going
Past	I was walking	I was going
Future	I shall (will) be walking	I shall (will) be going
PERFECT		
Present	I have walked	I have gone
Past	I had walked	I had gone
Future	I shall (will) have walked	I shall (will) have gone

---

[1] There are in addition the emphatic forms with the auxiliary *do* or *did* (I *do go* there regularly).

In general, the **present tense** expresses present time, but there are exceptions. Compare the following:

> I *eat* lunch. (simple present tense—with the force of repeated action)
> I *am eating* lunch. (present progressive tense—present action)

> I *leave* for New York tomorrow. (present tense—future action)
> I *am leaving* in fifteen minutes. (present progressive tense—future action)

As the last two examples illustrate, the time expressed by the tense form is often determined by a word or a phrase.

Statements about the contents of literature and other works of art generally take the present tense (historical present).

> In Henry James's *The Turn of the Screw,* a governess *believes* that she sees ghosts.

Statements of natural truth or scientific law also take the present tense regardless of the controlling verb.

> In 1851, Foucault proved that the earth *rotates* on its axis.
> BUT
> Ancient Greeks *believed* that the earth *was* motionless.

The three **perfect tenses** indicate time or action completed before another time or action.

> PRESENT PERFECT WITH PRESENT
> I *have bought* my ticket, and I **am waiting** for the bus.

The controlling time word need not be a verb.

> I *have bought* my ticket **already.**

> PAST PERFECT WITH PAST
> I *had bought* my ticket, and I **was waiting** for the bus.
> I *had bought* my ticket before the bus **came.**

FUTURE PERFECT WITH FUTURE
I *shall have eaten* by the time we **go.** (The controlling word, *go,* is
    present tense in form but future in meaning.)
I *shall have eaten by* **one o'clock.**

The future perfect is rare. Usually the simple future tense is used
with an adverb phrase or clause.

RARE
I shall have eaten before you go.
MORE COMMON
I shall eat before you go.

In dialogue, the present tense is often used for the future or
the future perfect.

"When are you leaving?"
"We leave at dawn."

Relationships between verbs should be logical and consistent:

TWO PAST ACTIONS
The sailor *stood* on the shore and *threw* pebbles at the seagulls. (not
    throws)
He *turned* away when he *saw* me watching him.

TWO PRESENT ACTIONS
As the school year *draws* to a close, the students *are swept* into a
    whirl of activities.

FUTURE ACTIONS
Some *will go* to the sea for their vacations, some *will go* to the desert,
    but few *will go* to the city.

An infinitive (see **49**) generally takes the present tense when
it expresses action which occurs at the same time as that of the controlling verb.

NOT
I wanted *to have gone.*
BUT
I wanted *to go.*

NOT
I had expected *to have met* my friends at the game.
BUT
I had expected *to meet* my friends at the game.

NOT
I would have preferred *to have waited* until they came.
BUT
I would have preferred *to wait* until they came.

The perfect participle (see **49**) expresses an action which precedes another action.

> *Having finished* the novel, the aged author stored it away in her safe with the others.

▶ Exercise 5
Underline the incorrect verb and write the correct verb above it. Write C to the left of correct sentences.

1. In looking back, public officials almost always say they would have preferred to have remained private citizens.

2. After having laid on the bottom of the bay for centuries, the Swedish ship was risen and placed in a museum.

3. Hundreds of dusty arrowheads and spearpoints were laying on the shelves in his study.

4. The actor opened the Bible and begins reading the Song of Solomon.

5. It was Goethe's feeling that genius was simply "consummate industry."

6. After it sets, concrete is a durable material for roads.

7. Joseph Conrad was well into his thirties before he begun to write his novels.

8. After one has already bidden at an auction, it is too late for him to change his mind.

9. After the *Titanic* had sank, the world at first found the tragedy difficult to believe.

10. The Puritans were in some ways narrow-minded, but they lead lives of deep devotion to what they believed.

---

5 Voice $\mathcal{VO}$

Use the active voice except when the context demands the passive.

A transitive verb is either active or passive. When the subject acts, the verb is active. When the subject is acted upon, the verb is passive. In most sentences the actor is more important than the receiver of the action. A weak passive verb may leave the actor unknown or seemingly ineffective.

> WEAK PASSIVE
> The huge iceberg *was rammed* into by the luxury liner.
> STRONG ACTIVE
> The luxury liner *rammed* into the huge iceberg.

> WEAK PASSIVE
> A good race *was run* by the Ferrari.
> STRONG ACTIVE
> The Ferrari *ran* a good race.

The active voice helps to create a more concise and vigorous style. The passive voice, however, is sometimes useful when the performer of an action is irrelevant or unimportant:

> The book about motorcycles *had been misplaced* among books about cosmetics.

The passive voice can also be effective when the emphasis is on the receiver, the verb, or even a modifier:

> The police *were* totally *misled.*

▶ Exercise 6
Change the voice of the verb when it is ineffective. Rewrite the sentence if necessary. Write E by sentences in which the verb is effective.

1. The bird's nest was flown into directly by the mother bird, which brought a worm to feed its young.

2. Some young people are learning the almost lost art of black-smithing and shoeing horses.

3. The horse lost the race because the shoe had been improperly nailed to the hoof.

4. Sharp curves are not well negotiated by many people just learning to drive.

5. The rare plants were not properly cared for by the gardener.

---

6 Subjunctive mood *mo*
In using the subjunctive mood, be guided by idiom.

The subjunctive in English has been traditionally employed to express commands, requests, wishes, and conditions which are improbable or contrary to fact. Today the subjunctive survives largely as a matter of idiom. In sentences like "I wouldn't do that if I *were* you," the choice of the subjunctive is natural and automatic. It is the idiom. Although a member of an organization still says, "I move that the meeting *be* adjourned," he is actually using a phrase which has frozen into the language. Some old subjunctives with *be* have disappeared (If I *be* right, that is a first edition). Occasionally "If this *be* true" is heard—but not often.

---

7 Subject and verb: agreement *agr*
Use singular verbs with singular subjects, plural verbs with plural subjects.

The *-s* or *-es* ending of the third person present tense of the *verb* indicates the **singular;** the *-s* or *-es* ending of a *noun* indicates the **plural.**

SINGULAR
The dog barks.
The ax cuts.
The ax does cut.

PLURAL
The dogs bark.
The axes cut.
The axes do cut.

7a   A compound subject with *and* takes a plural verb.

Two or more subjects connected by a coordinating conjunction are said to be compound.

Work and *play* **are** not equally rewarding.

Baseball and *swimming* **are** usually summer sports.

EXCEPTION Compound subjects connected by *and* but expressing a singular idea take a singular verb.

A gentleman and a scholar **is** a man of manners and breadth.

When the children are in bed, *the tumult and shouting* **dies.**

7b   After a compound subject with *or, nor, either . . . or, neither . . . nor, not . . . but,* the verb agrees in number and person with the nearer part of the subject.

NUMBER
Neither the *consumer* nor the *producer* **is** pleased by higher taxes.

Either *fans* or an *air conditioner* **is** necessary.

Either an *air conditioner* or *fans* **are** necessary.

PERSON
Neither *you* nor your *successor* **is** affected by the new regulation.

Colloquially, a plural verb may be used to express a plural idea with *neither . . . nor.*

Neither *television* nor the *press* **are** unduly censored.

7c Intervening phrases or clauses not introduced by coordinating conjunctions do not affect the number of a verb.

Connectives like *as well as* and *along with* are not coordinating conjunctions but prepositions; they do not form compound subjects. Other such words and phrases include *in addition to, together with, with, plus,* and *including.*

The *engine* as well as the wings **was** destroyed in the crash.

The *pilot* along with all his passengers **was** rescued.

7d A collective noun takes a singular verb when referring to a group as a unit, a plural verb when the members of a group are thought of individually.

A collective noun names a class or group: *family, flock, jury, congregation,* and so on. Meaning often determines number, but generally in American usage the collective noun is treated as singular.

The *family* **is** going on vacation to Florida and the Caribbean. (whether all together or some to Florida and some to the Caribbean)

To avoid the unidiomatic "The family *are* going . . ." and to clarify the meaning, it would be better to rewrite.

Jean and I **are** vacationing in Florida; the boys are going to the Caribbean.

7e   Most nouns plural in form but singular in meaning take a singular verb.

Economics and *news* are considered singular; *trousers* and *scissors* are treated as plural except when used after *pair*. When in doubt, consult a dictionary. *Data* is considered singular or plural; the singular form, *datum,* is rare.

Economics **is** often thought of as a science.

The *news* of the defeat **is** disappointing.

Tactics **is** the art of maneuvering military forces.

British and American military *tactics* **were** different.

The *trousers* **are** unpressed and frayed about the cuffs.

An old *pair* of trousers **is** essential for the Bohemian.

The *scissors* **are** dull.

That *pair* of scissors **is** dull.

7f   Indefinite pronouns, such as *each, either, neither, one, no one, everyone, someone, anyone, nobody, everybody, somebody, anybody,* usually take singular verbs.

Neither of his themes **was** acceptable.

Everybody **has** trouble choosing a subject for an essay.

Each student **has** chosen a subject for his report.

A plural verb with words like *each* is gaining some acceptance in colloquial English.

Each of the divers **are** allowed to follow their individual styles.

7g   Some words, such as *none, some, part, all, half* (and other fractions), take a singular or a plural verb, depending on the meaning of the noun or pronoun which follows.

singular
Some of the sugar **was** spilled on the floor.

plural
Some of the apples **were** spilled on the floor.

singular
Half of the money **is** yours.

plural
Half of the students **are** looking out the window.

None is considered sometimes singular, sometimes plural:

None of those accused **was** really responsible.

None of those accused **were** really responsible.

The number is usually singular:

The number of people in the audience **was** never determined.

A number is considered equivalent to the adjective *some,* and the noun or pronoun which follows controls the verb:

A *number* of the *guests* **were** whispering.

7h In sentences beginning with *there* or *here* followed by verb and subject, the verb is singular or plural depending on the subject.

There and *Here* are devices (**expletives**) sometimes used when the subject follows the verb.

There **was** a long *interval* between the two discoveries.

There **were** thirteen *blackbirds* perched on the fence.

Here **is** a *thing* to remember.

Here **are** two *things* to remember.

The singular *There is* may be used to introduce a compound subject when the first noun is singular.

There is a *swing* and a *footbridge* in the garden.

In sentences beginning with *It,* the verb is singular.

It **was** many years ago.

7i A verb agrees with its subject, not with a subjective complement.

His horse and *his dog* **are** his main source of pleasure.

His main *source* of pleasure **is** his horse and his dog.

7j After a relative pronoun (*who, which, that*) the verb has the same person and number as the antecedent.

antecedent ⟶ relative pronoun ⟶ verb of relative pronoun

We   who   **are** about to die salute you.

The *costumes which* **were** worn in the ballet were dazzling.

He was the *candidate who* **was** able to carry out his campaign pledges.

He was one of the *candidates who* **were** able to carry out their campaign pledges.

BUT
He was *the* only *one* of the candidates *who* **was** able to carry out his campaign pledges.

7k A title is singular and requires a singular verb even if it contains plural words and plural ideas.

The Canterbury Tales **is** a masterpiece of comedy.

"Prunes and Prisms" **was** a syndicated newspaper column on grammar and usage.

▶ Exercise 7
Correct any verb which does not agree with its subject. If a sentence is correct, write C next to it.

1. The sound of hammers mingle with the screech of seagulls and the crash of waves on the beach.

2. In O'Neill's *Long Day's Journey into Night,* Mary's smiles and laughter are increasingly forced, her resentment more obvious, and her journey into night more plainly marked.

3. D. H. Lawrence's *Sons and Lovers* are a landmark among the novels of the time.

4. A large number of students are now moving away from housing provided by universities and colleges.

5. Suspended from the ceilings of the palace were a variety of chandeliers, some of sparkling crystal, others of gleaming brass.

6. Ethics are the study of moral philosophy and standards of conduct.

7. Molasses were used in a great number of early New England recipes.

8. This tribal custom is enforced by strict taboos, the violation of which bring immediate death.

9. Childish sentences or dull writing are not improved by a sprinkling of dashes.

10. Neither money nor power satisfy the deepest human needs of those who seek to fulfill themselves.

▶ Exercise 8
Follow the instructions for Exercise 7.

1. For a certain kind of American, a vacation of at least two weeks have come to be looked upon as a panacea.

2. All year long, the worker who is shackled to his job look forward to the time when he can lounge in endless ease upon the shore of a mountain lake or the white sands by the sea.

3. It is highly improbable that either the white sands or the mountain lake are the answer for this tense city-dweller.

4. Anybody who live a life of quiet desperation for months or even years can hardly expect to forget anxieties at once.

5. Nevertheless, realizing an extreme need to slow down, the American vacationer, along with his entire family, set out.

6. Plan after plan have been made; nothing can go wrong.

7. The trouble is that the family have made too many plans.

8. Father is *determined* to relax; he somehow fails to see that relaxation and two weeks of feverish activity is not compatible.

9. This man's situation, like that of thousands of others, are the result of his desire on the one hand to slow down and on the other to forget himself, to escape the thoughts that haunts him for fifty weeks of the year.

10. To relax physically and at the same time to escape his frustrations are impossible for him.

11. He thus returns to his job more weary or more worried or both than when he left.

12. The roots of this man's problem goes very deep, and he must seek deep within himself for the solution.

13. He must learn to stop frequently and to take account of himself and his values.

14. He must identify himself with a standard of values which have been proved lasting.

15. Above all, he must learn that there is much worse fates than falling behind the Joneses.

Pronouns: agreement and reference *agr/ref* **8b**

8 Pronouns: agreement and reference *agr/ref*

Use singular pronouns to refer to singular antecedents, plural pronouns to refer to plural antecedents. Make a pronoun refer to a definite antecedent.

8a In general, use a plural pronoun to refer to a compound antecedent with *and*.

The *owner* and the *captain* refused to leave **their** distressed ship.

If two nouns designate the same person, the pronoun is singular.

The *owner and captain* refused to leave **his** distressed ship.

8b After a compound antecedent with *or, nor, either . . . or, neither . . . nor, not only . . . but also,* a pronoun agrees with the nearer part of the antecedent (see 7b).

Neither the *Secretary* nor the *Undersecretary* was in **his** seat.

Neither the *Secretary* nor his *aides* were consistent in **their** policy.

A sentence like this written with *and* is less stilted.

The Secretary and his aides were not consistent in their policy.

Colloquially, a plural pronoun may be used to express a plural with *neither . . . nor.*

Neither *Nicholas* nor *Alexandra* lost **their** dignity under pressure.

Sentence errors and grammar 27

8c   A singular pronoun follows a collective noun antecedent when the members of the group are considered as a unit; a plural pronoun, when they are thought of individually (see 7d).

A UNIT
The student *committee* presented **its** report.

INDIVIDUALS
The *committee* filed into the room and took **their** seats, some of **them** defiant.

8d   Such singular antecedents as *each, either, neither, one, no one, everyone, someone, anyone, nobody, everybody, somebody, anybody* usually call for singular pronouns.

Not *one* of the linemen felt that **he** had had a good day.

Everyone who is a mother wonders what **her** children will be like as adults.

NOTE   When a singular pronoun refers to persons of both sexes (as *his* has been used in the past to refer to a man or a woman), there is now no simple solution: *his* to refer to a person when the sex is not known may raise objections; *his or her* is still ungainly. The best practice may be to avoid the problem.

UNGAINLY
Each young rider successfully rode *his or her* horse.
OBJECTIONABLE TO SOME
Each young rider successfully rode *his* horse.
ALTERNATE CHOICE
The young riders successfully rode *their* horses.

Use of a singular pronoun to refer to a singular antecedent is sometimes awkward.

Everybody cheered. I was pleased to hear him.

In informal speech, *to hear them* is acceptable.

8e *Which* refers to animals and things. *Who* refers to persons, but may be used with animals and some things called by name. *That* refers to animals or things and sometimes to persons.

The *boy* **who** was fishing is my son.

The *dog* **which (that)** sat beside him looked listless.

Sometimes *that* and *who* are interchangeable.

A child *that* (*who*) sucks his thumb is often insecure.
A person *that* (*who*) giggles is often insecure.

NOTE *Whose* (the possessive form of *who*) is often used to avoid the awkward *of which,* even in referring to animals and things.

The *car* **whose** right front tire blew out crashed and burned.

8f Pronouns should not refer vaguely to an entire sentence or clause or to unidentified people.

Many fuzzy references result from starting a sentence without foreseeing problems that will come up.

Some people worry about wakefulness but actually need little sleep.
This is one reason they have so much trouble sleeping.

This could refer to the worry, to the need for little sleep, or to psychological problems or other traits which have not even been mentioned in the sentence.

CLEAR
Some people have trouble sleeping because they lie awake and worry about their inability to sleep.

They, them, it, and *you* are sometimes used as vague references to people and conditions which need more precise identification.

VAGUE
They always get *you* in the end.

The problem here is that the pronouns *they* and *you* and the sentence are so vague that the writer could mean almost anything pessimistic. The sentence could be referring to teachers, deans, government officials, or even all of life.

NOTE In informal writing especially, experienced writers sometimes let *this, which,* or *it* refer to the whole idea of an earlier clause or phrase when no misunderstanding is likely.

The grumbler heard that his boss had called him incompetent. *This* made him resign.

8g Make a pronoun refer clearly to one antecedent, not uncertainly to two.

UNCERTAIN
Melville visited Hawthorne while he was American consul in Liverpool.
CLEAR
While Hawthorne was American consul in Liverpool, Melville visited him.

► Exercise 9

Revise sentences that contain errors in pronoun agreement. Write C to the left of correct sentences.

1. The captain of the damaged plane let each member of the crew decide whether they wanted to remain with the ship or bail out.

2. On or before April 15, most American citizens file their income tax returns.

3. No matter what the detergent commercials say, no woman is really jubilant at the prospect of mopping their dirty kitchen floor.

4. The drifter, along with his many irresponsible relatives, never paid back a cent they borrowed.

5. Neither the batter nor the fans hesitated to show his ardent disapproval of the umpire's decision.

6. Every man remembers the glamorous days of their childhood.

7. The League of Nations failed because they never received full support from the member countries.

8. Not every Victorian lady was as prudish as popular opinion would have them be.

9. Neither of the two old ladies ever admitted their guilt, but the

police strongly suspected one of them of poisoning several magazine salesmen.

10. The group of several hundred students asked the president of the student body to speak to the dean on its behalf.

▶ Exercise 10
Revise sentences that contain vague or faulty pronoun references.

1. Your average factory worker is now well paid, but they have not been able to do much about the boredom.

2. They tell you that you must pay taxes, but most of the time you do not know what they use your money for.

3. In the highly competitive world of advertising, those who do not have it are soon passed over for promotions.

4. They use much less silver now in coins; so they are worth less in themselves as well as in what they buy.

5. Mail service has not improved over the years though it has gone up.

▶ Exercise 11
Revise sentences that contain errors in pronoun reference. Write C *to the left of correct sentences.*

1. The lifeguard which saved the two children did not learn to swim until she was eighteen.

2. Many people are wildly searching for a panacea; this is why they are frustrated.

3. Lawyers generally charge their clients a standard fee unless they are unusually poor.

4. David fought Goliath although he was much smaller in size and he was an experienced warrior and he was not.

5. Some people claim that it is almost meaningless to send greeting cards, but others believe that it is worth preserving.

6. On the night of July 14, the patriots stormed the doors of the jails, and they were immediately smashed open.

7. Luck is a prerequisite to riches, which is why few people are rich.

8. The poet is widely admired, but it is very difficult indeed to make a living at it.

9. The osprey feeds on fish, which it captures by diving into the water.

10. At present there are thousands of people trying to escape unemployment, yet they cannot find it in their cities.

9 Case *c*

Use correctly the case forms of pronouns and the possessive case forms of nouns.

To determine case, find how a word is used in its own clause—for example, whether it is a subject or a subjective complement, a possessive, or an object.

9a Use the subjective case for subjects and subjective complements.

SUBJECTS

This month *he and I* **have** not been inside the library. (never *him and me*)

It looked as if *he and I* **were** going to be blamed. (never *him and me*)

SUBJECTIVE COMPLEMENTS

The two guilty ones who went unpunished **were** *you and I.*

In conversation *you and me* is sometimes used instead of *you and I* for the subjective complement. In speech *it's me* is almost universally accepted. *It's us, it's him,* and *it's her* are also common.

9b Use the objective case for the object of a preposition.

FAULTY

The manager had to choose *between* **he and I.**

RIGHT

The manager had to choose *between* **him and me.**

Between you and me presents essentially the same problem. *Between* is a preposition and therefore demands an object.

Be careful about the case of pronouns in constructions like the following:

FAULTY
A few *of* **we girls** learned how to cook.
RIGHT
A few *of* **us girls** learned how to cook.

When in doubt, test by dropping the noun (not *of we,* but *of us*).

9c Use the objective case for the subject of an infinitive.

subject

The reporter considered **him** *to be* the best swimmer in the pool.

9d Give an appositive and the word it refers to the same case.

Pronoun appositives take different cases depending on the case of the word they refer to.

SUBJECTIVE
Two *members* of the committee—**Bill and I**—were appointed by the chairman.
OBJECTIVE
The chairman appointed two *members*—**Bill and me.**

9e The case of a pronoun after *than* or *as* in an elliptical (incomplete) clause should be the same as if the clause were completely expressed.

understood
↓
No one else in the play was as versatile as **she** (*was*).

understood
↓
The director admired no one else as much as (*he did*) **her.**

9f Use the possessive case for most pronouns preceding a gerund. A noun before a gerund may be possessive or objective.

My *driving* does not delight my father.
The **lumberman's** *chopping* could be heard for a mile.

The noun is objective in certain instances:
1. when a phrase intervenes

Regulations prevented the **family** of a sailor *meeting* him at the dock.

2. when a noun preceding the gerund is plural

There is no rule against **men** *working* overtime.

3. when a noun is abstract

I object to **emotion** *overruling* judgment.

4. when a noun denotes an inanimate object

The crew did object to the **ship** *staying* in port.

When the verbal is a participle and not a gerund, the noun or pronoun preceding it is in the objective case.

> I heard **him** _singing_ loudly.
> I hear **you** _calling_ me.

9g Use an _of_ phrase to indicate the possessive of abstractions or inanimate objects.

INCONGRUOUS
The building's construction was delayed.
PREFERRED
The construction of the building was delayed.

There are well-established exceptions: _a stone's throw, for pity's sake, a month's rest, heart's desire, a day's work._

9h The possessive forms of personal pronouns do not have an apostrophe; the possessive forms of indefinite pronouns do have an apostrophe.

PERSONAL PRONOUNS
yours, its, hers, his, ours, theirs

INDEFINITE PRONOUNS
everyone's, other's, one's, anybody else's

NOTE Contractions such as _it's_ (_it is_), _he's,_ and _she's_ require an apostrophe.

9i The case of an interrogative or a relative pronoun is determined by its use in its own clause.

Interrogative pronouns (used in questions) are _who, whose, whom, what, which._ Relative pronouns are _who, whose, whom,_ *what, which, that,* and the forms with *-ever,* such as *whoever* and *whosoever.* Those which give difficulty through change in form are *who* and *whoever* (subjective) and *whom* and *whomever* (objective).

The case of these pronouns is clear in uncomplicated sentences.

Who *defeated* Richard III?

But when something (usually a subordinate clause) intervenes between the pronoun and the rest of the clause, its function is sometimes obscured:

Who do the history books say *defeated* Richard III?

Use two simple ways to tell the case of the pronoun in such sentences.

1. Mentally cancel the intervening words:

Who ~~do the history books say~~ defeated Richard III?

2. Rearrange the sentence in declarative order, subject—verb—complement:

The history books do say who defeated Richard III.

A similar procedure will work in determining when *whom* should be used.

NOTE At the beginning of a sentence in speech, *who* is usually the form used.

Who were you talking *to* over there?

The case of a relative pronoun is determined by its use in its own clause, not by the case of its antecedent. Use these three easy steps to check this usage:

1. Pick out the relative clause and draw a box around it.

This is the withered old man (**who, whom**) the artist said was his model.

2. Cancel intervening expressions (*he says, it is reported,* and so on).

This is the withered old man (**who, whom**) ~~the artist said~~ was his model.

3. Find the verb in the relative clause.

This is the withered old man ~~who~~ **whom** was his model.

subject   *verb*

NOTE Do not confuse the function of the relative pronoun in its clause with the function of the clause as a whole.

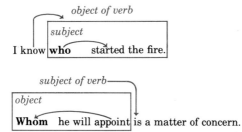

I know **who** started the fire.

object of verb
subject

Whom he will appoint is a matter of concern.

subject of verb
object

Try to avoid writing sentences with elaborate clauses using *who* and *whom*.

▶ Exercise 12
Underline the correct form in each of the following sentences.

1. No one knows the penalty for cheating better than (he, him).

2. On the platform stood the man (who, whom) they all believed had practiced witchcraft.
3. On the platform stood the man (who, whom) they all accused of practicing witchcraft.
4. The speaker defended his right to talk critically of (whoever, whomever) he pleased.
5. He (who, whom) would be great of soul must first know poverty and suffering.
6. Wise spending is essential to (us, we) poor music teachers.
7. On skid row is a little mission which gives (whoever, whomever) comes a hot meal, a dry place to sleep, and a word of encouragement.
8. Will the delegate from the Virgin Islands please indicate (who, whom) she wants to support?
9. It was (her, she) who discovered the human fossils in the Olduvai Gorge.
10. Truth is there for (whoever, whomever) will seek it.

▶ Exercise 13
Underline the incorrect forms of pronouns and nouns, and write in the correct forms.

1. The director said that the stunt man and himself were the ones most afraid of the white water on the trip down river.

2. The Navajo and the woman tourist walked behind the display booth. After much discussion between he and she, it was finally agreed that the first chance to buy the turquoise bracelet was her's.

3. No one was able to make more intricate sand designs than him.

4. "You and me," the bearded Old Chinese man said, "will construct intricate fireworks which will burst into colorful designs."

5. The mayor chose two aldermen—Mercival Wen and me—to select the person whom was to make the speech.

6. It was a good days work to repair the house's roof.

7. Deep thinkers have motives and secrets that us ordinary people can never fathom.

8. Who's theory was it that matter can be neither created nor destroyed?

9. Its true that the Potomac got it's name from the Indians.

10. I apologized because I wanted no ill feelings between she and I.

---

10 Adjectives and adverbs *adj / adv*

Adjectives modify nouns and pronouns. Adverbs modify verbs, adjectives, and other adverbs.

Most adverbs end in *-ly,* whereas only a few adjectives (*lovely, holy, manly, friendly*) have this ending. Some adverbs have two forms, one with *-ly* and one without: *slow* and *slowly, loud* and *loudly.* Most adverbs are formed by adding *-ly* to adjectives: *warm, warmly; pretty, prettily.*

Choosing correct adjectives and adverbs in some sentences is no problem.

> They stood *close.*
> The barber gave him a *close* shave.
> Study the text *closely.*

Avoid using adjectives to modify verbs, other adjectives, or adverbs. Distinguish between *sure* and *surely, easy* and *easily, good* and *well, real* and *really, some* and *somewhat.*

NOT
A *real* **good** high jumper *soars* over the bar **easy.**

BUT
A *really* **good** high jumper *soars* over the bar **easily.**

10a Form the comparative and superlative degrees of most short adjectives and some adverbs by adding *-er* and *-est.* Use *more* and *most* (or *less* and *least*) before long adjectives, participles, and most adverbs.

	COMPARATIVE	SUPERLATIVE
ADJECTIVES		
dear	dearer	dearest
pretty	prettier	prettiest
BUT		
pitiful	more pitiful	most pitiful
grasping	more grasping	most grasping
ADVERBS		
slow	slower	slowest
BUT		
rapidly	more rapidly	most rapidly

Certain adjectives and adverbs have irregular comparative and superlative forms: *good, better, best; well, better, best; little, less, least; bad, worse, worst.*

Strictly speaking, some adjectives and adverbs are absolute; that is, they cannot be compared (*dead, perfect, complete, unique*). A thing cannot, logically, be more or less dead, or perfect, or unique (one of a kind). In formal writing, use *more nearly perfect.*

10b Use the comparative to refer to two things; the superlative, to more than two.

Both cars are fast, but the small car is (the) faster.
All *three* cars are fast, but the small car is (the) fastest.

10c Use a predicate adjective, not an adverb, after a linking verb such as *be, seem, become, look, appear, feel, sound, smell, taste.*

He feels **bad.** (He is ill or depressed.)

He *reads* **badly.** (*Reads* expresses an action; it is not a linking verb.)

The *tea* tasted **sweet.** (*Sweet* describes the tea.)

She *tasted* the tea **daintily.** (*Daintily* tells how she tasted the tea.)

10d Use an adjective, not an adverb, to follow a verb and its object when the modifier refers to the object, not to the verb.

Verbs like *keep, build, hold, dig, make, think* can have an object plus a modifier of the object or verb. After verbs of this kind, choose the adjective or the adverb form carefully.

Keep your *clothes* **neat.** (adjective—modifies the object)

Keep your clothes **neatly** in the closet. (adverb—modifies verb)

Make my *bed* **soft.**

Make my bed **carefully.**

▶ Exercise 14
Underline unacceptable forms of adjectives and adverbs, and write the correct form. If a sentence is correct, write C *next to it.*

1. Socrates thought deep about the nature and purpose of humanity.

2. Even though one may feel bad about past acts, they can never be changed.

3. The young coach was real angry about the controversial decision to fine her.

4. It sure cannot be denied that Tennyson was one of the popularest poets of his time.

5. The ambassador spoke so rapid that no one interpreted him accurate.

6. The computer, a real complicated mechanical mind, is the most unique instrument of modern civilization.

7. The golfer's score was only average, but since he had often done poorly, he felt good about it.

8. Of the two colleges, which has the most majors in physical education?

9. In times of tribulation, you must think clear.

10. The manager, a man of indecision, never knew which of two possibilities was the best.

Sentence Structure

11 Excessive coordination *co*

Do not string together a number of short independent clauses.

Wordiness and monotony derive from brief independent clauses connected by coordinating conjunctions (*and, and so, but, or, nor, for, yet, so*). Excessive coordination fails to show precise relationships between thoughts. English is rich in subordinating connectives, and skillful writers use them.

STRINGY

Sugarloaf Mountain is four thousand feet high, and it is surrounded by fields and forests, and the air currents are favorable for hang gliding, and many gliding enthusiasts go there in the summer.

Make the last clause the central idea, and condense the sentence by using subordinating elements.

IMPROVED

Surrounded by fields and blessed with air currents favorable for hang gliding, four-thousand-foot-high Sugarloaf Mountain attracts many gliding enthusiasts in the summer.

▶ Exercise 1

Eliminate excessive coordination in the following sentences by subordinating some of the ideas.

1. Pagodas are temples or sacred buildings, and they are found in several Eastern countries, and they often have many stories and upward-curving roofs.

2. Sharks are ferocious, and they attack many bathers each year, but they seldom kill; so their reputation as killers is in part undeserved.

3. Some vacationers leave home in search of quiet; so they find a place without a telephone or television, but other people want complete isolation, but they discover that it is difficult to find a state park that is not crowded with trailers and tents.

4. The instructor gave the new student an assignment, and he had to write just one sentence, but he could not think of an interesting subject, and so he did not do the required work.

5. Famous books are not always written by admirable people, for some authors are arrogant, and some are even immoral.

6. The manta ray has a wide, flat body, and it is a member of the same class of fish as the shark.

7. Headhunters still exist in remote areas of the world, but they are rapidly disappearing, and today we seldom hear of them.

8. Computers calculate rapidly, and they do more work than a human being in the same time, and they threaten many jobs, but we must use them.

9. Women have been discriminated against, and they have been patient, but now they are complaining, and their cause is just.

10. Benjamin Franklin was an American, but he was at home wherever he went, and so he gained wide popularity in France, and he was also well known in England.

---

12 Subordination *sub*

Use subordinate clauses accurately and effectively to avoid excessive coordination and also to achieve variety and emphasis.

Insufficient or excessive subordination may ruin style or create excessively long and stringy sentences (see also **11**). Selection of the proper thought to subordinate reveals the relative importance of ideas in a sentence.

12a   Express main ideas in independent clauses, less important ideas in subordinate clauses.

An optimistic sociologist, who might wish to stress progress despite crime, would write:

> Although the crime rate is very high, society has progressed in many ways.

A pessimistic sociologist might wish the opposite emphasis:

> Although society has progressed in many ways, the crime rate is very high.

Putting the main idea in a subordinate clause is called "upside-down" subordination.

12b   Avoid excessive overlapping of subordinate constructions.

Monotony and even confusion can result from a series of clauses with each depending on the previous one.

OVERLAPPING

A watch is an intricate mechanism

which measures time,

which many people regard as the gift

that is most precious.

IMPROVED

A watch is an intricate mechanism made to measure time, which many people regard as the most precious gift.

▶ Exercise 2
The following is an exercise in thinking and relationships, designed to point up differences in meaning that result from subordination. Read the pairs of sentences carefully, and answer the questions.

1. A. After the Roman Empire was considerably weakened, corruption in high places became widespread.
   B. After corruption in high places became widespread, the Roman Empire was considerably weakened.

   Which of these sentences would a historian writing on the causes of Rome's fall be more likely to write?

2. A. Although a lifetime is short, much can be accomplished.
   B. Although much can be accomplished, a lifetime is short.

   Which of these sentences expresses more determination?

3. A. When in doubt, most drivers apply the brakes.
   B. When most drivers apply the brakes, they are in doubt.

   With which drivers would you prefer to ride?

4. A. In spite of the fact that he had a speech defect, Cotton Mather became a great preacher.
   B. In spite of the fact that he became a great preacher, Cotton Mather had a speech defect.

   In which sentence did he possibly overcome the defect?
   In which sentence did the defect remain noticeable?

5. A. While taking a bath, Archimedes formulated one of the most important principles in physics.
   B. While formulating one of the most important principles in physics, Archimedes took a bath.

   Which sentence indicates accidental discovery?
   In which sentence does Archimedes take a bath for relaxation?

▶ Exercise 3
   Rewrite the following sentences to avoid overlapping subordination.

1. *Hamlet* is a play by Shakespeare that tells of a prince who has difficulties making up his mind to avenge the murder of his father.

2. Each musician who plays in the orchestra which performs in the club that is on the side of the lake has at least fifteen years of professional experience.

3. Lobster Newburg is a dish which consists of cooked lobster meat which is heated in a chafing dish which contains a special cream sauce.

4. Few people who smoke realize that the tobacco used in ordinary cigarettes is of the same family as nightshade, which is poisonous.

5. Between the sixth and seventh floors the elevator stuck that had the board member who could have cast a vote that would have changed the future of the corporation.

---

13 Completeness *inc*
Make your sentences complete in structure and thought.

Sentences should be clear, and every element should be expressed or implied clearly enough to prevent misunderstanding. Do not omit necessary verbs, conjunctions, and prepositions.

13a Make constructions with *so, such,* and *too* complete.

To avoid misunderstanding, be sure that the idea is expressed completely.

NOT CLEAR
The boy was too short. (Too short for what?)
CLEAR
The boy was too short to play center.

NOT CLEAR
Those coins were so rare. (So rare that what?)
CLEAR
Those coins were so rare that even an expert could not identify them.

13b Do not omit a verb or a preposition which is necessary to the meaning of the sentence.

Idiom (see **37e**) sometimes demands two different forms:

NOT
He was simultaneously *repelled* and *drawn* **toward** the city.
BUT
He was simultaneously *repelled* **by** and *drawn* **toward** the city.
BETTER
He was simultaneously *repelled* **by** the city and *drawn* **toward** it.

NOT
In the confusion the *silver coins* **were** scattered and the *paper money*
stolen. (Paper money *were* stolen?)
BUT
In the confusion the *silver coins* **were** scattered, and the *paper money*
was stolen.

However, when the same form is called for in both elements, it
need not be repeated:

To err is human; to forgive, divine.

13c Omission of *that* sometimes obscures meaning.

OBSCURE
The systems analyst found a happy worker is more efficient.
CLEAR
The systems analyst found *that* a happy worker is more efficient.

14   Comparisons   *comp*

Make comparisons logical and clear.

Compare only similar terms.

The *laughter* of a loon is more frightening than an **owl.**

This sentence compares a sound and a bird. A consistent sentence would compare sound and sound or bird and bird.

The *laughter* of a loon is more frightening than the **hoot** of an owl.

A *loon* is more frightening than an **owl.**

The word *other* is often needed in a comparison:

ILLOGICAL
The Sahara is larger than any desert in the world.
RIGHT
The Sahara is larger than any *other* desert in the world.

Avoid awkward and incomplete comparisons.

AWKWARD AND INCOMPLETE

The lily is *as white* if not whiter **than** any other flower. (*As white* requires *as,* not *than.*)
BETTER
The lily is *as* white **as** any other flower, if not whiter. (*Than any other* is understood.)

AWKWARD AND INCOMPLETE
Yellowstone National Park is one of the most beautiful if not the most beautiful national park. (After *one of the most beautiful,* the plural *parks* is required.)
BETTER
Yellowstone National Park is one of the most beautiful national parks, if not the most beautiful.
OR
Yellowstone is one of the most beautiful national parks.

AMBIGUOUS
After many years my teacher remembered me better than my roommate. (Better than he remembered my roommate, or better
than my roommate remembered me?)

CLEAR
After many years my teacher remembered me better than my roommate did.

OR
After many years my teacher remembered me better than he did my
roommate.

FEEBLE
Catch-22 is different.

CLEAR
Catch-22 is different from other war novels of its time.

▶ Exercise 4
*Correct any errors in completeness and comparisons. Write C to
the left of correct sentences.*

1. When Alexander the Great was young he swore to hate Rome more

   than any man.

2. Visitors to New Lawson discover that the summers there are as hot

   if not hotter than any they have ever experienced.

3. People go to Florida every winter because they feel that the winter

   climate there is better than any state.

4. This sentence is a little different.

5. The baboons ate more of the bananas than the ants.

6. Happy workers always have and still do produce the best results.

7. The veterinarian read a learned article proving that horses like dogs better than cats.

8. For one's health, plain water is as good if not better than most liquids.

9. The lighthouse stood as a symbol and guide to safety.

10. Some parents are so lax that they allow their children almost unlimited freedom.

▶ Exercise 5
Follow the instructions for Exercise 4.

1. The flooding river was so wide, so powerful, and so uncontrollable.

2. The telephone is one of the most useful if not the most useful instruments in modern life.

3. The editors say that the headlines have been written and the type set.

4. The children enjoyed singing songs about how we go over the fields and the woods.

5. The gardener knew a plant which grows in the air without roots requires little attention.

15 Consistency *cons*

Write sentences which maintain grammatical consistency.

Unnecessary changes in grammatical forms are misleading and annoying.

15a Avoid unnecessary shifts between past and present tense.

Shifts in tense most frequently occur in narration.

NEEDLESS SHIFT FROM PAST TO PRESENT
The architect *plans* the new stadium, and then the mayor *decided* not to build it.

In writing about literature, avoid shifting between past tense and the historical present.

NEEDLESS SHIFT FROM PRESENT TO PAST
The social worker in the novel *makes* extensive plans to accomplish reforms, but all her efforts *came* to nothing.

Also avoid needless shifts between conditional forms (*should, would, could*).

NOT
Exhaustion after a vacation *could be* avoided if a family *can* plan better. (Use either sequence, *could . . . would,* or *can . . . can.*)

15b Avoid careless shifts in person.

In felling a tree, *a good woodsman* [**3rd person**] first cuts a deep notch near the bottom of the trunk and on the side toward which *he* [**3rd person**] wishes the tree to fall. Then *you* [**2nd person**] saw on the other side, directly opposite the notch. (The second sentence should read *Then he saws. . . .* Or the first, *you first cut . . . toward which you wish. . . .*)

15c Avoid unnecessary shifts in mood.

$$\overset{\textit{subjunctive}}{\downarrow} \qquad \overset{\textit{indicative}}{\downarrow}$$

SHIFTS
It is necessary that the applicant *fill* in this form and *mails* it.
CONSISTENT SUBJUNCTIVE
It is necessary that the applicant *fill* in this form and *mail* it.

SHIFTS
$$\overset{\textit{imperative}}{\downarrow} \qquad\qquad\qquad \overset{\textit{indicative}}{\downarrow}$$
First *mail* the application; then the applicant *will go* for an interview.
CONSISTENT IMPERATIVE
First *mail* the application; then *go* for an interview.

15d Avoid unnecessary shifts in voice.

POOR
The chef *cooks* (**active**) the shrimp casserole for thirty minutes and then it is *allowed* (**passive**) to cool.
BETTER
The chef *cooks* the shrimp casserole for thirty minutes and then *allows* it to cool.

15e Avoid unnecessary shifts from one relative pronoun to another.

SHIFT

She went to the cupboard *that* leaned perilously forward and *which* always resisted every attempt to open it.

CONSISTENT

She went to the cupboard *which* leaned perilously forward and *which* always resisted every attempt to open it. (or, *that* . . . *that*)

15f Avoid a shift from indirect to direct discourse in the same construction.

Indirect discourse paraphrases the speaker's words; direct discourse quotes exactly.

MIXED

←——————————*indirect*——————————→
The censor says that the book is obscene and

←——————————*direct*——————————→
why would anyone wish to read it?

INDIRECT

The censor says that the book is obscene and asks why anyone would wish to read it.

DIRECT

The censor says, "The book is obscene. Why would anyone wish to read it?"

► Exercise 6
Correct the shifts in grammar in the following sentences. Write C to the left of correct sentences.

1. The representative rose slowly, cleared her throat, and moved that the motion be tabled and that the meeting is adjourned.

2. A boy who writes an appealing letter to his girl friend will seem to have personality, but the next time you see her you must be as interesting in person as you are when you write.

3. The failures in the experiments will be avoided this time if the assistants would follow the instructions precisely.

4. The retreating actor backed out of the door, jumped on a horse, and rides off into the sunset.

5. The economics professor was dismayed because at the end of last year seven students still cannot define the law of supply and demand.

16 Position of modifiers *po*

Place modifiers so that they clearly attach to the right word or element in the sentence.

A poorly placed modifier which attaches to the wrong word can cause confusion, misunderstanding, or absurdity. Usually a modifying adjective precedes its noun, whereas an adverb may precede or follow the word it modifies. Prepositional phrases (see Glossary) usually follow closely, but may precede; adjective clauses follow closely; and adverbial phrases and clauses may be placed in many positions.

16a Avoid dangling modifiers.

Many danglers are verbal phrases at the beginning of a sentence.

DANGLING PARTICIPLE

Running along the street, my *nose* felt frozen. (A participle at the
first of a sentence usually modifies the subject. Here *running*
seems to modify *nose.)*
CLEAR
Running along the street, I felt as if my nose were frozen.
OR
As I ran along the street, my nose *felt* frozen. (The participial
phrase has been changed to an adverbial clause which modifies
felt.)

DANGLING GERUND

After **searching** around the attic, a *halloween mask* was discovered.
(The passive voice in the main clause causes the modifier—a
preposition and a gerund—to attach wrongly to the subject.)
CLEAR
After **searching** around the attic, I discovered a halloween mask.

DANGLING INFINITIVE

To enter the house, the *lock* on the back door was picked. (*To enter
the house* refers to no word in this sentence.)
CLEAR
To enter the house, he picked the lock on the back door.

DANGLING PREPOSITIONAL PHRASE

In old age, my father's *impatience* with new ideas became intolerable. (In whose old age? Impatience's? Of course not; my
father's.)

CLEAR

In **his** old age, *my father's* impatience with new ideas became intolerable.

DANGLING ELLIPTICAL CLAUSE

While still sleepy and tired, the *counsellor* lectured me on breaking rules.

CLEAR

While I was still sleepy and tired, the counsellor lectured me on breaking rules.

Loosely attaching a verbal phrase to the end of a sentence is ineffective:

WEAK

Students in a cooperative program may work part of the time **earning enough for all their expenses.**

Often simple coordination is a good way to revise a sentence of this kind.

BETTER

Students in a cooperative program may work part of the time and earn enough for all their expenses.

NOTE Some verbal phrases need not refer to a single word in the sentence.

Strictly speaking, does this sentence contain a dangling construction?

To tell the truth, it does not.

The phrases are sentence modifiers.

16b Avoid misplaced modifiers.

The placement of a modifier in a sentence affects meaning.

He enlisted after he married *again*.
He enlisted *again* after he married.

Almost any modifier which comes between an adjective clause and the word it modifies can cause awkwardness or misunderstanding:

Wordsworth addressed a passage to his friend Coleridge in *The Prelude,* who collaborated with him in writing *Lyrical Ballads*.
Some insecticides are still used on crops that are suspected of being dangerous.

The first sentence is awkward though its intent is clear; the second is actually misleading.

In *The Prelude* Wordsworth addressed a passage to his friend Coleridge, who collaborated with him in writing *Lyrical Ballads*.
Some insecticides that are suspected of being dangerous are still used on crops.

16c A modifier placed between two words so that it seems to modify either word is said to "squint."

UNCLEAR
The horse which was pawing *violently* kicked its owner.
CLEAR
The horse which was *violently pawing* kicked its owner.
OR
The horse which was pawing *kicked* its owner *violently*.

▶ Exercise 7
Correct the faulty modifiers in the following sentences.

1. Dangling by one leg from a pair of tweezers, the little boy held the huge moth far out in front of him.

2. The courageous patient was able to walk about two weeks after the accident.

3. This computer is seldom used even though it is most effective because of the high cost.

4. To be absolutely certain, the answer must be checked.

5. The restaurant offers special meals for children that are inexpensive.

6. Serve one of the melons for dessert at lunch; keep one of them for the picnic in the refrigerator.

7. The carpenter inspected the board before sawing for nails.

8. At the age of five my grandfather told me about his life as a soldier.

9. Having been found guilty of drunken driving, the judge sentenced the young man to ninety days in jail.

10. The woman who was writing hastily rose from the desk and left the room.

▶ Exercise 8
Follow the instructions for Exercise 7.

1. The forester identified every kind of tree in the forest enabling the new plantation owner to select the best trees to cut.

2. Without shoes, the rough stones cut the feet of the hikers.

3. Although grumbly and rebellious, the bridge was still built by the workers.

4. To taste really good, the chef should prepare a dressing precisely suitable to the raw spinach salad.

5. The editor only told me that lighthearted columns would be accepted for the children's page.

---

17   Separation of elements   *sep*

Do not unnecessarily or excessively separate closely related elements.

Separation of subject and verb, parts of a verb phrase, or verb and object can be awkward or misleading.

AWKWARD
Wild dogs had, *for several sleet-ridden and storm-ravaged winter days when food was scarce and the marrow seemed to freeze in the bones,* been seen on the hills.

IMPROVED
For several sleet-ridden and storm-ravaged winter days when the marrow seemed to freeze in the bones and food was scarce, wild dogs had been seen on the hills.

LUDICROUS
She is the man who owns the service station's wife.
ACCURATE
She is the wife of the man who owns the service station.

Do not divide a sentence with a quotation long enough to cause excessive separation.

AVOID
Stephen Crane's view of the place of man in the world,
>   A man said to the universe:
>   "Sir, I exist!"
>   "However," replied the universe,
>   "The fact has not created in me
>   A sense of obligation,"
is pessimistic.

Split infinitives occur when a modifier comes between *to* and the verb form, as in *to loudly complain.* Some grammarians ban them without exception. Others insist that some split infinitives are more graceful than possible alternatives. To avoid objections, you would be wise not to split infinitives.

18 Parallelism //

Use parallel grammatical forms to express elements which are parallel in thought. Constructions should be parallel in form if they are connected by coordinating conjunctions (*and, but, or, nor*) or by correlative conjunctions (*either . . . or, neither . . . nor, not . . . but, not only . . . but also, both . . . and*).

Words go with similar words, phrases with similar phrases, clauses with similar clauses.

NOT PARALLEL
The braggart was characterized by all talking and no action.
PARALLEL
The braggart was characterized by all talk and no action.

NOT PARALLEL

The collector promises
{
to buy a copy of the rare book
and
that the cost will not be excessive.
}

PARALLEL

The collector promises
{
that she will buy a copy of the rare book
and
that the cost will not be excessive.
}

AWKWARD CORRELATIVES   *verb*   *pronoun*

The reactionary *not only* supported tyranny *but also* he became a tyrant.

PARALLEL   *verb*   *verb*

The reactionary *not only* supported tyranny *but also* became a tyrant.

Do not make elements parallel in a structure when they are not parallel in thought.

MISLEADING PARALLELISM

At the end of the season the management quietly closed the hotel, boarded up its windows, and burned a month later.

▶ Exercise 9

Revise any sentences with faulty parallelism. Write C to the left of correct sentences.

1. The ideal piecrust is tender, flaky, and, of course, tastes good.

2. Advertisements promise that small foreign cars are economical and how easy they are to park.

3. Adjusting to a large college is very difficult for a person who has

always attended a small school and being used to more individual attention.

4. Roaming through the great north woods, camping by a lake, and getting away from crowds are good ways to forget the cares of civilization.

5. To be a good listener, one must have a genuine interest in people, a strong curiosity, and discipline oneself to keep the mind from wandering.

6. *Death of a Salesman* is a play about a man who wasted his life and which teaches the need for self-discovery.

7. A good trial lawyer must be well educated in the profession and something of an actor.

8. The delegation found it impossible either to see the governor or even her secretary.

9. Most slow readers could read much faster and better if they would not glance back over lines they have passed and also moving their lips when they read.

10. The jaguar is swift, quiet, and moves with grace.

19   Variety *var*

Vary sentences in length, structure, and order.

Length   An unbroken series of short sentences may become monotonous and fail to indicate such relationships as cause, condition, concession, time sequence, and purpose.

CHOPPY
Overpopulation is becoming a problem. Alaska is not thickly populated. Many people may move there. It has vast open lands.

These sentences can be combined into one complex sentence which shows more exactly the relationships of the thoughts.

IMPROVED
Alaska, a relatively unpopulous state, has vast open lands which may attract many people in this time of overpopulation.

Structure   Do not overuse one kind of sentence structure. Write simple, compound, and complex patterns; and vary your sentences between loose, periodic, and balanced forms.

A **loose sentence,** the most frequently used kind, makes its main point early and then adds refinements. In contrast, a **periodic sentence** withholds an element of the main thought until the end to create suspense and emphasis.

LOOSE
Boys are wild animals, rich in the treasures of sense, but the New England boy had a wider range of emotions than boys of more equable climates.

HENRY ADAMS

LOOSE
Uncle Tom's Cabin is a very bad novel, having, in its self-righteous, virtuous sentimentality, much in common with *Little Women.*

JAMES BALDWIN

PERIODIC

Under a government which imprisons any unjustly, the true place
  for a just man is also a prison.

HENRY DAVID THOREAU

PERIODIC

There is one thing above all others that the scientist has a duty to
  teach to the public and to governments: it is the duty of
  heresy.

J. BRONOWSKI

A **balanced sentence** has parts which are similar in structure and length and which express parallel thoughts. Indeed, balance is simply another word for refined and extended parallelism.
(For a discussion of parallel structure see **18**.) The following
sentence has perfect symmetry:

Marriage has many pains, but celibacy has no pleasures.

SAMUEL JOHNSON

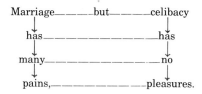

A sentence can also be balanced if only parts of it are symmetrical:

Thus the Puritan was made up of two different men, the one all
  self-abasement, penitence, gratitude, passion; the other proud,
  calm, inflexible, sagacious.

THOMAS BABINGTON MACAULAY

> Thus
> the Puritan
> was made up
> of two different men,
>
> the one————the other
> all self-abasement,——— proud,
> penitence,————calm,
> gratitude,————inflexible,
> passion;————sagacious.

Order If all sentences follow the normal order of subject-verb-complement, the effect can be monotonous. For interest and emphasis invert the order occasionally, and do not always tack dependent clauses and long phrases on at the end. Study the variations in the following sentences.

NORMAL ORDER
subject   verb   object   modifiers
   ↓   ↓   ↓
She attributed these *defects* in her son's character to the general
    weaknesses of mankind.

SENTENCE BEGINNING WITH DIRECT OBJECT
These *defects* in her son's character she attributed to the general
    weaknesses of mankind.

SENTENCE BEGINNING WITH PREPOSITIONAL PHRASE
To the general weaknesses of mankind she attributed the defects in
    her son's character.

SENTENCE BEGINNING WITH ADVERB
Quickly the swordfish broke the surface of the water.

INVERTED SENTENCE BEGINNING WITH CLAUSE USED AS OBJECT
That the engineer tried to avert the catastrophe, none of them would
    deny.

INVERTED SENTENCE BEGINNING WITH DEPENDENT ADVERBIAL
CLAUSE
If you wish to create a college, therefore, and are wise, you will seek to
    create a life.

WOODROW WILSON

SENTENCE BEGINNING WITH PARTICIPIAL PHRASE
Flying low over the water for hours, the plane searched for survivors.

In climactic order, the elements of a series are arranged according to increasing importance. Ordering by decreasing importance may result in anticlimax and loss of emphasis.

UNEMPHATIC
The hurricane left thousands of people homeless, ruined the crops, and interrupted transportation.

CLIMACTIC
The hurricane interrupted transportation, ruined the crops, and left thousands of people homeless.

▶ Exercise 10
Make one sentence out of each of the groups below.

1. At the age of seventeen I went to debate at a high school.
Three girls went with me.
It was the fall of my senior year.
The high school was over a hundred miles away.

ADAPTED FROM JOHN UPDIKE

2. There is, indeed, much wrong with cities.
Big ones and little ones have problems.
They should not be abandoned.
We should not rebuild them on abstract principles.

ADAPTED FROM ROBERT MOSES

3. Philadelphia is one of America's most historic cities.
   At present it is involved in a program of urban renewal.
   This program is already showing substantial results.

4. Van Gogh was a Dutch painter.
   He belonged to the Impressionist School.
   Van Gogh once cut off his ear with a razor.
   At that time he was in one of his frequent fits of depression.

5. Some people think mountain climbing is silly.
   They do not really understand.
   A mountain climber is meeting a challenge.
   It is a symbolic challenge.
   The mountain represents the seemingly invincible obstacles of life.

▶ Exercise 11
Rewrite the following sentences and make them periodic. If you consider a sentence already periodic, put a check mark next to it.

1. One machine, the typewriter, revolutionized business practices and had a profound influence on the style of many authors.

2. A sense of humor is one quality no great leader can be without.

3. Selfishness, some philosophers maintain, is the reason behind every action of any person.

4. The blue whale is the largest known creature on earth.

5. He studied when all other possible methods of passing the course

proved unworkable.

▶ Exercise 12
*Rewrite the following sentences to give them balanced con-
structions. If a sentence already has a balanced construction,
put a check mark next to it.*

1. The rewards of youth are obvious, but much more subtle are the

rewards of age.

2. A successful advertisement surprises and pleases, but not all

advertisements are successful because some are merely boring and

irritating.

3. Realists know their limitations; romantics know only what they

want.

4. A politician is concerned with successful elections whereas the fu-

ture of the people is foremost in the mind of a statesman.

5. A trained ear hears many separate instruments in an orchestra,

but the melody is usually all that is heard by the untutored.

▶ Exercise 13
Rewrite the following sentences according to the principles of climactic order.

1. Our space ship brought back from the strange planet a large animal, two small green people, and a soil sample.

2. John Quincy Adams served in more than seven political offices; he was, among other things, President of the United States, a Senator, and a Congressman.

3. Plagues in the Middle Ages were probably the greatest kind of national disaster; millions of people suffered death, great pain, and economic losses.

4. Cities are faced with countless problems, such as crime in the streets, littering, pollution, and traffic jams.

5. Although the controversial speaker tried to proceed, stones thrown at the platform, annoying catcalls, and a barrage of rotten fruit brought an end to the meeting.

▶ Exercise 14
Rewrite the following passage so that it is more varied in sentence structure.

An Italian, Cristoforo Colombo, discovered America. Another, Amerigo Vespucci, gave it his name. Neither Italians as a people nor Italy as a country had a significant place in the early history of the United States. During the colonial period, a few men from the Italian peninsula settled in America. They lived in the cities along the Atlantic seaboard. This sprinkling of Italians left no noteworthy mark on the life of the English colonies. In 1621, a small group of Italian glassmakers lived in Jamestown. They made an impression. It was negative. According to the secretary of that colony, "A more damned crew hell never vomited."

The largest group of Italians to settle in North America consisted of about two hundred. They were Protestants. They had lived in the valleys of Piedmont. They were usually called "Waldensians" after Peter Waldo of Lyon. He was a merchant. He founded their sect. They suffered persecution and massacre at home. Then they fled to Holland. From there they sought refuge in the New World. They arrived in New Amsterdam in the spring of 1657. A few weeks after their arrival, they moved on to Delaware. There Dutch Protestants purchased land for them. The Italians organized the first government of New Amstel. Later it was called New Castle. Historians know little about these settlers and their movements. They do know they were Italians. They spoke and kept their records in French. They know too that a small band of them also established a settlement at Stony Brook, New York.

ADAPTED FROM ALEXANDER DE CONDE,
*Half Bitter, Half Sweet: An Excursion
into Italian-American History*

Punctuation

20 The comma ,

Use commas to reflect structure and to clarify the sense of the sentence.

The **comma** is chiefly used (1) to separate equal elements, such as independent clauses and items in a series, and (2) to set off modifiers or parenthetical words, phrases, and clauses. Elements which are set off within a sentence take a comma both *before* and *after*.

NOT
This novel, a best seller has no real literary merit.
BUT
This novel, a best seller, has no real literary merit.

20a Use a comma to separate independent clauses joined by a coordinating conjunction.

Nice is a word with many meanings, and some of them are opposite to others.

Sherlock Holmes had to be prepared, for Watson was full of questions.

NOTE The comma is sometimes omitted when the clauses are short and there is no danger of misreading.

The weather was clear and the pilot landed.

20b Use a comma between words, phrases, or clauses in a series.

The closet contained worn clothes, old shoes, and dusty hats.

The final comma before *and* in a series is sometimes omitted.

The closet contained worn clothes, old shoes and dusty hats.

But the comma must be used when *and* is omitted.

The closet contained worn clothes, old shoes, dusty hats.

And it must be used when the final elements could be misread.

An old chest in the corner was filled with nails, hammers, a hacksaw and blades, and a brace and bit.

Series of phrases, of dependent clauses, or of independent clauses are also separated by commas.

PHRASES

We hunted for the letter in the album, in all the old trunks, and even under the rug.

DEPENDENT CLAUSES

Finally we guessed that the letter had been burned, that someone
else had already discovered it, or that it had never been
written.

INDEPENDENT CLAUSES

We left the attic, Father locked the door, and Mother suggested that
we never unlock it again.

In a series of independent clauses, the comma is not omitted before
the final element.

▶ Exercise 1
Insert commas where necessary in the following sentences.

1. Some prominent women authors took masculine pen names in the
   nineteenth century for they felt that the public would not read
   novels written by women.

2. A good orator should prepare well for a talk speak clearly enough
   to be understood and practice the art of effective timing.

3. The markings on the wall of the cave were not as ancient as others
   but none of the experts could interpret them.

4. The hamper was filled with cold cuts mixed pickles bread and
   butter.

5. Some government documents are classified secret for the safety of
   the country must be preserved.

6. The sensitive child knew that the earth was round but she thought that she was on the inside of it.

7. The instructor said that the class had not been doing very well that obviously everyone had failed to take notes and that she wanted to see some improvement.

8. For breakfast he served us bacon and eggs toast and jelly and hot coffee.

9. Careless driving includes speeding stopping suddenly making turns from the wrong lane of traffic going through red lights and so forth.

10. Driving was easy for a great part of the way was paved and traffic was light.

> **20c** Use a comma between coordinate adjectives not joined by *and.* Do not use a comma between cumulative adjectives.

Coordinate adjectives modify the noun independently. Cumulative ones modify not only the noun, but the whole cluster of intervening adjectives. Note the difference:

COORDINATE
Madame de Stael was an attractive, gracious lady.

Ferocious, vigilant, loyal dogs were essential to safety in the Middle Ages.

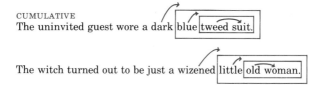

CUMULATIVE
The uninvited guest wore a dark blue tweed suit.

The witch turned out to be just a wizened little old woman.

Two tests are helpful.

Test one *And* is natural only between coordinate adjectives.

an attractive *and* gracious lady
ferocious *and* vigilant *and* loyal dogs
BUT NOT
dark *and* blue *and* tweed suit
wizened *and* little *and* old woman

Test two Coordinate adjectives are easily reversible.

a gracious, attractive lady
loyal, vigilant, ferocious dogs
BUT NOT
tweed blue dark suit
old little wizened woman

The distinction is not always clear-cut, however, and the sense of the cluster must be the deciding factor.

She was wearing a full-skirted, low-cut velvet gown.   (a velvet gown that was full-skirted and low-cut, not a gown that was full-skirted and low-cut and velvet)

NOTE A comma is not used before the word modified:

NOT	BUT
gracious, lady	gracious lady
ferocious, dogs	ferocious dogs

▶ Exercise 2
Punctuate the following. When in doubt apply the tests described above. Write C to the left of those which require no comma.

1. a graceful agile cat

2. large glass front doors

3. a little black recipe book

4. a high-crowned lemon-yellow felt hat

5. a wrinkled brown paper bag

6. a hot sultry depressing day

7. the gloomy forbidding night scene

8. straight strawberry-blond hair

9. a woebegone ghostly look

10. beautiful imported Persian rugs

20d Use a comma after a long introductory phrase or subordinate clause.

LONG PHRASE
With this bitter part of the ordeal behind him, the trapper felt more
confident.
LONG CLAUSE
When this bitter part of the ordeal was behind him, the trapper felt
more confident.

When the introductory element is short and there is no danger of
misreading, the comma is often omitted.

SHORT PHRASE
After this bitter ordeal the trapper felt more confident.
SHORT CLAUSE
When this ordeal was over the trapper felt more confident.

Commas after these introductory elements would be acceptable.
Use of the comma may depend on personal taste.

Introductory participial, infinitive, and gerund phrases, however, are usually set off by commas.

PARTICIPLE
Living for centuries, redwoods often reach a height of three hundred
feet.

INFINITIVE
To verify or correct his hypothesis, a scientist performs an experiment.

GERUND
After surviving this ordeal, the trapper felt relieved.

A phrase or a clause set off by a comma at the beginning of a
sentence may not require a comma if it is moved to the end of the
sentence.

BEGINNING
Because of pity for creatures that must live in small cages, some people refuse to go to the zoo.

END
Some people refuse to go to the zoo because of pity for creatures that must live in small cages.

20e Use commas to set off nonrestrictive appositives, phrases, and clauses.

A **nonrestrictive modifier** describes and adds information but does not point out or identify; omit the modifier, and the sentence loses some meaning but does not change radically or become meaningless.

NONRESTRICTIVE
Shakespeare's last play, *The Tempest*, is optimistic and even sunny in mood.
Taxicabs, *which are always expensive*, cost less in New York than elsewhere.
Oil, *which is lighter than water*, rises to the surface.

In these sentences the italicized modifiers add information, but they are not essential to the meaning of the sentence.

NOTE *That* never introduces a nonrestrictive clause.
A **restrictive modifier** points out or identifies its noun or pronoun; remove the modifier, and the sentence radically changes in meaning or becomes nonsense.

RESTRICTIVE
Taxicabs *that are dirty* are illegal in some cities.
Water *which is murky in appearance* should always be boiled before drinking.
The play *Macbeth* has been a scholar's delight for over three hundred years.

In all these sentences, the italicized expressions identify the words they modify; to remove these modifiers is to change the meaning radically or to make the sentence false.

Some modifiers can be either restrictive or nonrestrictive, and use or omission of the commas changes the sense.

> The coin which gleamed in the sunlight was a Spanish doubloon.
> (There were several coins.)
> The coin, which gleamed in the sunlight, was a Spanish doubloon.
> (There was only one coin.)

In speech a nonrestrictive modifier is usually preceded by a pause, whereas a restrictive modifier is not.

▶ Exercise 3

The following pairs of sentences illustrate differences in meaning which result from use of commas to set off modifiers. Answer the questions about each pair of sentences.

1. A. Her marriage to the architect Warren White ended in divorce.
   B. Her marriage, to the architect Warren White, ended in divorce.

   In which sentence had the woman been married only once?

2. A. The hitchhiker leaning against the post seemed totally indifferent about getting a ride.
   B. The hitchhiker, leaning against the post, seemed totally indifferent about getting a ride.

   How many hitchhikers are there in sentence A?
   Sentence B?

3. A. The compulsory school law, which has just been passed, strongly insures educational training for all children.
   B. The compulsory school law which has just been passed strongly insures educational training for all children.

Which sentence refers to a place which has never before had a compulsory school law?

4. A. Young drivers, who are not well trained, cause most of our minor automobile accidents.
   B. Young drivers who are not well trained cause most of our minor automobile accidents.

   Which sentence shows a prejudice against young drivers?

5. A. Anthropologists, who respect native ways, are welcome among most tribes.
   B. Anthropologists who respect native ways are welcome among most tribes.

   Which sentence reflects confidence in anthropologists?

▶ Exercise 4
   Insert needed commas for nonrestrictive modifiers; circle all unnecessary commas. Write C to the left of correct sentences.

1. The name Rover was often associated with dogs which were stupid and happy.

2. Barbers, who are bald, are frequently the ones who are most authoritative in discussing baldness with their customers, who are worrying about losing their hair.

3. The wealthy who keep their expensive jewelry in bank vaults sometimes hire people to wear their pearls for them so that the gems will not lose their luster.

4. Vests which were once very popular were out of vogue for several decades.

5. Adam's son Abel was a shepherd.

6. Abel Adam's son was a shepherd.

7. Across the bay lived Alan J. Allen the millionaire, and only three or four hundred yards away was the palatial home of Osgood England the soap king.

8. The brothers of Jacob's son Joseph sold him to some Midianites who in turn sold him into Egypt.

9. Sherwood Anderson's book, *Poor White*, is one of the author's strongest expressions of the recurrent theme, that industrialism has caused human frustrations never felt before.

10. Tom and his wife Daisy traveled over the world, moved from one place to another, and finally settled down in a huge mansion in East Egg which is on Long Island.

20f Use commas with sentence modifiers, conjunctive adverbs, and sentence elements out of normal word order.

Sentence modifiers like *on the other hand, for example, in fact, in the first place, I believe, in his opinion, unfortunately,* and *certainly* are set off by commas.

Only a few poets, unfortunately, make a living by writing.
Wells's early novels, I believe, stand the test of time.

Commas are frequently used with conjunctive adverbs, such as *therefore, moreover, consequently, nevertheless.*

optional

BEFORE CLAUSE
The secretary checked the figures once more; therefore, the mistake
was discovered.

optional

WITHIN CLAUSE
The secretary checked the figures once more; the mistake, therefore,
was discovered.

Commas always separate the conjunctive adverb *however* from the rest of the sentence.

The auditor found the error in the figures; however, the books still
did not balance.
The auditor found the error in the figures; the books, however, still
did not balance.

Commas are not used when *however* is an adverb meaning "no matter how."

However fast the hare ran, he could not catch the tortoise.

Use commas if necessary for clearness or emphasis when part of a sentence is out of normal order.

Aged and infirm, the President governed through loyal ministers.
OR
The President, aged and infirm, governed through loyal ministers.
BUT
The aged and infirm President governed through loyal ministers.

20g Use commas with degrees and titles and with elements in dates, places, and addresses.

DEGREES AND TITLES
William Snipes, M.A., came to the reception.
Charles Morton, Jr., Chairman of the Board, departed.

DATES
Sunday, May 31, is my birthday.
August 1973 was very warm. *or* August, 1973, was very warm. (Either is acceptable.)
December 7, 1941, will never be forgotten. (Use commas *before* and *after*.)
She was born 31 December 1970. (Use no commas.)
The year 1968 was eventful. (Restrictive; use no commas.)

PLACES
Cairo, Illinois, is my home town. (Use commas *before* and *after*.)

ADDRESSES
Write the editor of *The Atlantic*, 8 Arlington Street, Boston, Massachusetts 02116. (Use no comma before the zip code.)

20h Use commas for contrast or emphasis and with short interrogative elements.

The pilot had been forced to use an auxiliary landing field, not the city airport.
The field was safe enough, wasn't it?

20i Use commas with mild interjections and with words like *yes* and *no*.

Well, I did not think it was possible.
No, it proved to be quite simple.

20j Use commas with words in direct address and after the salutation of a personal letter.

Mary, have you seen the portrait?
Dear John,
    It has been some time since I've written. . . .

20k Use commas with expressions like *he said, she remarked,* and *she replied* when used with quoted matter.

"I am planning to give up Latin," she remarked, "at the beginning of next term."
He replied, "It's all Greek to me."

20L Set off an absolute phrase with commas.

An **absolute phrase** consists of a noun followed by a modifier. It modifies the sentence as a whole, not any single element in it.

    ←*absolute phrase*→
Our journey over, we made camp for the night.

    ←——*absolute phrase*——→
The portrait having dried, the artist hung it on the wall.

20m Use commas to prevent misreading or to mark an omission.

After washing and grooming, the pup looked like a new dog.
When violently angry, elephants trumpet.
Beyond, the open fields sloped gently to the sea.

verb omitted

To err is human; to forgive, divine.

▶ Exercise 5

*Add necessary commas. If a sentence is correct as it stands,
write C to the left of it.*

1. Inside the convention hall resembled a huge, overcrowded barn.

2. A few hours before he was scheduled to leave the mercenary visited his father who pleaded with him to change his mind and then finally said quietly "Good luck."

3. Seeing a nightingale the American ornithologist recognized its resemblance to other members of the thrush family.

4. Seeing a nightingale for the first time is disappointing; hearing one for the first time unforgettable.

5. History one would think ought to teach people not to make the same mistakes over again.

6. Despite the old saying to the contrary you can sometimes tell a book by its cover.

7. The Vandyke beard according to authorities was named after Sir Anthony Van Dyck a famous Flemish painter.

8. Only after reading a book either very carefully or more than once should a critic write a review.

9. While burning cedar has a distinct and strong odor.

10. The cloverleaf a road arrangement that looks somewhat like a four-leaf clover permits traffic to flow easily between two intersecting expressways.

▶ Exercise 6
Follow the instructions for Exercise 5.

1. The hippopotamus has a stout body very short legs and a large head and muzzle.

2. Contrary to popular belief the tarantula a large hairy spider is not highly venomous.

3. Before students can understand the principles of quantum physics they must master simple algebra.

4. The ancient urn mysteriously dated 6/00 had stood in the corner of the garden and the honeysuckle vines almost hid it from view.

5. While the mystery writer was working on the first part of his last novel *The Tiger's Eye* he received a note warning him not to write about anyone he knew in the Orient.

6. "Although the prairies are reputed to be flat" Rebecca Haille a professor of geography said "you dwellers in the hills and mountains I tell you that there is indeed much variety in the terrain of the prairies at some places."

7. "Yes" she continued with a little too much of the manner of a dramatic orator "Red Cloud Nebraska is a place of some geographic variety."

8. Having surprised many in her audience the speaker said "People you must develop a feeling for place must refuse to condemn a world about which you are uninformed."

9. Not even the presider of the meeting herself made a single contradictory or disputatious statement.

10. Towers domes and stadiums provided little contrast with the low overhanging clouds.

▶ Exercise 7
Add necessary commas. Write C *to the left if no commas are needed. (The authors wrote these sentences as a series of three paragraphs.)*

1. Sunday morning December 7 1941.

2. Clouds rushed overhead as six big aircraft carriers escorted by a

pair of fast battleships three cruisers and a covey of destroyers slammed through heavy seas at 24 knots.

3. Their course was due south their destination a point in the ocean 275 miles north of Pearl Harbor close enough to launch an air strike on this main base of the U.S. Pacific Fleet. [end of paragraph]

4. Leading the left-hand column of three flattops was the veteran *Akagi* pride of the Imperial Japanese Navy.

5. Behind her was her near-sister *Kaga* followed by the *Hiryu*.

6. Leading the right-hand column was the *Soryu* the smallest of the six at 15900 tons displacement.

7. Behind *Soryu* were the new twins *Shokaku* and *Zuikaku*.

8. This task force comprised all of the first-line attack carriers of the Japanese Navy.

9. Also it was the strongest carrier task force ever assembled.

10. Never before had six flattops embarking more than 400 planes in their air groups sailed on a war mission. [end of paragraph]

11. Commanding the Pearl Harbor attack force called the First Air

Fleet was a gray-haired stoutish veteran seaman Vice Admiral Chuichi Nagumo.

12. Nagumo was not a flyer himself.

13. His only prior aviation experience had been as a light-carrier skipper in 1929.

14. Moreover he disapproved of the Pearl Harbor operation and during the planning stages had opposed it as being too risky.

15. He considered his carriers to be extremely vulnerable ships loaded as they were with an antithetical combination of volatile aviation gas and high-explosive bombs and ammunition.

16. Any enemy hit short of a dud might blow one up.

17. Nevertheless Nagumo had accepted the command of the First Air Fleet and had decided to press home the attack.

18. Rear Admiral Ryunosuke Kusaka his Chief of Staff was confident that the air crews would find eight battleships in Pearl Harbor.

19. That was enough for Nagumo.

20. If his flyers could sink or disable the battle wagons of the U.S. Pacific Fleet he would have scored a success.

ADAPTED FROM JAMES H. BELOTE AND
WILLIAM M. BELOTE, *Titans of the Seas*

▶ Exercise 8

Add necessary commas. Write C to the left if no commas are needed. (The author wrote these sentences as two paragraphs.)

1. The chief deity of the Aegeans was—like that of many Asiatic cults—feminine.

2. She was the *Great Goddess* the Universal Mother in whom were united all the attributes and functions of divinity.

3. Above all she symbolized fertility and her influence extended over plants and animals as well as humans; all the universe was her domain.

4. As celestial goddess she regulated the course of the heavenly bodies and controlled the alternating seasons.

5. On earth she caused the products of the soil to flourish gave men riches protected them in battle and at sea guided them on their adventurous voyages.

6. She killed or tamed fierce beasts; and finally she also reigned over the Underworld. [end of paragraph]

7. The Great Goddess is represented depending on the epoch either crouching or standing.

8. Sometimes she is nude sometimes dressed like a Cretan woman.

9. In the latter case she wears a flounced skirt and her bosom is either entirely bare or covered with a corsage which leaves her breasts exposed.

10. Her head-dress varies: the hair may be free knotted with a simple fillet; it may be covered by a sort of turban decorated with flowers or aigrettes or by a conical tiara in the Oriental manner or again by a very tall tiara in the shape of a topless cone.

ADAPTED FROM FELIX GUIRANDS,
Greek Mythology

21 Unnecessary commas *no* ,
Do not use too many commas.

A comma at every pause within a sentence is not necessary.

21a Do not use a comma between subject and verb, between verb or verbal and complement, or between an adjective or an adverb and the word it modifies.

NOT
The guard with the drooping mustache, snapped to attention.
Some students in the class, admitted, that they had not read,
    "Mending Wall."
The stubborn, mischievous, child refused to respond.

A phrase set off by two commas may be used between subject and verb.

> The malamute, an Alaskan work dog, can survive extraordinarily cold weather.

21b Do not use a comma between two compound elements, such as verbs, subjects, complements, or predicates, except for contrast or emphasis (see 20h).

UNNECESSARY
He *left* the scene of the accident, and *tried* to forget that it had happened.

21c Do not use a comma before a coordinating conjunction joining two dependent clauses, except for contrast or emphasis.

UNNECESSARY
The contractor testified that the house was completed, and that the work had been done properly.

See **20a** for the use of commas to separate independent clauses.

21d Do not use a comma before *than* in a comparison or between compound conjunctions like *as . . . as, so . . . as, so . . . that.*

AVOID
John Holland was more delighted with life on the Continent, than he had thought he could be.

21e Do not use a comma after *like, such as,* and similar expressions.

A comma is used before *such as* only when the phrase is nonrestrictive.

      comma here   not here

Some languages, such as Latin and Anglo-Saxon, are still studied but no longer spoken.

21f Do not use a comma with a period, a question mark, an exclamation point, or a dash. These marks stand by themselves.

AVOID
"Did you get the job?", her roommate asked.

21g A comma may be used after a closing parenthesis, but not before an opening parenthesis.

         no comma here

When he had finished reading *The Pilgrim's Progress* (the most pop-
       comma here
ular allegory in the language), he turned next to *The House of the Seven Gables*.

21h A comma is not required after most introductory adverbial modifiers if they are short and essential or after coordinating conjunctions (see **20d**).

OPTIONAL
After he had slept, he felt more confident.

NOT
Thus, he passed the examination.
But, some people are excessively tolerant.

21i Do not use commas to set off restrictive clauses, phrases, or appositives (see **20e**).

NOT
People, who live in glass houses, should not throw stones.

21j Do not use a comma between adjectives which are not coordinate (see **20c**).

FAULTY
The tired, old, work horse.

▶ Exercise 9
Circle all unnecessary commas, and be prepared to explain your decisions.

1. Soccer is a popular sport in Great Britain, where it is sometimes called, football.

2. The secretary bird is so named, because, on its crest, it has feathers which resemble quill pens.

3. Restaurants, that serve excellent food at modest prices, are always

popular among local people, though tourists seldom know about them.

4. After several long, expensive visits to the dentist, (especially if they are painful), people, who have always taken their teeth for granted, will probably brush more regularly, and more carefully.

5. "My secret of long life?", the old mountaineer responded. "Why I just do not worry about dying, like most people do."

6. Communities, near large airports, have become increasingly aware that noise pollution can be just as unpleasant as impurities in the air, or in streams.

7. The way, of celebrating certain holidays, has changed over the years, but these occasions can still be meaningful.

8. Once, huge movie houses were fashionable, but now these palaces are like dinosaurs, extinct giants, curious reminders, of the past.

9. The Olympic runner was disqualified, after he ran out of his lane, but he would not have won a gold medal, anyway.

10. The gardener vowed that he would never work for the millionaire again, and that he would go back to his small farm.

22 The semicolon ;

Use a semicolon between independent clauses not joined by coordinating conjunctions (*and, but, or, nor, for, so, yet*) and between coordinate elements with internal commas.

Failure to use a semicolon between independent clauses may result in a comma splice or a fused sentence (see 2).

22a Use a semicolon between two independent clauses not connected by a coordinating conjunction.

WITH NO CONNECTIVE
For fifteen years the painting stood in the attic; even Mr. Kirk forgot it. "It needed cleaning, and the frame was cracked," he explained later; "we just stored it away."

WITH A CONJUNCTIVE ADVERB
In 1976 a specialist from the museum arrived and asked to examine it; then all the family became excited.

See **20f** for use of commas with conjunctive adverbs, such as *however, therefore, moreover, then, consequently, nevertheless,* and so on.

WITH A SENTENCE MODIFIER
The painting was valuable; in fact, the museum offered five thousand dollars for it.

See **20f** for use of commas with sentence modifiers, such as *on the other hand, for example, in fact, in the first place,* and so on.

22b Use a semicolon to separate independent clauses which are long and complex or which have internal punctuation.

In many compound sentences either a semicolon or a comma may be used.

COMMA OR SEMICOLON
Moby-Dick, by Melville, is an adventure story, (*or;*) and it is also one of the world's great philosophical novels.

SEMICOLON PREFERRED
Ishmael, the narrator, goes to sea, he says, "whenever it is a damp, drizzly November" in his soul; and Ahab, the captain of the ship, goes to sea because of his obsession to hunt and kill the great albino whale, Moby Dick.

22c Use semicolons in a series between items which have internal punctuation.

The old farmer kept a variety of poultry: chickens, for eggs and Sunday dinners; turkeys, for very special meals; and peacocks, for their beauty.

22d Do not use a semicolon between elements which are not coordinate.

FAULTY   *dependent clause*   *independent clause*
After the tugboat had signaled to the barge twice; it turned toward the wharf.

▶ Exercise 10
Circle unnecessary semicolons and commas, and insert necessary ones. Write C to the left of sentences which are correct.

1. In Greek mythology Proteus was a sea god; one that could change his shape, whenever he wished.

2. The stipulations of the agreement were; that each company would keep its own name that profits would be evenly divided and that, no employees would lose their jobs; because of the merger.

3. An advanced civilization is guided by enlightened self-interest; however, it is also marked by unselfish good will.

4. The sound of the banjo drifted up from the floor below, it blended with the chatter of typewriters; and the droning of business conferences.

5. After a prolonged and severe economic depression; people are hesitant to spend money freely; because they are afraid hard times will recur.

6. The hallway was long, and dark; and at the end of it hung a dim, obscure painting representing a beggar; in eighteenth-century London.

7. The mutineers defeated the loyal members of the crew; took command of the ship; and locked the captain and other officers in the brig.

8. Winning is important, and rewarding; but sportsmanship is more essential in building character.

9. Fortunetelling still appeals to many people even when they realize it is superstitious nonsense; they will continue to patronize charlatans, like palm readers.

10. The making of pottery, once a necessary craft as well as an art, has again become popular, and hundreds of young people, many of them in the country, are discovering the excitement of this form of creativity.

---

23 The colon :

Use a colon as a formal and emphatic mark of introduction.

$23a$ Use a colon before quotations, statements, and series which are introduced formally.

Some of the buildings in the county were unusual: antebellum two-storied homes, built mainly in the 1840's; smaller houses, which had long open hallways; and stores, some of which had two stories with porches.

A colon may be used to introduce a quotation formally when there is no verb of saying:

The warden began the short statement with a sharp reminder: "Gentlemen, you are now almost free; but some of you will not remain free for long."

23b Use a colon between two independent clauses when the second explains or amplifies the first.

> Music is more than something mechanical: it is an expression of deep feeling and ethical values.

23c Use a colon before formal appositives, including those introduced by such expressions as *namely* and *that is*.

> There are three sources of belief: reason, custom, inspiration.
>   BLAISE PASCAL
> One element is missing from some contemporary styles: good taste.

NOTE The colon comes before *namely* and similar expressions, not after.

> After a sleepless night the senator reached his decision: namely, that he would not seek re-election.

23d Use a colon between hours and minutes to indicate time, after the salutation of a formal letter, and between city and publisher in bibliographical entries.

> 12:15 P.M.
> Dear Dr. Tyndale:
> Boston: Houghton, 1929

23e Do not use a colon after a linking verb or a preposition.

FAULTY

Some chief noisemakers are: automobiles, airplanes, and lawn
mowers.

His friend accused him of: wiggling in his seat, talking during the
lecture, and not remembering what was said.

24 The dash —

Use a dash to introduce summaries and to indicate interruptions, informal breaks in construction, parenthetical remarks, and special emphasis.

In typescript a dash is made by two hyphens (--) with no space
before or after.

FOR SUDDEN INTERRUPTIONS

She replied, "I will consider the—No, I won't either."

FOR SPECIAL EMPHASIS

Great authors quote one book more than any other—the Bible.

FOR SUMMARY

Attic fans, window fans, air conditioners—all were ineffective that
summer.

25 Parentheses ( )

Use parentheses to enclose loosely related comment or explanation or to enclose figures which number items in a series.

The oil well (the company had drilled it only as an experiment) produced a thousand barrels a day.

Mary McCauley (1754?–1832) was called Molly Pitcher because she
used a pitcher to carry water to wounded soldiers.

The oil company refused to buy the land because (1) the owner had no
clear title, (2) it was too remote, and (3) it was too expensive.

A parenthetical sentence within another sentence has no period or capital, as in the first example above. A freestanding parenthetical sentence between sentences requires parentheses, a capital, and a period.

26 Brackets *[ ]*

Use brackets to enclose interpolations within quotations.

In the opinion of Arthur Miller, "There is no more reason for falling down in a faint before his [Aristotle's] *Poetics* than before Euclid's geometry."

Sometimes parentheses within parentheses are replaced by brackets ([ ]). Usually it is best to avoid a construction which calls for this intricate punctuation.

27 Quotation marks *" "*

Use quotation marks to enclose the exact words of a speaker or writer and to set off some titles.

Most American writers and publishers use double quotation marks (". . .") except for internal quotations, which are set off by single quotation marks ('. . .').

27a Use quotation marks to enclose direct quotations and dialogue.

DIRECT QUOTATION
At a high point in *King Lear,* the Duke of Gloucester says, "As flies to wanton boys, are we to the gods."

In dialogue a new paragraph marks each change of speaker.

DIALOGUE

"What is fool's gold?" the explorer asked.

"Really," the geologist told him, "it's pyrite, which has the color of gold."

In typescript, indent and single-space quotations which are one hundred words or longer. Do not use quotation marks to enclose these blocked quotations.

Poetry is single-spaced and centered between the left and right margins. The lines should be copied exactly as written.

> If you would keep your soul
> From spotted sight or sound,
> Live like the velvet mole;
> Go burrow underground.

Short quotations of poetry may be written like the regular text, not set off. Used in this way, they are put in quotation marks, and a slash (with a space before and after it) is used between lines.

Elinor Wylie satirically advises, "Live like the velvet mole; / Go burrow underground."

27b Use single quotation marks to enclose a quotation within a quotation.

The review explained: "Elinor Wylie is ironic when she advises, 'Live like the velvet mole.'"

27c Use quotation marks to enclose the titles of essays, articles, short stories, short poems, chapters (and other sub-

divisions of books or periodicals), television programs, paintings, and short musical compositions.

D. H. Lawrence's "The Rocking-Horse Winner" is a story about the
need for love.
Chapter VII of *Walden* is entitled "The Beanfield." (For titles of
books, see **30a**.)
My younger brother likes to watch "Sesame Street."
A cheap reproduction of van Gogh's "Sunflowers" hung on the wall
above the desk.

27d Do not use quotation marks around the title of your
own theme.

27e Do not use quotation marks to emphasize or change
the usual meanings of words or to justify slang, colloqui-
alisms, or attempts at humor.

AVOID
Some of the old politician's opponents were hoping that he would
"kick the bucket" before the next election.
The beggar considered himself a "rich" man.

27f Follow established conventions in placing other
marks of punctuation with quotation marks.

Periods and **commas** are placed *inside* quotation marks in
American usage.

All the students had read "Lycidas."
"Amazing," the professor said.

Semicolons and **colons** are always placed *outside* closing quotation marks.

> The customer wrote that she was "not yet ready to buy the first edition"; it was too expensive.

A **question mark** or an **exclamation point** is placed *inside* quotation marks only when the quotation itself is a direct question or an exclamation. Otherwise, these marks are placed *outside*.

> He asked, "Who is she?" (Only the quotation is a question.)
> "Who is she?" he asked. (Only the quotation is a question.)
> Did he ask, "Who is she?" (The quotation and the entire sentence are questions.)
> Did he say, "I know her"? (The entire sentence asks a question; the quotation makes a statement.)
> She screamed, "Run!" (Only the quotation is an exclamation.)
> Curse the man who whispers, "No"! (The entire statement is an exclamation; the quotation is not.)

After quotations, never use a comma and an exclamation point or a question mark together.

NOT
"When?", I asked.

NOT
"Help!", I cried.
BUT
"Help!" I cried.

28   End punctuation   . ?/

End a declarative sentence with a period, an interrogative sentence with a question mark, and an exclamatory sentence with an exclamation point.

These marks of punctuation also have special uses within a sentence.

28a Use a period after a sentence which makes a statement or expresses a command.

Some modern people claim to practice witchcraft.
Water the flowers.
The gardener asked whether the plant should be taken indoors in
winter. (This sentence is a statement even though it expresses
an indirect question.)

28b Use periods after most abbreviations.

Periods follow such abbreviations as Mr., Dr., Pvt., Ave., B.C., A.M., Ph.D., e.g., ibid., and many others. In British usage periods are often omitted after titles (Mr).

Abbreviations of governmental and international agencies often are written without periods (FCC, TVA, UNESCO, NATO, HEW, and so forth). Usage varies. When in doubt, consult your dictionary.

A comma or another mark of punctuation may follow the period after an abbreviation, but at the end of a sentence only one period is used.

After she earned her M.A., she began studying for her Ph.D.

But if the sentence is a question or an exclamation, the end punctuation mark follows the period after the abbreviation.

When does she expect to get her Ph.D.?

28c Use three spaced periods (ellipsis dots) to show an omission in a quotation.

Notice how the source below is shortened with ellipsis marks in the quotation that follows it.

SOURCE
"He [the Indian] had no written record other than pictographs, and his conqueror was not usually interested, at the time, in writing down his thoughts and feelings for him. The stoic calm of his few reported speeches and poems gives only a hint of the rich culture that was so soon forgotten."

ROBERT E. SPILLER

QUOTATION WITH ELLIPSIS

ellipsis not necessary at   *one period to end sentence*
beginning of quotation   *and three for ellipsis*
The Indian had no written record other than pictographs. . . . The
    stoic calm of his . . . speeches and poems gives only a hint of
spaces and three periods for ellipsis
    the rich culture. . . ."
four at end of sentence

28d The title of a theme, a book, or a periodical has no period, but some titles may include a question mark or an exclamation point.

The Sound and the Fury   "What Are Years?"
Westward Ho!   *Ah*! *Wilderness*

28e Use a question mark after a direct question.

Do teachers file attendance reports?
Teachers do file attendance reports? (a question in the form of a declarative sentence)

Question marks may follow separate questions within a single interrogative sentence.

Do you recall the time of the accident? the license numbers of the cars involved? the names of the drivers?

28f Use a question mark within parentheses to show that a date or a figure is doubtful.

Pythagoras, who died in 497 B.C. (?), was a mathematician.

NOTE Do not use a question mark or an exclamation point within a sentence to indicate humor or sarcasm.

NOT
The comedy (?) was a miserable failure.

28g Use an exclamation point after a word, a phrase, or a sentence to signal strong exclamatory feeling.

Wait! I forgot my lunch!
Stop the bus!
What a ridiculous idea!

Use exclamation points sparingly. After mild exclamations, use commas or periods.

NOT
Well! I was discouraged!
BUT
Well, I was discouraged.

▶ Exercise 11
Supply quotation marks as needed in the following passage, and indicate new paragraphs when necessary by inserting the sign ¶.

Alex Tilman, young, vigorous, and alert, walked briskly beside the little stream. As he neared the pond, which the diligent beavers had made generations before, he thought of Thoreau's essay Walking and the sense of calm that pervaded nature. An old man was fishing with a pole on the bank of the pond. Knowing that fishermen dislike noisemakers, Alex strolled quietly up to the old man and said, How's your luck today? Oh, about like every other day, except a little worse, maybe. Do you mean you haven't caught anything? Well, I did catch a couple of bream. But they're small, you know. Before I left home my wife said to me, If you don't catch any sizable fish today, you might as well give it up. And I'm beginning to wonder if she hasn't got something there. Alex watched the water for a little while, now and then stealing a glance at the unshaved fisherman, who wore baggy breeches, a faded old flannel shirt, and a slouchy hat. Then he dreamily said, Well, I guess most people don't really fish just for the sake of catching something. The old gentleman looked up at him a little surprised. His eyes were much brighter and quicker than Alex had expected. That's right, he said, but, you know, that's not the kind of wisdom you hear these days from young folks. You new around here, son? Yes. My wife and I just bought the old Edgewright place. Oh! Well, maybe you can come fishing with me sometime. I'm usually around about this time during the day. Alex was not eager to accept an invitation from a creature quite so shabby as this one, but he was moved by a sudden sympathy. Yes. Maybe. Say, if you need any work, I might be able to find something for you to do around our place. My wife and I are trying to get things cleaned up. A slight smile came over the old fellow's face, and he said warmly, Much obliged, but I've got more work now than I know what to do with. So I come out here and hum Lazy Bones and fish. On the way back to his house, Alex asked a neighbor who that old tramp was fishing down by the pond. Tramp! his friend repeated. Good heavens, man, that was no tramp. That was Angus Morgan, one of the wealthiest men in the country.

▶ Exercise 12
Add quotation marks where needed; circle unnecessary ones.
Also make all necessary changes in punctuation. Where new
paragraphs are needed insert the sign ¶.

1. "Failure is often necessary for humanity", Professor Xavier said.

   Without failure, he continued, how can we retain our humility and

   know the full sweetness of success? For, as Emily Dickinson said,

   Success is counted sweetest / By those who ne'er succeed.

2. Madam, said the talent scout, I know that you think your daughter

   can sing, but, believe me, her voice makes the strangest sounds I

   have ever heard. Mrs. Audubon took her daughter "Birdie" by the

   hand and haughtily left the room wondering "how she could ever

   have been so stupid as to expose her daughter to such a 'common'

   person."

3. Your assignment for tomorrow, said Mrs. Osborn, is to read the fol-

   lowing (to use Poe's own term) tales of ratiocination: The Purloined

   Letter, The Murders in the Rue Morgue, and The Mystery of Marie

   Roget. When you have finished these stories you might read ahead

   into the next assignment.

4. The boy and his great-uncle were "real" friends, and the youngster

listened intently when the old man spoke. Son, he would say, I remember my father's words: You can't do better than to follow the advice of Ben Franklin, who said, One To-day is worth two To-morrows.

5. The expression population explosion suggests the extreme rapidity with which the world's "population" is increasing.

6. A recent report states the following: The marked increase in common stocks indicated a new sense of national security; however, the report seems to imply "that this is only one of many gauges of the country's economic situation."

7. Chapter IV, The National Mind, develops one of the most optimistic views of the country's future to be found in "modern" studies of economics.

8. One of Mark Twain's most famous letters, addressed to "Andrew Carnegie," reads as follows:

"You seem to be in prosperity. Could you lend an admirer $1.50 to buy a hymn-book with? God will bless you. I feel it; I know it. So will I."

"N.B.—If there should be other applications, this one not to count".

9. In a "postscript," Mark Twain added, Don't send the hymn-book; send the money; I want to make the selection myself. He signed the letter simply Mark.

10. The conversation between Aunt Hattie and the door-to-door salesman went something like this. Madam, you have been very highly recommended to us. As an advertising venture, will you allow us to put a set of these books in your home? No. But I don't think you understand. No. What I mean is, there is no charge at all for—No. For the books themselves. No! Good-day, young man. Slam!

Mechanics

29 Manuscript and letter form *ms*

Follow correct manuscript form in your papers and business letters.

Themes Use white paper 8½ by 11 inches for typescript, ruled paper for longhand. Do not use onionskin. Use blue or black ink. When typing, double-space. In longhand skip every other line. Write or type on one side of the paper only. Center the title and leave extra space between title and text.

Leave ample and regular margins at the top and bottom of the page, and leave at least an inch on each side. Indent the first line of each paragraph uniformly—about one inch in longhand and five spaces in typescript.

Number all pages except the first with an Arabic numeral in the upper right corner (2, *not* II). On the first page the number should be omitted or centered at the bottom of the page.

Example of Correct Manuscript Form

Up through the last century only the well-to-do could afford

the luxury of travel; therefore, traveling took on a kind of snob

appeal. If people were financially able to take trips abroad or

even long journeys to other parts of their own country, they usu-

ally did so because all the best families were doing it. Travel

became a sign of affluence and culture. Wealthy young people

took what used to be called the "grand tour"--an extended trip

over the European continent--in order to complete their educa-

tion. A mark of the lower classes and the uneducated was lack of

travel experience.

As the cost of traveling came within the financial range of

more and more people, they began to overrun the favorite tourist

cities of Europe. Americans seemed almost frantic to see as much

of another part of the world as possible in a short period of

time. The name of a modern motion picture satirically expressed

this frenzied activity of Americans traveling on tight schedules:

If It's Tuesday, This Must Be Belgium. So inexpensive did tour-

ing become that a book called Europe on Five Dollars a Day became

a guide for countless travelers on limited budgets. Youths on

motorcycles and even on bicycles began to turn up in foreign

cities with empty pockets and with sleeping bags, eager to see

the great places of history.

A Business Letter and Envelope

```
                              Box 1122  ←————————— Address of writer
                              Cedar Falls, Iowa  50613
                              March 1, 1977 ←——————————————— Date



                    _____  Name and title of addressee,
                    ↓                          6 spaces below date
Mr. James Costello, Principal
Elm Street Elementary School ⌐
1315 Elm Street              | ←————————————————— Full address
Centerville, Kansas  66014   ⌐

Dear Mr. Costello: ←——————┌————— Salutation: Use name when possible
←————————————————————————————————————————— Blank line
┌——→ In June I shall graduate from the University of
|  Northern Iowa with a Bachelor of Science degree in
|  elementary education.  I am particularly interested
|  in teaching the fifth grade.
|_____ Indentation possible
    ↓  If you will have an opening for a teacher of my  but not necessary
   qualifications in September, I wish to file an
   application.
←————————————————————————————————————————— Blank line
                    Sincerely yours, ←————— Complimentary close

Signature, handwritten → Mary L. Jones

                    Mary L. Jones ←——— Name, typed
                                        Optional for married women:
                                        Mary L. Jones
                                        (Mrs. Arthur B. Jones)
                                        or
                                        (Mrs.) Mary L. Jones
```

Before submitting any paper, read over the final draft two or three times, at least once aloud for sound. (For methods of revising, see page xvii.) If possible, allow some time between readings. Watch especially for misspellings, typographical errors, faulty punctuation, and omissions made in revising or copying.

Revising papers after they have been read and marked by your instructor is often required and always helpful.

```
Mary L. Jones
Box 1122
Cedar Falls, IA  50613




                    Mr. James Costello, Principal
                    Elm Street Elementary School
                    1315 Elm Street
                    Centerville, KS  66014



```

Business letters In writing a business letter follow the conventional form. All essential parts are included in the example on page 122. The letter should be typewritten if possible, single-spaced, with double-spacing (one blank line) between paragraphs. Paragraphs may be indented or may begin at the left margin without indentation.

Business letters are usually written on stationery 8½ by 11 inches. Fold horizontally into thirds to fit a standard-sized business envelope. For smaller envelopes fold once horizontally and twice the other way.

It is wise to determine the title and the name of the addressee, but sometimes a letter must be addressed to an organization rather than to a particular person. If an unknown recipient turns out to be a woman, she may be slightly annoyed by *Gentlemen* or *Dear Sir*. These traditional salutations may be omitted if the addressee is unknown.

30 Underlining for italics *ital*

Underline to represent italics in titles of independent publications (books, magazines, newspapers) and occasionally for emphasis.

Italic type slants (*like this*). Underline words individually (like this), or underline both words and spaces (like this).

30a Underline titles of books (except the Bible and its divisions), periodicals, newspapers, motion pictures, musical compositions, plays, and other works published separately.

Be precise: watch initial articles (*A*, *An*, *The*) and any punctuation.

BOOKS
Adventures of Huckleberry Finn (*not* The Adventures . . .)
An American Tragedy (*not* The American Tragedy)

PERIODICALS
The Atlantic Monthly and the American Quarterly

NEWSPAPERS
New York Times

MOTION PICTURES
Citizen Kane

MUSICAL COMPOSITIONS
Bizet's Carmen
Beethoven's Mount of Olives

PLAYS
The Cherry Orchard

30b Underline names of ships and trains.

the Queen Elizabeth II   the U.S.S. Hornet   the Zephyr

30c Underline foreign words used in an English context, except words which have become part of our language.

Consult a dictionary to determine whether a word is still considered foreign or has become Anglicized.

Fried grasshoppers were the pièce de résistance of the meal.

BUT

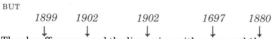

The chauffeur garaged the limousine with verve and élan. (The dates
show when these words [all from French] came into English,
according to the *Oxford English Dictionary*. Long accepted,
they are not italicized or underlined.)

30d Underline words, letters, and figures referred to as such.

The word puppy usually has delightful connotations.
Don't forget to dot your i's.

NOTE Occasionally quotation marks are used instead of underlining.

30e Avoid excessive underlining for emphasis.

Weak writing is seldom improved by mechanical tricks. Do not sprinkle a page with underlinings, dashes, or exclamation points.

30f Do not underline the title of your own theme.

31 Spelling *sp*

Spell correctly; use a dictionary to look up words you are unsure of.

Spelling is troublesome in English because many words are not spelled as they sound (*laughter, slaughter*); because some distinct pairs and triplets sound the same (*capital, capitol; there, they're, their; to, too, two*); and because many words are pronounced with the vowel sound "uh," which gives no clue to spelling (*sensible, capable, defiant*).

Many misspellings are due to the omission of syllables in habitual mispronunciations (*accident-ly* for *acciden-tal-ly*); the addition of syllables (*disas-ter-ous* for *disas-trous*); or the changing of syllables (*prespiration* for *perspiration*).

There are no infallible guides to spelling in English, but the following are helpful.

ie or *ei*?

Use *i* before *e*
Except after *c*
Or when sounded as *a*
As in *neighbor* and *weigh*.

WORDS WITH IE
believe, chief, field, grief, piece

WORDS WITH EI AFTER C
receive, receipt, ceiling, deceit, conceive

WORDS WITH EI SOUNDED AS A
freight, vein, reign

EXCEPTIONS TO MEMORIZE
either, neither, leisure, seize, weird, height

Drop final silent *e*?

DROP		KEEP	
When suffix begins with		*When suffix begins with*	
a vowel		*a consonant*	
curse	cursing	live	lively
come	coming	nine	ninety
pursue	pursuing	hope	hopeful
arrange	arranging	love	loveless
dine	dining	arrange	arrangement

TYPICAL EXCEPTIONS	TYPICAL EXCEPTIONS
courageous	awful
noticeable	ninth
dyeing (compare *dying*)	truly
singeing (compare *singing*)	argument

Change *y* to *i*?

CHANGE		DO NOT CHANGE	
When y *is preceded by*		*When* y *is preceded by*	
a consonant		*a vowel*	
gully	gullies	valley	valleys
try	tried	attorney	attorneys
fly	flies	convey	conveyed
apply	applied	pay	pays
party	parties	deploy	deploying

		When adding -ing	
		try	trying
		fly	flying
		apply	applying

Double final consonant?

If the suffix begins with a consonant, do not double the final consonant of the base word (*man, manly*).

If the suffix begins with a vowel:

DOUBLE
When final consonant is preceded by single vowel

Monosyllables

pen	penned
blot	blotted
hop	hopper
sit	sitting

Polysyllables accented on last syllable

defér	deferring
begín	beginning
omít	omitting
occúr	occurring

DO NOT DOUBLE
When final consonant is preceded by two vowels

| despair | despairing |
| leer | leering |

Words ending with two or more consonants preceded by single vowel

| jump | jumping |
| work | working |

Polysyllables not accented on last syllable after addition of suffix

defér	déference
prefér	préference
devélop	devéloping
lábor	lábored

Add *s* or *es*?

ADD S
For plurals of most nouns

| girl | girl s |
| book | book s |

For nouns ending in o *preceded by a vowel*

| radio | radios |
| cameo | cameos |

ADD ES
When the plural has an extra syllable

| church | church es |
| fox | fox es |

Usually for nouns ending in o *preceded by a consonant (consult your dictionary)*

potato es
Negro es

BUT
flamingos *or* flamingoes

NOTE The plurals of proper names are generally formed by adding *s* or *es* (*Darby*, the *Darbys*; *Jones*, the *Joneses*).

Words frequently misspelled

Following is a list of over two hundred of the most commonly misspelled words in the English language.

absence	business	discipline
accidentally	calendar	dissatisfied
accommodate	candidate	dormitory
accumulate	category	eighth
acquaintance	cemetery	eligible
acquitted	changeable	eliminate
advice	changing	eminent
advise	choose	encouraging
amateur	chose	environment
among	commission	equipped
analysis	committee	especially
analyze	comparative	exaggerate
annual	coming	excellence
apartment	compelled	exhilarate
apparatus	conceivable	existence
apparent	conferred	experience
appearance	conscience	explanation
arctic	conscientious	familiar
argument	control	fascinate
arithmetic	criticize	February
ascend	deferred	fiery
athletic	definite	foreign
attendance	description	formerly
balance	desperate	forty
beginning	dictionary	fourth
believe	dining	frantically
benefited	disappearance	generally
boundaries	disappoint	government
Britain	disastrous	grammar

grandeur
grievous
height
heroes
hindrance
hoping
humorous
hypocrisy
immediately
incidentally
incredible
independence
inevitable
intellectual
intelligence
interesting
irresistible
knowledge
laboratory
laid
led
lightning
maintenance
maneuver
manufacture
mathematics
may
maybe
miniature
mischievous
mysterious
necessary
Negroes
ninety
noticeable

occasionally
occurred
omitted
opportunity
optimistic
parallel
paralyze
pastime
performance
permissible
perseverance
personnel
perspiration
physical
picnicking
possibility
practically
precede
precedence
preference
preferred
prejudice
preparation
prevalent
privilege
professor
pronunciation
prophecy
prophesy
probably
quantity
quiet
quite
quizzes
recede

receive
recognize
recommend
reference
referred
repetition
restaurant
rhythm
ridiculous
sacrifice
salary
schedule
secretary
seize
separate
sergeant
severely
shining
siege
similar
sophomore
specifically
specimen
stationary
stationery
statue
succeed
successful
supersede
surprise
studying
temperamental
tendency
their
thorough

to	unanimous	villain
too	undoubtedly	weather
tragedy	until	weird
tries	usually	whether
truly	village	writing
tyranny		

▶ Exercise 1

According to a recent newspaper article, the twenty most misspelled words, as listed in the American Heritage Dictionary, *are as follows. Choose the correct spelling of each.*

1. battalion, battallion
2. coolly, cooly
3. desiccate, desicate
4. disservice, diservice
5. disippate, dissipate
6. embarrass, embarass
7. Filipino, Fillippino
8. friccasee, fricassee
9. harrass, harass
10. hypocrisy, hypocricy
11. inoculate, innoculate
12. knicknack, knickknack
13. loneliness, lonliness
14. liquify, liquefy
15. mayonaise, mayonnaise
16. medallion, medalion
17. moccasin, mocasin
18. parrafin, paraffin
19. sacriligious, sacrilegious
20. supercede, supersede

32 Hyphenation and syllabication –

Use a hyphen in certain compound words and in words divided at the end of a line.

32a Consult a dictionary to determine whether a compound is hyphenated or written as one or two words.

HYPHENATED	ONE WORD	TWO WORDS
one-way	droplight	drop leaf (noun)
white-hot	whitewash	white heat
water-cool	watermelon	water system

32b Hyphenate a compound of two or more words used as a single modifier before a noun.

HYPHEN	NO HYPHEN AFTER NOUN
She is a *well-known* executive	The executive is *well known*.

A hyphen is not used when the first word of such a group is an adverb ending in -*ly*.

HYPHEN	NO HYPHEN
a *half-finished* task	a *partly finished* task

32c Hyphenate spelled-out compound numbers from *twenty-one* through *ninety-nine*.

32d Follow accepted syllabication in hyphenating a word at the end of a line.

When in doubt, consult a dictionary. Hyphenate only between syllables, and place the hyphen only at the end of the first line, not at the beginning of the next.

Do not divide monosyllables even if they are long (*thought, strength, cheese*), and do not set off a single letter (*a-bout, might-y*). Prefixes and suffixes may be set off, though it is preferable not to carry over a two-letter suffix (*straight-ened,* not *straighten-ed*). Compounds normally written with a hyphen (*self-satisfied*) should not be divided elsewhere at the end of a line (not *self-satis-fied*).

33 The apostrophe '

Use the apostrophe to form the possessive case of many nouns, to form contractions, to show omissions, and to indicate some plurals.

Use 's to form the possessive of nouns not ending in s.

SINGULAR
child's, man's, deer's, lady's, mother-in-law's
PLURAL
children's, men's

Use 's or ' without s to form the possessive of singular nouns ending in s.

Charles's, Watts's, Dickens's, waitress's, actress's

NOTE When 's added to a singular noun ending in s causes a difficulty in pronunciation, add only the apostrophe.

the actress' success, Dickens' stories

Use ' without s to form the possessive of plural nouns ending in s.

the Joneses' car, the Dickenses' home, waitresses' tips

Use 's to form the possessive of indefinite pronouns.

anybody's, everyone's, somebody else's, neither's

NOTE Use no apostrophe with personal pronouns like *his, hers, theirs, ours, its* (meaning "of it"). *It's* means "it is."

Use 's with only the last noun for joint possession in a pair or a series.

Marge and Jack's bicycle (The two jointly own one bicycle.)
Marge's and Jack's bicycles (Each owns a bicycle.)

Use ' to show omissions or to form contractions.

the roaring '20's, o'clock, jack-o'-lantern
we'll, don't, can't, it's (meaning "it is")

Use 's to form the plural of numerals, letters, and words referred to as words.

three 7's (but *three sevens*), four *a*'s, six *the*'s

---

34   Capital letters   *cap*

Use a capital letter to begin a sentence and to designate a
proper noun—the name of a particular person, place, or thing.

Capitalize the first word of a sentence, the pronoun *I*, and the
interjection *O*.

How, **O** ye gods, can **I** bear this misfortune?

Capitalize first, last, and important words in titles, including
the second part of hyphenated words.

Across the River and into the Trees
"The Man Against the Sky"
"After Apple-Picking"

NOTE Articles (*a, an, the*), short prepositions, and conjunctions are not capitalized unless they begin or end a title.
Capitalize first words of direct quotations and words capitalized by the author.

Carlyle said, "Meanwhile, we will hate Anarchy as Death, which it
is. . . ."

Capitalize titles preceding a name.

President Truman

Capitalize titles of high rank.

The President is not expected to veto the measure.

Capitalize titles used specifically as substitutes for particular names.

Lieutenant Yo pleaded not guilty; the Lieutenant was found innocent.

NOTE A title not followed by a name is usually not capitalized.

The stockholders sat down, and the president called for order.

Titles which are common nouns that name an office are not capitalized.

A college president has more duties than privileges.
A lieutenant deserves a good living allowance.

Capitalize degrees and titles after a name.

Jeffrey E. Tyndale, Sr., Ph.D., J.D.
Abraham Lincoln, Attorney at Law

NOTE Do not capitalize names of occupations used as appositives or as descriptions.

Abraham Lincoln, a young lawyer from Springfield, took the case.

Capitalize words of family relationship used as names when not preceded by a possessive pronoun.

After Father died, Mother carried on the business.
BUT
After my father died, my mother carried on the business.

Capitalize proper nouns and their derivatives.

	BUT
Plato, Platonic, Platonism	pasteurize
Venice, Venetian blind	a set of china
the West, a Westerner	west of the river
the Republican Party	a republican government
the Senior Class of Ivy College	a member of the senior class
Clifton Street	my street
the Mississippi River	the Mississippi and Ohio rivers

Capitalize months, days of the week, and holidays.

April, Friday, the Fourth of July, Labor Day

NOTE Do not capitalize seasons and numbered days of the month unless they name holidays.

spring, the third of July

Capitalize movements, periods, and events in history.

the Romantic Movement
the Civil War

NOTE Do not capitalize the name of a century as such.

the twentieth century

Capitalize B.C., A.D., words designating the Deity, religious denominations, and sacred books.

in 273 B.C.
the Messiah, our Maker, the Trinity, Yahweh, Allah, Buddha, Jesus

"Praise God from Whom all blessings flow."
Catholic, Protestant, Presbyterian
the Bible, the Koran

NOTE Pronouns referring to the Deity are usually capitalized.

From Him all blessings flow.

Capitalize names of specific courses.

I registered for Sociology 101 and Chemistry 445.

NOTE Do not capitalize studies (other than languages) which do not name specific courses.

I am taking English, sociology, and chemistry.

---

35 Abbreviations *ab*
Avoid most abbreviations in formal writing.

Abbreviations are short cuts. A few are accepted in all kinds of writing; most are not. The following are acceptable in any context.
Use abbreviations before names.

Mr., Mrs., Ms., Messrs., Mmes., Dr., St. *or* Ste. (for *Saint,* not *Street*), Mt., Rev. (but only with a first name: *the Rev. Ernest Jones,* not *Rev. Jones*)

Use abbreviations after names.

M.D. (and other degrees), Jr., Sr., Esq.

Use abbreviations in footnotes and bibliographies. See **48.**

Use abbreviations without periods for many agencies and organizations.

TVA, NAACP, FBI

Use abbreviations with dates and time.

B.C. and A.D. (with dates expressed in numerals, as *500 B.C.*)
A.M. and P.M. or a.m. and p.m. (with hours expressed in numerals, as *4:00 A.M.*)

Spell out names of days, months, units of measurement, and (except in addresses) states and countries.

/ Friday (*not* Fri.)
February (*not* Feb.)
pounds (*not* lbs.)
Sauk Centre, Minnesota (*not* Minn.)

EXCEPTION Washington, D.C.

---

36 Numbers *num*

Spell out numbers that can be written in one or two words.

twenty-three, one thousand

Use figures for other numbers.

123    $1^{13}/_{16}$ $1,001.00

NOTE Newspapers and government publications generally use figures for numbers above ten.

EXCEPTIONS
Never use figures at the beginning of a sentence. Spell out the number or recast the sentence.

Use numerals for figures in a series and for tabulations and statistics.

One polar bear weighed 200 pounds; another, 526; the third, 534.

Use figures for dates, street numbers, page references, percentages, and hours of the day used with A.M. or P.M.

USE FIGURES	SPELL OUT
July 3, 1776 (*not* 3rd)	the third of July
1010 State Street	Fifth Avenue
See page 50.	The book has fifty pages.
He paid 8 per cent interest.	
The concert begins at 6 P.M.	The concert begins at
(or 6:00 P.M.)	six o'clock.

Diction and Style

Use Standard English except on special occasions, and consult your dictionary on questions of usage. Use a style appropriate to your subject.

The language in generally accepted use in the English-speaking countries is known as **Standard English.** It may be characterized as the language of educated persons. Though it varies in some details from one country to another, as is indicated by such labels as *U.S.* or *Brit.* in dictionaries, it is the common language of the great majority of those who communicate in English, and that is why it is taught in schools and colleges. **Nonstandard,** correspondingly, refers to usages, spellings, or pronunciations not usually found in the speech or writing of educated persons.

Diction is the choice and use of words. Consult your dictionary for definitions of the status or usage labels it employs (for example, *Slang, Dialect, Vulgar, Poetic, Informal, Obsolete,* and so on). **Colloquial** or informal language, which is appropriate in certain situations (though usually not in college themes), does not include regional language or dialect. The best sources of information are dictionaries which record usage both current and past. The question is "What is appropriate?" rather than "What is correct?" A dictionary is not prescriptive; it does not tell you what is "right." Rather, it describes usage; it tells who uses what and lets you make your own choices. In minor matters dictionaries do not always agree. In current dictionaries, for example, you will find disagreement about *cooperate, co-operate,* and *coöperate.*

Particularly useful at the college level are the following desk dictionaries:

The American Heritage Dictionary of the English Language, New College Edition. Boston: Houghton Mifflin Company.
The Random House College Dictionary. New York: Random House.
Webster's New Collegiate Dictionary. Springfield, Mass.: G. & C. Merriam Company.
Webster's New World Dictionary of the American Language. Cleveland: Collins-World Publishing Company.

Style is manner of writing, the way writers express their thoughts in language. Effective writing always involves the choice of words and expressions, the arrangement of words in sentences, and variety in the patterns of sentences. Sentences which express similar ideas may have vastly different effects, and much of the difference is a matter of style. Writing may be whimsical, poetic, terse, flippant, imaginative, literal, and so on. Develop the habit of noticing the style and tone of what you read and what you write. Your style should be appropriate to your subject and to your own personality.

37a Use slang only when nothing else will serve as well.

Slang is a colorful nonstandard language usually invented by special groups. The main objection to slang is that it is too often an easy, popular rubber stamp which only approximates exact thought. A person who said "He's a jerk" would not communicate much. What precisely does this mean, except that he is in some vague and unspecified way unattractive?

Another objection to slang in student papers is that it may turn out to be unintentionally funny. Slang expressions are particularly out of place in a context that is otherwise more dignified.

> The violin virtuoso's performance on the cello was a *real bomb*.
> When Macbeth recoiled at the thought of murder, Lady Macbeth urged him not to *chicken out*.

Slang which is vivid and useful sometimes becomes standard. "Skyscraper," "bus," and "mob" were once slang; and because no other word was found to convey quite the same meanings as "date," it is no longer slang.

37b Avoid illiteracies and (except for special purposes) dialect.

Illiteracies, which are found in the language of uneducated people, should be avoided in speech and writing.

NOT
She *ain't* ready yet. Would you care to *set* awhile?

Words and usages peculiar to one section of the country are **dialect,** which should be avoided except to give the flavor of local speech. Similarly, the speech and linguistic patterns of a particular social group, especially an ethnic minority, are often termed dialect.

There is no reason to erase all dialectal characteristics from your language. They are a cultural heritage and a continuing source of richness, flavor, and variety. But in general communication it is wise to avoid expressions which are not widely understood or which reflect ignorance of standard usage.

37c Avoid archaic words.

Archaisms, out-of-date words, are seldom appropriate in modern speech or writing. *Oft, yon,* and *holp* (past tense of *help*) are examples.

▶ Exercise 1
Using your own judgment, point out and label any slang words and expressions, illiteracies, dialectal words, and archaisms in the following sentences.

1. Overdue books always gross out librarians.

2. What cooked his goose was a clue that the police discovered in his apartment.

3. She was instructed to tote the taters back to the produce department and to follow the manager to his office.

4. The suit in the window was the best set of threads in the store, but it wasn't no use trying to buy it because the price was too high.

5. Methinks times have changed considerable since I set there as a student.

6. Pipe smoking just ain't as popular as it used to be, but some devoted pipe freaks are still around.

7. The award went to a little-known actress who played good the part of a raving beauty who married a deformed dwarf.

8. I reckon the plane will arrive betimes, provided of course that the runways are not congested.

9. He couldn't do nothing without the supervisor giving him the eyeball and coming down on him.

10. Before the rain ceased, the group of tourists were besprinkled, but their enthusiasm was not dampened.

37d Avoid improprieties. Use words in their correct functions and meanings.

A **functional impropriety** is the use of a word as the wrong part of speech. Many nouns, for example, may not also serve as adjectives or verbs. Thus it is not Standard English to write *orchestra selection* for *selection by the orchestra* or *orchestral selection*. *Cliché* is a noun; *clichéd* would be an impropriety.

The following list contains examples of the most common kinds of improprieties.

IMPROPRIETIES	PROPER FORMS
psychology approach	*psychological* approach
(noun for adjective)	
suspicioned	*suspected*
(noun made into verb)	

IMPROPRIETIES	PROPER FORMS
an *invite*	an *invitation*
(verb for noun)	
good *eats*	good *eating,* good *food*
(verb for noun)	
stagnate waters	*stagnant* waters
(verb for adjective)	
surprising great number	*surprisingly* great number
(adjective for adverb)	

The wrong meaning for a word can also be an impropriety. See **37h.**

37e   Use correct idioms.

An **idiom** is a proper language habit, the right way to join together a group of associated words. Separated, the words do not suggest the meaning of the idiom. (Such expressions as *run for office* or *down and out* cannot be understood literally.) A wrong word in an idiomatic expression causes an error in meaning or awkwardness. Many English idioms are verb phrases, for example, *put out, put out about* (or *by*), *put up, put in, put down. Differ from* means "to be unlike"; *differ with* means "to disagree with." Many common errors in English idiom occur in the use of prepositions after verbs. A good dictionary lists idiomatic uses of all kinds; consult one if you are in doubt whether a phrase is idiomatic.

Study the following list of common idioms.

UNIDIOMATIC	IDIOMATIC
according with	according to
capable to	capable of
conform in	conform to (*or* with)
die from	die of
ever now and then	every now and then
excepting for	except for
identical to	identical with
in accordance to	in accordance with

UNIDIOMATIC	IDIOMATIC
incapable to do	incapable of doing
in search for	in search of
intend on doing	intend to do
in the year of 1976	in the year 1976
off of	off
on a whole	on the whole
plan on	plan to
prior than	prior to
similar with	similar to
superior than	superior to
try and see	try to see
type of a	type of

▶ Exercise 2
Mark the improprieties or the incorrect idioms in each of the following groups.

1. her advise and consent, her advice and consent
2. accede to, with, for, about
3. preposition phrase, prepositional phrase
4. inferior of, from, about, to
5. the statue on the square, the statute on the square, the stature on the square
6. abide with, by, for
7. agree to, on, with, for
8. food, the eats, victuals
9. oblivious of, to, about
10. society problems, social problems, societal problems.

37f Avoid specialized vocabulary in writing for the general reader.

All specialists from cook to engineer to philosopher have their own vocabularies. Some technical words find their way into general use; most do not. We know the plastic *lucite,* but not its chemical name, the acrylic resin *polymethyl methacrylate.*

Trouble comes when specialists either cannot or do not see the need to express their ideas in language for the general reader. The following passage, for instance, would not be addressed to a general group or a wide audience.

> The neonate's environment consists in primitively contrasted perceptual fields weak and strong: loud noises, bright lights, smooth surfaces, compared with silence, darkness and roughness. The behavior of the neonate has to be accounted for chiefly by inherited motor connections between receptors and effectors. There is at this stage, in addition to the autonomic nervous system, only the sensorimotor system to call on. And so the ability of the infant to discriminate is exceedingly low. But by receiving and sorting random data through the identification of recurrent regularity, he does begin to improve reception. Hence he can surrender the more easily to single motivations, ego-involvement in satisfactions.
>
> JAMES K. FEIBLEMAN, *The Stages of*
> *Human Life: A Biography of Entire Man*

Contrast the foregoing passage with the following, which is on the same general subject of the infant but which is written so that the general reader—not just a specialized few—can understand it.

> Research clearly indicates that an infant's senses are functional at birth. He experiences the whack from the doctor. He is sensitive to pressure, to changes in temperature, and to pain, and he responds specifically to these stimuli. . . . How about sight? Research on infants 4–8 weeks of age shows that they can see about as well as adults. . . . The difference is that the infant cannot make sense out of what he sees. Nevertheless, what he sees does register, and he begins to take in visual information at birth. . . . In summary, the neonate (an infant less than a month old) is sensitive not only to internal but also to external stimuli. Although he cannot respond adequately, he does take in and process information.
>
> IRA J. GORDON, *Human Development:*
> *From Birth through Adolescence*

The only technical term in the passage is *neonate;* and unlike the writer of the first passage, who also uses the word, the second author defines it for the general reader. Special vocabularies may obscure meaning. Moreover, they tempt the writer into the use of inflated and vague words instead of plain ones—a style sometimes known as *gobbledygook* or *governmentese* because it flourishes in bureaucratic writing. Harry S. Truman made a famous statement about the presidency: "The buck stops here." This straightforward assertion might be written by some bureaucrats as follows: "It is incumbent upon the President of the United States of America to uphold the responsibility placed upon him by his constituents to exercise the final decision-making power."

▶ Exercise 3

Many of the following expressions can be used at more than one level of style or usage, depending on context. Select ten; identify each with an appropriate label—Standard, Nonstandard, Formal, Informal, Colloquial, Slang, and so on. (Note: there is no universal system of usage labels. Read the preliminary pages in your dictionary, and be sure you understand its particular system. Use your dictionary and your own judgment.)

ain't	gobbledygook
beak (nose)	goober
blockhead	greenhorn
brainpan	Hibernia
bunk (nonsense)	high-hat
bunk (to occupy a bed)	in-depth
clove (past tense)	kid (child)
drag race	kine (cows)
edifice	loco (insane)
exam	loser (a failure)
fardel	mad (angry)
faux pas	mayhap
feist	nugatory
freak out	octane
fresh (presumptuous)	off the beam
ghetto	pad (apartment)

pep	steed
peekaboo	traumatic
rattle (to confuse)	trip (hallucinations)
shades (sunglasses)	TV
shipshape	y-clept
sidle	zany

37g Avoid triteness. Strive for fresh and original expressions.

Clichés are stock phrases and figures of speech once striking but used so often that they have lost their suggestive value. *A bull in a china shop* was once vivid and funny, but it has been used so many times that we no longer visualize the careening animal and the flying porcelain. Examples of triteness are innumerable: *it is interesting to note, flat as a flounder, pandemonium reigned, true blue, apple of his eye, tired but happy, quick as lightning, quick as a flash, an ax to grind,* and so forth.

37h Be exact. Use words in their precise meanings.

Knowledge of idiom, use of a dictionary, and awareness of the ways words are used—all these are necessary for precision in writing. The misuse of a word like *preservation* for the more exact *conservation* results in vagueness and confusion. Correct use of words usually derives from good habits with language rather than from rules. The misused words in the following sentences express wrong meanings.

> She was *overtaken* by the heat. (*Overcome* was intended.)
> *Foremost,* both librarians lost their patience. (Was *immediately* intended? or *first?*)
> She *parallels* the love she feels with the permanence of a tree. (*Compares* would be better.)

Misuse of one word for another that is somewhat like it can make a sentence ridiculous. See **37d**.

> Her dishonesty hurt her conscious. (The word is *conscience*.)
> Hamlet wished to get *avenge* for the murder of his father. (*revenge*)
> As the sun beams down upon the swamp, no different varieties of color are reflected, only the unreal grayish color of dead *vegetarian*. (*vegetation*)

Other examples are *climatic* for *climactic, statue* for *stature* (or vice versa), *incidences* for *incidents,* and *course* for *coarse*. Nonwords should never be used: for example, *interpretate* for *interpret* and *predominately* for *predominantly*.

▶ Exercise 4
Point out clichés and inexact words and expressions in the following sentences.

1. It goes without saying that the value of a college education cannot be measured in money, but tuition is high as a kite.
2. The meal was fabulous, and the service was fantastic.
3. Although the model claimed she wanted to marry a strong, silent type, she tied the knot with a man who could talk the horns off a brass billygoat.
4. Holidays always repress some people.
5. On the outskirts of the small town a sign was erected that renounced that this was the home of the one and only Fitz Fritzsimmons.
6. The survivor was weak as a kitten after eight days on the ocean, but his overall condition was unbelievable.
7. The brothers were as different as night and day, but each drank like a fish.
8. The eager young attorney jumped to her feet and cried, "That is irrevalent and immaterial."
9. At the retirement dinner the corporation president toasted the old

janitor and told him that his daily presents in the building would be soarly missed.

10. As he looked back, the farmer thought of those mornings as cold as ice when the ground was hard as a rock and when he shook like a leaf as he rose at the crack of dawn.

37i Add new words to your vocabulary.

Good writers have large storehouses of words, and they know the precise ones they need to express their meanings. Your vocabulary reflects your mentality, your education, and some aspects of your various abilities.

In reading pay careful attention to words you have never seen before. Look them up in a dictionary. Remember them. Recognize them the next time you see them, and learn to use them. Your knowledge of words measures not only your vocabulary but your abilities as a thinker and a writer.

▶ Exercise 5
Vocabulary Test: Underline the letter of the word or phrase you think is nearest in meaning to the key word. A score of nineteen to twenty correct is excellent, sixteen to eighteen is good, and thirteen to fifteen is fair. Notice that Exercise 5 consists entirely of monosyllables and that Exercise 6 has words of more than one syllable. (From It Pays to Increase Your Word Power *by Peter Funk.)*

1. brook (brŏŏk): (a) to put up with, (b) bridge, (c) deny, (d) resent
2. vie (vī): (a) to covet, (b) compete, (c) stimulate, (d) surpass
3. eke (ēk) (eek): (a) to dilute, (b) supplement, (c) coax, (d) revive
4. brunt (brŭnt): (a) abrupt, (b) impact, (c) insult, (d) malice
5. roil (roil) (roy'l): (a) to confuse, (b) curl, (c) amuse, (d) irritate
6. sloth (slawth): (a) clumsiness, (b) sadness, (c) stupidity, (d) idleness

7. cull (kul): (a) to win over, (b) till, (c) select, (d) memorize
8. prate (prāt) (prate): (a) to prance, (b) babble, (c) brag, (d) argue
9. bode (bōd): (a) foreshadow, (b) wait, (c) dwell, (d) endure
10. qualm (kwom): (a) warmth, (b) misgiving, (c) duty, (d) peace
11. moot (mōot): (a) gloomy, (b) ugly, (c) debatable, (d) spiritless
12. bane (bān): (a) banter, (b) mystery, (c) affliction, (d) exile
13. deign (dān): (a) to condescend, (b) pretend, (c) disparage, (d) refuse
14. tryst (trist): (a) appointment, (b) coyness, (c) faith, (d) ruse
15. irk (urk): (a) to scold, (b) make a wry face, (c) urge, (d) annoy
16. glut (glŭt): (a) glue, (b) to be lewd, (c) disembowel, (d) overfill
17. drone (drōn): (a) talk monotonously, (b) complain, (c) be idle, (d) stretch
18. mere (mēr): (a) nothing but, (b) humble, (c) only one, (d) weak
19. deem (dēm): (a) to consider, (b) speculate, (c) acknowledge, (d) consent
20. loll (lŏl): (a) to cuddle, (b) flatter, (c) lounge, (d) soothe or quiet

▶ Exercise 6
Follow the instructions for Exercise 5. (*From* It Pays to Increase Your Word Power *by Peter Funk.*)

1. semantics (si man′ tiks): (a) study of word meanings, (b) science of sounds, (c) sleight of hand, (d) origin of words
2. fiat (fī′ at): (a) power, (b) contradiction, (c) command, (d) end
3. platitude (plăt′ ĭ tōod): (a) rule of life, (b) wise saying, (c) flat surface, (d) trite remark
4. nomadic (nō măd′ ĭk): (a) adventuresome, (b) fixed, (c) romantic, (d) roaming
5. welter (wĕl′ ter): (a) confusion, (b) heat, (c) wilting, (d) swelling
6. hurtle (hur′ t′l): (a) to throw away, (b) jump over, (c) trip, (d) rush headlong
7. punitive (pŭ′ nĭ tiv): (a) pertaining to punishment, (b) insignificant, (c) stimulating, (d) repulsive
8. cavil (kăv′ ĭl): (a) to make fun of, (b) find fault, (c) insult, (d) whine
9. heinous (hā′ nus) (hay-): (a) insulting, (b) ugly, (c) wicked, (d) dark

10. preempt (prē empt'): (a) to appropriate, (b) order bluntly, (c) contradict, (d) obstruct
11. augment (og měnt') (awg-): (a) to increase, (b) urge, (c) lose, (d) dispute
12. insidious (in sid' ē ŭs): (a) of doubtful origin, (b) secret, (c) serious, (d) designed to entrap
13. exonerate (ĕg zŏn' er āt) (-ate): (a) to praise, (b) absolve, (c) elevate, (d) daydream
14. inure (in ūre'): (a) to hurt, (b) accustom, (c) deprive, (d) confine
15. complicity (kŏm plis' ĭ tē): (a) sharing in wrongdoing, (b) calmness, (c) state of well-being, (d) clarity
16. obtuse (ŏb tūs'): (a) stubborn, (b) profound, (c) stupid, (d) blunt in manner
17. supervene (sōō per vēn'): (a) to follow closely upon, (b) overcome, (c) force out, (d) come between
18. endue (en dū'): (a) endow, (b) saturate, (c) be patient, (d) await
19. fortuitous (for tū' ĭ tus): (a) sudden, (b) accidental, (c) lucky (d) courageous
20. mawkish (mawk' ĭsh): (a) obstinate, (b) clumsy, (c) dumb, (d) sentimental

▶ Exercise 7

In each of the following passages select from the alternatives in parentheses the word or phrase which you think the author used. The choices involve exactness in meaning, idiom, triteness or originality, level of diction, and just plain good taste. If more than one choice is acceptable, base your decision on the choice of words and phrases in the rest of the passage. Be prepared to defend your selections. The following is a description by a modern biographer of life in a Russian prison as it was experienced by the novelist Feodor Dostoevsky in the nineteenth century.

1. Life in prison was life still. It asserted itself in this bleak place like grass (growing, thrusting its way) between slabs of granite. The

brutal severity of the regimen was to some degree mitigated (for, by, with) incredible laxity. The (convicts, jailbirds, criminals) were not permitted to do any work for themselves to earn money. Nevertheless, as soon as the doors were locked for the night the barracks would turn into a humming workshop. Many pursued (a hobby, a craft, an art), some engaged in buying and selling and in financial transactions of sorts, and there were those who hired themselves out to their mates as entertainers, lookout men, (factotums, stooges, cronies). All managed to earn something and were able to secure certain (amenities, goodies, luxuries). Some ate other than prison food. Cards, (nicotine, tobacco, pot), vodka were strictly (forbidden, taboo), yet gambling, smoking, and drinking thrived, and the more enterprising even got themselves (ladies, broads, women) by (bribing, greasing the palms of) the guards. Money was precious as a symbol of freedom, the dream even of "lifers." Yet they used it in the most spendthrift fashion, fearing that it would be (violently requisitioned, purloined, snatched) from them before they could enjoy it, and also in order to secure the respect of their fellows by a splurge. Of course, all infringements of discipline were committed at the peril of reprisals. Eight Eyes would descend like the wolf on the fold, goods and money would be confiscated, and the offenders (flogged, flagellated, chastised).

Only Christmas and Easter were days of (amusement, leisure, revelry), and on these occasions relaxation of discipline was, if not sanctioned, at least connived at. New Year's Eve (in the year of 1852, somewhere around 1852, 1852) was marked by a unique event: the convicts, under Dostoevsky's (direction, bossing, tyranny), staged a comedy, a farce, and a musical pantomime. The (spectacular, happening, spectacle) was attended not only by the inmates but also by the prison officials and other (big shots, "noble and highborn persons," VIPs), for whose benefit a playbill was posted. There were no theatricals in the city and the show was a huge success.

AVRAHM YARMOLINSKY, *Dostoevsky:*
Works and Days

2. Shakespeare, who thought (a lot, a great deal, a whole lot) about the relations of fathers and children, makes this problem the subject of several of his (best, fine) plays. He shows us a father who, with vast dexterity and (push, ginger, vinegar, energy), has won himself a (good job, great position). The (dad, forebear, father) loves his (boy, progeny, son), and hopes that he will share the (loot, rewards, prizes) and (privileges, responsibilities, love) of power. The (kid, brat, son, boy) is (keen, talented, smart) and (cute, charming, sweet), brave and (peppy, energetic, pushy). It would be (easy, a push-over), one would think, and (fun, pleasant) for him to (throw in with, amalgamate with, join) his (sire, old man, father). (There's, There is) no compulsion. He can do (as he liketh, whatever he likes). He may sit at home playing shove-ha'penny if he (selects, wants to, chooses); or hunt all week during the season; or (diddle around, waste time harmlessly) in other ways. But he chooses to become a (mobster, gangster). He is only an amateur, but he is on the fringe of the (pro, professional) crooks. His best (chum, friend, pal) is a broken-down old (villain, ruffian, codger) who has drunk (most, almost) all his gifts (away, down, up) and is living (by, off, on) the (balance, remainder) of his (head, mind, wits). He (sees far more of, runs around more with) Falstaff than he does (of, with) his father, King Henry IV. He makes Falstaff into a (sort of, sort of a) (substitute, second-string, sub) father, (carrying on, laughing) with him as he (can't, cannot) with his father, tricking and (joshing, befooling) him as he would like to (belittle, run down) his father. As the play goes on, it is (harder and harder, tougher and tougher) to understand (what's, what is) wrong with Hal. Why should he throw away his chances? Why does he want to hurt his father? He *says* he is doing it (so, so that) he can get more praise for reforming later; but this is not the real (answer, reason), and it never comes up after his (reform, going straight) takes place. The real reason (appears, shows up) when his father is in genuine danger and when Hal himself is challenged by a rival of his own age. Then he rushes to help the king's cause, and kills his challenger, Hotspur.

GILBERT HIGHET, The Art of Teaching

3. One of the reasons that country (folks, hicks, folk), with limited experience, are nevertheless so much better (pals, companions, associates) for (an artist, a longhair, an artiste) or a (Ph.D., thinker, brain) than city (slicks, people) of the same (class, category), is that the former have always kept for themselves a little free time to sit still and (breed, cogitate, brood), whittling wood around a winter fire, or bent impassively over a fishing pole, watching the trout's (canny, sharp, smart) (movements, flirtations, cavortings). The city worker (maybe, may be) better read; but the countryman is more (intelligent, intellectual, reflective): such experience as he has (experienced, encountered, met) he has (saved, salted down, preserved).

LEWIS MUMFORD, Faith for Living

---

38 **Wordiness** $\mathcal{w}$

Omit needless words and irrelevant ideas.

Conciseness increases the force of writing. Do not pad your paper with words merely to complete an assignment.

Use one word for many.

The love letter was written by somebody who did not sign a name. (13 words)
The love letter was anonymous (*or* was not signed). (5 or 6 words)

Use the active voice for conciseness (see **5**).

The truck was overloaded by the workmen. (7 words)
The workmen overloaded the truck. (5 words)

Revise sentence structure for conciseness.

Another element which adds to the effectiveness of a speech is its emotional content. (14 words)
Emotional content also makes a speech more effective. (8 words)

NOTE Avoid constructions with *It is . . .* and *there are . . .*

NOT
It is truth which will prevail.
BUT
Truth will prevail.

Use one word, not two with the same meaning (tautology).

Basic and fundamental principles. (4 words)
Basic principles. (2 words)

Study your sentences carefully and make them concise by using all the preceding methods. Do not, however, sacrifice concreteness and vividness for conciseness and brevity.

EXCESSIVELY CONCISE
The garden has steps at both ends.
CONCRETE AND VIVID
At each end of the sunken garden, worn granite steps, flanked by large magnolia trees, lead to formal paths.

▶ Exercise 8
Express the following sentences succinctly. Do not omit important ideas.

1. The custom which has always been so popular in the country of waving to strangers as you pass them is gradually fading out.

2. There are several reasons why officers of the law ought to be trained in the law of the land, and two of these are as follows. The first of these reasons is that policemen can enforce the law better if they are familiar with it. And second, they will be less likely to

violate the rights of private citizens if they know exactly and accurately what these rights are.

3. Although the Kentucky rifle played an important and significant part in getting food for the frontiersmen who settled the American West, its function as a means of protection was in no degree any less significant in their lives.

4. Some television programs assume a low level of public intelligence and present their shows to the public as if the audience were made up of morons.

5. The distant explosion was audible to the ear.

6. The Japanese beetle is a beetle which was introduced into America from Japan and which thrives on fruits and roots of grass.

7. In modern warfare every nation which is engaged in the war broadcasts over radio and television information which is intended to convince the people in the enemy country that their cause is wrong.

8. It is not true that he is guilty.

9. It is a pleasure for some to indulge in eating large quantities of food at meals, but doctors of medicine tell us that such pleasures can only bring with them unpleasant results in the long run of things.

10. The essay consists of facts which describe vividly many of the events in the life of a typical juggler. In this description the author uses a vocabulary which is easy to understand. This vocabulary is on neither too high a level nor too low a level, but on one which can be understood by any high school graduate.

---

39 Repetition *rep*

Avoid redundancy—careless repetition of words, phrases, sounds, and ideas.

Unintentional repetition is seldom effective. Avoid repetition by (1) using synonyms, (2) using pronouns, and (3) condensing sentences and omitting words.

REPETITIOUS

Consideration of others is really the main *quality* of a gentleman. This *quality* comes from the heart.

CONDENSED

Consideration of others, which is really the main quality of a gentleman, comes from the heart.

39a Do not use several different words for the same meaning.

EXCESSIVE SYNONYMS

Consideration of others is really the main *quality* of a *gentleman.* A *man* who has this *trait* is sincere.

CONDENSED

Sincere consideration of others is really the main quality of a gentleman.

39b Avoid unpleasant repetition of sounds.

Devices like rhyme, meter, and repetition of sounds are a vital part of poetry and of some kinds of creative prose, but they are generally to be avoided in expository writing.

RHYME

The biologist again *checked* the charts to determine the *effect* of the poison on the *insect.*

CORRECTION

The biologist again studied the charts to determine the effect of the poison on the moth.

REPETITION OF CONSONANTS

The *desp*erate *dep*ression of that *dec*ade *d*oomed many people.

CORRECTION

The severe depression of that time ruined many people.

39c Repeat a word or a phrase only for emphasis or for clarity.

Purposeful repetition of a word or a phrase often gains emphasis. Frequently repetition is used with aphorisms or axioms or in sentences that make statements about principles and abstractions.

Books and libraries preserve the *wisdom* of the ages, but not all *wisdom* comes from *books and libraries.*
Consistency may be regarded as a mark of *integrity,* but many a person of *integrity* does not define *consistency* as a great virtue.

► Exercise 9
Rewrite the following passage. Avoid wordiness and undesirable repetition.

A large number of people enjoy reading murder mysteries regularly. These people are not themselves murderers as a rule, nor would these people really ever enjoy seeing someone commit an actual murder, nor would most of them actually enjoy trying to solve an actual murder. They probably enjoy reading murder mysteries because of this reason: they have found a way to escape from the monotonous, boring routine of dull everyday existence.

To such people the murder mystery is realistic fantasy. It is realistic because the people in the murder mystery are as a general rule believable as people. They are not just made-up pasteboard figures. It is also realistic because the character who is the hero, the character who solves the murder mystery, solves it not usually by trial and error and haphazard methods but by exercising a high degree of logic and reason. It is absolutely and totally essential that people who enjoy murder mysteries have an admiration for the human faculty of logic.

But murder mysteries are also fantasies. The people who

read such books of fiction play a game. It is a game in which they suspend certain human emotions. One of these human emotions that they suspend is pity. If the reader stops to feel pity and sympathy for each and every victim that is killed or if the reader stops to feel terrible horror that such a thing could happen in our world of today, that person will never enjoy reading murder mysteries. The devoted reader of murder mysteries keeps uppermost in mind always and at all times the goal of arriving through logic and observation at the final solution to the mystery offered in the book. It is a game with life and death. Whodunits hopefully help the reader to hide from the hideous horrors of actual life and death in the real world.

---

40 Vagueness *vag*

Do not write vaguely. Choose words that are as specific and as concrete as your meaning requires.

Avoid sentences which can have many different meanings.

The weather was undesirable.

The preceding sentence could mean several things:

Heavy rains caused a flash flood.
The baseball game was rained out.
During the long drought all the crops failed except the peanuts.

Writing which is not specific can cause misunderstanding. Abstract language draws general concepts from specific instances. The diagram below is a simple illustration; each step to the right represents a further abstraction.

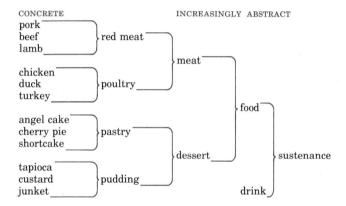

Without the power to abstract, we would be bound to the immediate object or experience. We could never talk about "a meal," but only "roast beef and a baked potato." Increasingly abstract concepts like *meat, food, meal,* and *sustenance* allow us to group large numbers of objects, ideas, and experiences and to combine abstractions in order to discover still more relationships—in short, to think.

Abstractions like *food, drink,* and *sustenance* derive from concrete experience. High-level abstractions like *integrity, morality, freedom, goodness, love, justice,* and *democracy* are further removed from specific acts and objects. An abstraction of this kind may cause difficulty because it means something a little different to almost everyone who uses the word. Many abstractions (*democ-*

racy and *liberty,* for example) are not simple sums of concrete facts; instead, they are built on a complex of other abstractions. Because such words are hard to define, use them only with great care. Notice how the following passage improves as it becomes more specific and concrete.

GENERAL

Mankind needs to recognize the geographical limitations of communities and the advantages of changes in environment. This is a principle which is evident in the movements and migrations of the creatures of nature.

MORE SPECIFIC

For the improvement of one's health, a change of environment is advisable. It is fortunate that no one place encompasses the world. The vegetation and birds of one place do not exist in another. Migratory birds are more cosmopolitan than people; they eat their meals each day in a different part of the country. Even some animals follow the seasons.

VERY SPECIFIC

To the sick the doctors wisely recommend a change of air and scenery. Thank Heaven, here is not all the world. The buckeye does not grow in New England, and the mockingbird is rarely heard here. The wild goose is more of a cosmopolite than we; he breaks his fast in Canada, takes a luncheon in the Ohio, and plumes himself for the night in a southern bayou. Even the bison, to some extent, keeps pace with the seasons, cropping the pastures of the Colorado only till a greener and sweeter grass awaits him by the Yellowstone.

HENRY DAVID THOREAU, *Walden*

▶ Exercise 10
Change words and details in the following sentences so that they become exact, concrete, specific.

1. He consumed the food.
2. She went across the street.

3. The sunset was colorful.
4. The vegetation was thick.
5. The furniture was damaged.

▶ Exercise 11
Write your personal definition of one of the following abstract terms in a paragraph of about two hundred words. Give concrete examples from your experience.

wisdom   love   patriotism   wit

41 Connotation *con*

Choose words with connotations appropriate to tone and content.

In addition to dictionary or denotative meanings, many words carry special associations or suggestions—**connotations.** The **denotation** of a word is its precise meaning, the exact definition given in a dictionary. Denotatively, a dog is a four-legged carnivorous domesticated mammal. Literally the word *dog* arouses no emotional response of any kind, no hatred, no affection.

Connotations include emotional responses. What *dog* suggests to the reader or writer in addition to *four-legged carnivore* is connotation, which can be pleasant or unpleasant. To one person *dog* may suggest friendship; to another once attacked by a dog the word may connote terror.

A good writer uses connotations to evoke planned emotional reactions. To suggest sophistication, the writer may mention a *lap dog;* to evoke the amusing or the rural, *hound dog.* To connote a social or moral distinction, the writer may call someone a *cur.* Even this word may have different connotations: a social worker may react sympathetically to it; a snob, contemptuously. Consider the associations aroused by *canine, pooch, mutt, mongrel, puppy,* and *watchdog.* Even some breeds arouse different responses: *bloodhound, shepherd, St. Bernard, poodle.*

Words that are denotative synonyms may have very different connotative overtones. Consider the following:

> drummer—salesperson—field representative
> slender—thin—skinny
> resolute—strong-willed—stubborn

The exact writer avoids a word with unwanted connotations and chooses an appropriate synonym. Be sure that the words you choose give the suggestions you wish to convey. A single word with the wrong connotation can easily spoil a passage. Only one word has been changed in the following quotation:

> Let us never bargain out of fear. But let us never fear to bargain.

President Kennedy actually wrote:

> Let us never negotiate out of fear. But let us never fear to negotiate.

The word *bargain* ruins the tone of the statement even though it is a close synonym for *negotiate.*

▶ Exercise 12

Words which have approximately the same denotation frequently suggest responses that are quite different. The combinations below bring together words with different connotations. Rate each word for favorability of connotation, 1 for most favorable, 2 for second, 3 for least. Be prepared to defend your decisions and to explain the different shades of connotation.

1. diseased
   ill
   sick
2. fat
   overweight
   stout
3. economical
   stingy
   thrifty
4. job
   profession
   position
5. decay
   decompose
   rot
6. inexpensive
   cheap
   reasonable
7. remedy
   medicine
   cure-all
8. enthusiast
   extremist
   fanatic
9. garbage
   rubbish
   trash
10. impractical
    quixotic
    romantic
11. little
    petite
    small
12. innocent
    naive
    simple
13. stream
    gutter
    rivulet
14. famous
    notorious
    well-known
15. frolic
    clown
    cut up

42 Figurative language *fig*

Use fresh and imaginative figures of speech. Avoid mixed figures.

42a Use figurative comparisons.

Convey forceful impressions by comparing things that are not literally similar. Describe abstractions in concrete terms.

1. Write metaphors (implied comparisons).

Historians constantly stir the ashes of the past.
The mind is a house of many mirrors.

2. Write similes (comparisons stated with *like* or *as*).

The records of history are *like* the remains of burned-out fires.
The mind is *like* a house of many mirrors.

3. Personify.

the malicious whispers of gossip
the bearded oak

As you develop the habit of comparing things, good figures of speech may begin to come to you more easily.

42b Avoid mixed, worn out, or inappropriate figures of speech.

MIXED
These corporations lashed out with legal loopholes.

WORN OUT
The promising young broker was ruined by the fickle finger of fate and the long arm of the law.

INAPPROPRIATE
Then, like a thief in the night, my father passed away.

43 Flowery language ƒ ℓ

Avoid ornate or pretentious language.

Flowery language, often called **fine writing,** is frequently pompous and artificial. *These United States* rather than *the United States, in the year of 1978* rather than *in 1978, at this point in time* rather than *now,* for example, have the ring of affectation. *Green lawn*—or even *lawn*—is more natural then *verdant sward. Spade* or *shovel* is more natural than *simple instrument for delving into Mother Earth.* Sincerity disappears in the elaborate phrase that describes a teacher as *my fellow toiler in the long and arduous labors of pedagogy.*

The Process of
Composition

44 Clear and logical thinking *log*

Check any facts you use, and be certain of their accuracy. Some thinking involves reasoning which cannot be based on positive facts. For interpretations which cannot be scientifically proved right or wrong, use common sense to avoid the erroneous and the absurd.

44a Use only accurate and verified data.

Facts are demonstrable. They are the basis of judgments. A writer should distinguish carefully between the facts and the judgments derived from them and then explain how one comes from the other.

Errors of fact, ignorance, or dishonesty make the reader suspicious and lead to distrust and doubt. The following statements are immediately suspect because of errors of fact.

Arthur Wegelin testified that he had entered the country on June 31, 1976. ("Thirty days hath June.")

Only wealthy people buy original oil paintings. (The facts do not bear out this contention.)

44b Use reliable authorities.

Specialists in the same field may disagree. Therefore, in evaluating an authority you may use some of the following criteria and perhaps additional methods.

1. When was the work published? An old publication may contain superseded information.

2. Who published the work? University presses and well-established publishing houses employ well-informed consultants.

3. How has the work been evaluated by other authorities in bibliographies, reviews, and editorials?

4. Is the presumed authority writing about his or her own field? (An atomic scientist may not be an expert on world records in baseball.)

5. Are the language and the tone reasonable, or does the authority attempt to persuade by using ornate rhetoric or prejudiced and slanted words and terms?

6. Is the authority fair-minded enough to admit the existence of facts that seem contradictory?

7. Does the authority distinguish fact from opinion, or are abstractions obstinately elevated to the level of indisputable fact?

44c Avoid sweeping generalizations.

Generalize with great care. If you know that three of your friends oppose capital punishment, you should not assert that "Everyone wishes to have capital punishment abolished" or even that "Most people wish to have capital punishment abolished." These statements are too broad for the evidence on which they are based. Sweeping generalizations like the following may contain some element of truth, but it is lost in the extremity of the statements.

> A poor person cannot get a fair trial in America.
> Russian athletes are the best in the world.

Sweeping generalizations about nationalities and races are among the most illogical and pernicious. If you have not done extensive and conclusive research on your subject, qualify your opinions.

> Some poor people feel that they cannot get a fair trial in America.
> Many Russian athletes are among the best in the world.

It will help you to resist the temptation to claim too much if you remember that a sweeping generalization is very often a falsification.

44d Use enough specific and accurate evidence to support your argument.

Truth and accuracy depend on an adequate number of examples. Statistics and samplings of opinions, polls, and other kinds of data should be not only sufficiently extensive but also fairly and representatively chosen. Sometimes it is not enough that data should be picked at random. A public opinion poll taken from only one social, educational, or occupational group, for example, would probably be misleading.

44e Stick to the point.

Do not introduce irrelevancies or wander off the subject. First or last paragraphs of papers are sometimes especially irrelevant because they begin or end at a point too far removed from the subject. Digression is a sign of failure to focus attention on the problem at hand.

44f Do not ignore conflicting facts or evidence.

Be aware of facts and instances which seem to refute or qualify your views and conclusions. Deal with them fully and honestly. You can actually strengthen your case by taking opposing evidence into consideration.

44g Do not beg the question or reason in a circle.

A writer who begs the question assumes that something is true and writes as if it had been proved.

CIRCULAR REASONING
A large part of the taxpayer's educational dollar is spent on unnecessary items like school lunchrooms, classes for handicapped children, and instruction in art and music.

That the educational items mentioned are "unnecessary" ones is a debatable proposition which the writer does not establish but merely asserts. The writer is begging the question (arguing in a circle) by simply restating the proposition in terms of itself.

44h Do not omit essential steps in thought or draw false conclusions from unstated assumptions.

A **logical fallacy** results whenever the omission of a step in reasoning leads to a false conclusion. The argument that "He cannot be elected to Phi Beta Kappa because he is a football player" is based on a false assumption: that no football player ever makes good grades, or that Phi Beta Kappa will refuse to elect someone who plays football. Similar omissions of parts of the argument occur in the following sentences. What are the unstated assumptions, and why are the conclusions false?

> Since she made good grades in high school, she will undoubtedly be a good student in college.
> She will not make a good judge because she was once fined for speeding.
> He has a wonderful personality and will certainly be a successful salesman.

44i Do not substitute an appeal to emotions for an appeal to reason.

Name-calling is an appeal to prejudice. Calling an opponent a moron beclouds an issue. This is argument against a person rather than against a principle or a point of view.

"Loaded" words and **labels** attempt to shape an attitude through prejudice instead of reason. In loaded terms a government subsidy plan might become a "hand-out scheme that a bunch of radical do-gooders are trying to fasten on the taxpayers."

Flattery attempts to persuade through excessive praise. The political candidate who tells an audience that he knows they will vote for him because of their high intelligence is attempting to convince by flattering.

Snob appeal asserts that one should adopt a certain view because all the better people do—including, of course, the writer. The use of athletes, beauty queens, or motion picture stars in advertising is a form of snob appeal.

Mass appeal attempts to persuade by asserting that everyone follows a certain pattern. It suggests that one who does not follow the herd is in error (*everyone ought* to go to college; *everyone ought* to own a home).

44j Do not draw false conclusions about cause and effect.

When two things happen in sequence, the second is not necessarily caused by the first. If a man walks under a ladder and shortly thereafter loses his wallet, he should not assume that he lost his wallet *because* he walked under the ladder. To show a cause-and-effect relationship between two events, it is necessary to produce evidence of real causation.

44k Be moderate.

Be temperate in your judgments and in your choice of words. Overstatement, overemphasis, and dogmatic assertion not only irritate most readers but arouse doubt or even disbelief. The good writer knows better than to be cocksure and brash.

44L Allow for adequate alternatives.

On some questions it is false logic to assume that there are *two and only two* alternatives. Often other possibilities exist. If, for example, a father tells his son that he must go to college or fail in life, he has not recognized that his son may succeed without a college education.

▶ Exercise
Describe the errors in content and thought in each of the following.

1. The fact that the lexicographer wrote the publisher about his objections to the novel proves that as fiction it was not worth publishing.

2. Boys are good in mathematics and science; girls are good in English and the fine arts.

3. An interjection is a word or a clause used to express a strong emotion.

4. Russian medicine is far behind that in this country because Russia has so many young doctors.

5. The book which you reviewed favorably is trash, the kind of dirty garbage found on the cheapest shelves of pornographic bookstores.

6. Anyone who reaches the age of eighteen is old enough to make decisions without advice from other people.

7. John Quincy Adams, the second President of the United States, was respected for his idealism and great knowledge.

8. Nearly all the great monuments of this world are made of marble.

9. All college graduates are unusually intelligent; otherwise, they could not have passed the courses and completed their education.

10. The fact that you could espouse the cause of those rebels shows me that you are a coward and a degenerate.

11. After only one week at Reduso Spa, Mrs. Wentworth lost sixteen pounds. Enroll now if you really wish to lose weight.

12. My professor must be a good scholar; he is a member of the Modern Language Association.

13. Any young man should go to trade school before going to college because it is extremely difficult for a college graduate to get a good job unless he can do something with his hands.

14. Order our new device for restoring hair in your bald spots, and new hair will begin to grow within two weeks.

15. The only good kinds of narratives are fiction and autobiography.

16. Her parents deserted her when she was an infant. No wonder she has spent much of her life in prison.

17. The welfare system in this country makes the people who have

earned their money give it away to lazy good-for-nothings who are not willing to work for themselves.

18. Joseph Conrad was the greatest novelist who ever lived.

19. The Establishment has arrived at dependable rules of conduct; those who follow them will have no serious problems.

20. Freedom is a necessary ingredient in the life of every woman, and every woman should make her decisions without advice because of her need for liberation.

21. According to the high school chemistry text, the article in *Chemical Research Journal* cannot be correct.

22. Subscribe to *Now*, the intellectual's magazine, and join the most enlightened readers of the day.

23. Shakespeare did not write the plays attributed to him. This fact has been proved by a famous surgeon who recently retired from a medical career to which he had devoted almost all his energy.

24. Who says fortunetellers are fakes? Just as the palmist said, I went to Alaska three months after she told my fortune.

25. A good theme must be written in chronological order.

45 Writing good paragraphs *¶*

A **paragraph** usually develops one central purpose or idea. For the writer, careful paragraphing is an aspect of accurate thinking and logical organization. For the reader, clear and orderly paragraphs help comprehension by marking thought units and giving a sense of separation and progression. If sentences are the boards and bricks of the house of writing and the theme is the entire structure, paragraphs are the rooms. Some themes are written with such long paragraphs that they are like houses with few rooms. Other themes are so frequently divided that they are like houses with rooms no larger than closets.

45a Express the main idea of a paragraph in a topic sentence.

Most paragraphs contribute one block of thought within the theme, and usually that thought is summed up in one predominant sentence. The connection of that **topic sentence** to others like it in surrounding paragraphs should be easily apparent, and it should be clear how the other sentences in the paragraph are tied to the dominant sentence as well as how they are related to each other. Nearly always the topic sentence comes at the beginning of a paragraph because that is where the reader needs to know the direction of the paragraph. Topic sentences supply that direction. The other sentences add evidence, make refinements, develop the main idea, but as a rule they do not control the purpose of the paragraph or primarily reveal where the paper is going. Consequently, taken together the topic sentences of a paper are a sort of skeleton of the whole. Reading only the topic sentences should show a writer whether the lines of thought are clear in the paper. Usually the topic sentences will also enable a reader to scan a piece of writing and to see generally what its major points are.

Test your own papers by topic sentences. If they move logically and clearly through the main outlines of your work, that is a good sign. If not, you may have omitted ideas, arranged thoughts in the wrong sequence, or neglected to state purpose and direction. Then you may need to replan your paper, to move paragraphs about, to add new ones, and to rewrite topic sentences. When the basic structure seems effective, then you may begin to look more intently within the paragraph.

The following selection from an article on George Washington illustrates a skillful author's methods of writing good topic sentences and presenting the details that support them. The topic sentences are italicized.

At the simplest, most superficial level Washington's love of honor showed itself in a concern with outward appearances. His attachment to Mount Vernon, for example, did not stop at the desire to make a profit from it. He wanted the place and its surroundings to look right, to honor the owner by the way they looked; and this meant giving up the slovenly, though often profitable, agricultural practices of his neighbors. He stopped growing tobacco and turned to the rotation of cereal crops that were approved by the English agricultural reformers of the time. He tried, mostly in vain, to substitute handsome English hedgerows for the crude rail fences of Virginia. And he insisted that all weeds and brush be grubbed out of his plowed fields, not simply for the sake of productivity, but because the fields looked better that way. He would rather, he said, have one acre properly cleansed than five prepared in the usual way.

Similarly, as commander-in-chief, he wanted his soldiers to look well. Their uniforms must be kept in order and "well put on." Otherwise, he said, there would be "little difference in *appearance* between a soldier in rags and a soldier in uniform." Appearance mattered especially to him when French troops were coming: his army must not be dishonored by looking shabby or careless. Even the huts for winter quarters must be built of an identical size: "any hut not exactly conformable to the plan, or the least out of line, shall be pulled down and built again agreeable to the model and in its proper place." And when Washington became president, he showed the same concern for appearances in furnishing his house and decorating his coach in a plain but elegant style that he thought was appropriate for the head of a republican government.

But a man who craved honor could not gain it simply by putting up a good appearance. This was only a shade removed from vanity, and Washington from the beginning betrayed none of the vanity of a John Adams. Indeed his concern with appearances included a horror of appearing vain. He would not assist would-be biographers for fear, he confessed to a friend, of having "vanity or ostentation imputed to me." He would not even allow Arthur Young, the great English agricultural reformer with whom he corresponded, to publish extracts from the letters, for fear of seeming ostentatious or of giving occasion for some "officious tongue to use my name with indelicacy."

EDMUND S. MORGAN, "George Washington:
The Aloof American"

The paragraphs are related, and the italicized topic sentences indicate how the passage is about Washington's concern for order and for what the author calls "outward appearances"—even at the expense of utility. The first two paragraphs are arranged by Washington's concern for appearances in his different occupations—his farming and his serving as a military officer. The last sentence of the second paragraph shows how he carried the same quality on to other and higher offices. The third paragraph is more general; it shows how the characteristic discussed in all the paragraphs is a trait of the whole man, and it introduces a final and crucial point—that Washington was not really vain but rather was concerned that others might think he was. The three paragraphs are unified and coherent because each topic sentence introduces a unit of thought that contributes to an overall picture of the man.

45b   Write unified paragraphs. Be sure that each sentence is clearly related to the main idea.

Every sentence in a good paragraph bears on the main point. An irrelevant sentence first subtracts from the main point and then gives the reader difficulty in getting back to the subject. A good paragraph does not change its course and remain there or switch off to another point and then attempt to return. Notice how in the following paragraph the writer digresses less than halfway through and destroys unity:

> Groups of people often have something like a definable and single personality, and one group may differ markedly from another of a similar kind. For example, classes in college courses are often widely different in personality. As a group a class may be lazy or energetic, amenable or quarrelsome, bright or dull, and so on. The professor may hasten to one group with anticipation and drag his feet with dread as he goes to meet another. Of course, professors differ as much as their classes do. One may be generous with his time and truly concerned about his students. Another may be selfish and indifferent. I have known professors who disliked even talking with their own students. Different as groups like college classes are, it is almost impossible to define what causes the great divergences from one to another.

The writer of this paragraph set out to discuss the idea that groups of people seem to have a personality much as individuals do. Had the idea been sustained, it would have made an excellent paragraph. It does not succeed because the writer got off the track and addressed the subject of professors. The temptation to digress is often great when the mind runs ahead to other interesting thoughts. Consequently, mental discipline is one of the most important prerequisites in writing good paragraphs. The final sentence of the above paragraph turns to yet another subject—causes—and should almost certainly be the first sentence of a new paragraph instead of the last sentence of this one.

▶ Exercise 1

By deleting extraneous material, improve the paragraphs below that are not unified (as many as three sentences may be extraneous). Put a check next to paragraphs that are acceptable. Underline all topic sentences (some paragraphs may have more than one).

1. Sensible business people who deal in realities every day will often go out of their way on the street to avoid walking under a ladder.

Diners in restaurants throw salt over their shoulders to ward off bad luck when they spill a little. It is not at all unusual to see a perfectly sane adult knock on wood to insure continued good fortune. Many people moan over broken mirrors not because the accident will cost them the money to buy new mirrors but because they are worried that they may be in for seven years of bad luck. Superstitions, then, are many and various and still manifest themselves in the actions of a great many normal people.

2. The motion picture *All Quiet on the Western Front* was actually created as an antiwar protest. It deals with World War I from a German perspective. The hero has a professor he first admires but comes to distrust. Even though it is about the Germans, it does not glorify the German cause. It depicts the plight of the sensitive human spirit caught in the terrible grip of war. World War I started when Archduke Ferdinand was assassinated. Probably no one would have guessed that this incident would grow quickly into the greatest war the world had ever known. The theme of the picture is expressed in the ending, where the hero is killed while reaching for a flower he sees on the battlefield.

3. As the basic social unit the family is as important today in America as it ever was, though perhaps in a different way. Family coherence was essential in the early days of the country to insure the survival of the individual members. They helped each other and protected each other. Today people need their families not so much to insure physical survival as to help them through the perils of modern times, especially through such psychological perils as loss of identity. America is not all bad, however. It offers the greatest freedom of all countries for individual development. America is still the land of opportunity. The family gives one a sense of belonging, a sense of the past. When all else seems severed, the family can be the anchor to sanity.

4. A Saturday visit to the barber shop was once an exciting and meaningful experience for a boy. It offered an almost unique opportunity for a youngster to enter for a little while the adult masculine world. At school a boy had no opportunity to see this world. At home he was often with his father and perhaps his brothers, but that was not the same as sitting among men and listening to their jokes—often slightly off-color—and their strong opinions on people and politics and their stories, sometimes of violence and courage. If he were wise, the lad sat in the barber chair and listened carefully with silent respect, for he sensed that he was being given the rare opportunity of visiting a world he would someday enter.

5. Pollution is a more complex issue than it may appear to be on the surface. Consumers wish to have clean air, but they hesitate to pay more for the mechanism on cars that will help insure it. They want clean water, but they sometimes complain of the costs that are passed on to them of new sewage disposal plants. Yet the public is correct in its desire for more ecological controls, and at the same time its unwillingness to spend an increasingly large amount of money for them is understandable. Overpopulation is another threat to the future. The world population is growing at an alarming rate. If this fact is not recognized and if steps are not taken now to slow down population growth, our children's children may experience a frightening drop in the quality of life on earth. City dwellers would like to diminish noise pollution, but they are naturally hesitant to take steps that would eliminate such noise polluters as automobiles from their uptown streets. Pollution is thus not a simple problem to be overcome by a single act of legislation.

45c Avoid short, skimpy paragraphs.

Short paragraphs are sometimes standard and effective in news items, fiction, dialogue, and descriptions of dramatic action.

The length of a paragraph is usually decided by the importance and complexity of its central idea, the richness of detail that develops it, and even the number of words allowed in an assignment. Paragraphs in a theme of 600 words will generally be shorter and more uniform in length than those in a paper of 1500 to 2000 words. Thought should never be divided into paragraphs simply at mechanical intervals. In most expository prose a series of short, choppy paragraphs suggests undeveloped ideas or simply the writer's failure to put paragraph divisions at good places. Sometimes several short paragraphs can be combined under the one which has the strongest topic sentence, perhaps the only possible topic sentence in the group.

The following selection is chopped up excessively, and its divisions are not logical.

> But perhaps we should beware of taking evidence of this sort too tragically, or of deducing from detective stories nothing but a pessimistic moral. The condemnation of detective stories as drugs or cheap escapism may be pedantic.
>
> For, if they are a symptom, they can also be a cure. If we credit the Freudian view that socially dangerous impulses can be got rid of by removing them to the level of fantasy, then detective stories could be described as a harmless safety valve, a wholesome therapy serving a desirable social purpose.
>
> And yet one may wonder if this commonly accepted view is entirely correct, if fantasy and real life are actually so unrelated.
>
> To some extent we may build our real life around our fantasy and, if this is so, sensation literature may not so much rid us of dangerous drives as reinforce and reshape them.
>
> In any case, if detective stories are not so sinister as they at first appear from analysis, neither are they as frivolous as some critics have judged them.
>
> The drives they cater to are compelling and basic, and relate ultimately to the struggle for self-preservation. It is the universal nature of their theme which explains the size and variety of their reading audience. The intellectual, who scorns the cheap fantasies of the popular magazines, is not likely to be able to forgo the fantasies which give him hope for his survival in an alien world.
>
> Detective stories deal, in their own way and on their own

level, with the most essential and urgent problems in the human condition.

ADAPTED FROM WILLIAM O. AYDELOTTE,
"The Detective Story as a Historical Source"

Actually the above passage was written as two paragraphs, the second beginning with the sentence "In any case, if detective. . . ." Notice that this sentence makes an excellent transition: the first part looks back to the previous paragraph, and the rest introduces the new thought. When the passage is divided properly into two paragraphs, continuity is improved and the logic of the thought becomes clearer.

But perhaps we should beware of taking evidence of this sort too tragically, or of deducing from detective stories nothing but a pessimistic moral. The condemnation of detective stories as drugs or cheap escapism may be pedantic. For, if they are a symptom, they can also be a cure. If we credit the Freudian view that socially dangerous impulses can be got rid of by removing them to the level of fantasy, then detective stories could be described as a harmless safety valve, a wholesome therapy serving a desirable social purpose. And yet one may wonder if this commonly accepted view is entirely correct, if fantasy and real life are actually so unrelated. To some extent we may build our real life around our fantasy and, if this is so, sensation literature may not so much rid us of dangerous drives as reinforce and reshape them.

In any case, if detective stories are not so sinister as they at first appear from analysis, neither are they as frivolous as some critics have judged them. The drives they cater to are compelling and basic, and relate ultimately to the struggle for self-preservation. It is the universal nature of their theme which explains the size and variety of their reading audience. The intellectual, who scorns the cheap fantasies of the popular magazines, is not likely to be able to forgo the fantasies which give him hope for his survival in an alien world. Detective stories deal, in their own way and on their own level, with the most essential and urgent problems in the human condition.

45d Avoid excessively long paragraphs.

Very long paragraphs make it hard for a reader to digest meaning easily. To reduce excessive length it may be necessary to reduce the scope of the controlling idea—to limit purpose. But sometimes a paragraph can be trimmed simply by discarding material. You may not need ten examples to prove or illustrate a point. Four or five may do it just as well.

▶ Exercise 2

The authors divided the following passage into three paragraphs. Indicate the places where you believe they made the divisions, and underline the topic sentences.

Whereas most of us speak only to the relatively few people we meet face-to-face, reporters address an audience that ranges from a few hundred to several million. The average person can select subjects and wording to fit an individual listener, but the reporter ordinarily must write about actions and situations that interest large groups. And reporters must tell most of their stories in words that any reasonably literate person can understand. Professional reporters are the hired eyes, ears, legs, and brain of the reader, viewer, or listener. Everything they do is guided by the individual reader's interests. They are paid to survey a small fraction of the world's activities each day and tell the public what they find: what is happening, what is scheduled to happen, what people are saying about it, and (when they can be reasonably sure) what it means. If they do their job well, they supply much of the current information that each person needs to develop a workable picture of reality. If they do it poorly, they become responsible for part of the public's ignorance and prejudice. Continual awareness of this responsibility to the public marks the attitude of professional reporters. Reporters are individuals, but they also are vital elements in the social process of communication. By helping decide what constitutes news, how it should be written and to what length, they function as human valves and amplifiers in the vast machinery of mass communication. They select, reject, compile, interpret, explain, and highlight. But in so doing, they are geared more to the product than to the process. They do not serve simply as an open conduit between the reader and reality, as mechanical sifters of fact and opinion. If they are functioning properly, they are constantly attuned to the receiver. A reporter is a *thinking* agent of the reader.

JAMES M. NEAL AND SUZANNE S. BROWN,
Newswriting and Reporting

▶ Exercise 3
The author divided the following passage into five paragraphs. Indicate the places where you believe she made the divisions.

Almost two-thirds of American women live in cities. In relation to the total population, one-tenth of all white people are poor, but about one-third of all blacks are poor. Out of every ten poor persons, four are children. More than one family in ten is headed by a woman; there are 5.6 million such families in the United States, of which 43 per cent are headed by widows and 46 per cent by divorced or separated women. About two million of these families are below the poverty level. While the number of poor families headed by men dropped by half between 1959 and 1969, the number of poor families headed by women has remained virtually unchanged. The hardest hit family is the one headed by a black woman who works; 45 per cent of these families live in poverty compared to 16 per cent headed by a male black worker. Three-fifths of the 3.4 million families headed by a woman with children under 18 need some financial assistance. Most women hold a high school diploma. Of the women in the age group 20 to 24, 80 per cent were high school graduates in 1970, as were men in the same age group. But relatively few women have earned a college degree. In 1970 the per cent of all women over 21 who had been through four or more years of college was 9 per cent compared to 14 per cent for men. The widest gap, however, between men and women's education appears at the professional level. Only 9 per cent of all scientists are women, 7 per cent of all physicians, 3 per cent of lawyers and just 1 per cent of engineers and federal judges. The per cent of women on college faculties has declined from 28 per cent in 1922 to 22 per cent in 1940. In the 92nd Congress there was one female Senator. In the House twelve women held seats out of a possible 435; this is only two more than served in the 91st Congress and only one is a black woman. Early in 1969 eleven women were occupying federal judgeships by Presidential appointment. The number of women in state legislatures declined from 370 in 1965 to 318 in 1967, and now stands at about 300. Sixty-two per cent of American women are married. Most women marry young, on an average just before their 21st birthday. There is not only a rush to be a June bride but to be married by 21; after that a woman is an old maid capable only of feeling sorry for herself that she has failed somehow in the "sweepstakes of life." Approximately 27 per cent of American women marry younger than 21, between 14 and 19 years of age. It is not surprising then that the rate for disrupted marriages, those marriages ending in divorce or separation, is increasing and shows no immediate sign of declining. In 1970, 10 per cent of all married women were so affected. For young women between 20 and 24, the number of disrupted marriages has increased about 25 per cent since 1960.

JACQUELINE ST. JOHN, "Women's Legislative
Issues Today and Tomorrow"

45e Develop your paragraphs adequately.

Do not omit the examples, the proof, the explanations, the exceptions—in short, the finer and the fuller details that make good paragraphs. Instead of merely mentioning points, you should develop and clarify them for the reader. Details flesh out your ideas.

The following three topic sentences alone lack the fullness of good writing. The basic principles are introduced, but nothing is developed.

> Most of American history and much of American literature have been conditioned or influenced by the existence of a changing frontier.
> Until recently, a politician who had not been born in a log cabin was handicapped in any election.
> For Americans, the frontier has always been an ambivalent symbol.

In the paragraphs as they were originally written, the subject—the frontier—comes alive:

> Most of American history and much of American literature have been conditioned or influenced by the existence of a changing frontier. In our homes and in our schools many of our greatest stories and legends are about men like Captain John Smith, Lewis and Clark, Daniel Boone, Davy Crockett, and Kit Carson. We celebrate not only Washington's achievements as our Revolutionary leader and first President, but also his exploits as an Indian fighter and surveyor of the wilderness. We remember Andrew Jackson as Old Hickory, a frontier figure. We honor Abraham Lincoln as a son of the prairie woodland, a rail-splitter who read the Bible by light from a fireplace.
>
> Until recently, a politician who had not been born in a log cabin was handicapped in any election. Theodore Roosevelt gained glamor from his career as a cattleman and his fame as the organizer of the Rough Riders. Even a New Englander like Calvin Coolidge found it wise to visit the Black Hills of South Dakota and wear an Indian headdress for newspaper photographers. And in 1960 we elected as President another New Englander who promised us a "New Frontier."
>
> For Americans, the frontier has always been an ambivalent symbol. It has been considered a source of freedom and a place of danger; an exciting challenge, but also a cause of hardship and exhaustion; a place for heroism, but also an excuse for racism, sadism, and brutality; an inexhaustible mine of humor, but humor too often tinged with cruelty or false sentimentality. It has been idealized as a source of health, vitality, and nobility; but it has been condemned as rude, ugly, and barbaric.
>
> PHILLIP DURHAM AND EVERETT L. JONES,
> *The Frontier in American Literature*

In the first two paragraphs, the topic sentences are developed by references to typical and famous Americans related in some way to the frontier. In the last paragraph, interpretation is more significant, and the qualities in the men and the meaning of the frontier are the basis of development.

45f   Develop a paragraph by the method most appropriate for the central topic.

Paragraphs may develop their topics in many ways. They may define, classify, or move from cause to effect or effect to cause; from a generalization to the facts it interprets; or from a body of facts to a generalization about them. Usually the material on a subject so clearly dictates its pattern that the writer does not even have to decide to write a paragraph of a certain kind—definition, for example. He simply defines without deciding to do so, because defining is what the material demands. He thinks about the subject and material, and the method takes care of itself. There are, however, a few points to keep in mind.

Climactic order   Almost any list is more interesting if you begin with the least important item and end with the most important.

Comparison and contrast   Two basic methods can be used in developing a paragraph by comparison and contrast: writing everything about one point and then everything about the other (XXXX YYYY); or writing about alternating points throughout the paragraph (XY XY XY XY). Either method can be effective, but in long and complex comparisons and contrasts the alternating method is generally better.

Definition   Good expository definition tries to explain an abstraction clearly and accurately. The problem is to make the term sufficiently concrete in examples which do not excessively restrict the meaning. Intellectual definitions, of course, may be much more elaborate than the definitions given in dictionaries.

45g Use transitions to show relationships between sentences within paragraphs and between one paragraph and another.

Transitional devices help your reader see how and why you progress from one point to another and how your ideas are related.

Connective words and expressions

but	indeed	likewise
and	in fact	consequently
however	meanwhile	first
moreover	afterward	next
furthermore	then	in brief
on the other hand	so	to summarize
nevertheless	still	to conclude
for example	after all	similarly

Demonstratives

this   that   these   those

References to demonstratives must be clear.

Other pronouns

many   each   some   others   such   either

Repeated key words, phrases, and synonyms   Repetitions and synonyms are good signposts to guide the reader from sentence to sentence and paragraph to paragraph.

Transitional words in topic sentences can contribute materially to clarity, coherence, and the movement of the discussion. Some writers meticulously guide readers with a connector at the beginning of almost every paragraph. H. J. Muller, for example, begins a sequence of paragraphs about science as follows:

> In this summary, science . . .
> Yet science does . . .
> Similarly the basic interests of science . . .
> In other words, they are not . . .
> This demonstration that even the scientist . . .
> This idea will concern us . . .
> In other words, facts and figures . . .

Note how the connectors in the paragraphs in Exercise 4 help you to put the sentences in their correct order. All the paragraphs in Exercises 4–7 were taken from Dixon Wecter's *The Age of the Great Depression, 1929–1941*.

▶ Exercise 4
The sentences in the following paragraphs have been changed from their original sequence within each paragraph. Indicate their proper order.

1. A. Recordings of these speeches through the years show changes in Roosevelt's technique, from the old-fashioned sonorous style with oratorical pauses learned in preradio days, to a lower pitch and softer, relaxed, more engaging address better suited to the unseen audience.
   B. The New Deal's best radio propagandist was President Roosevelt himself, whose warm democratic salutation "My friends" had been adopted as early as his vain campaign for the vice-presidency in 1920.
   C. His direct, intimate appeal to the people built a personal leadership unprecedented in its influence; not infrequently fifty thousand letters a day followed a "fireside chat."

2. A. Based upon H. G. Wells's *War of the Worlds* and punctuated by announcements that should have carried reassurance, the sketch purported to describe a rocket-borne invasion of Martians, equipped with flame throwers and heat rays, who proceeded to ravage the New Jersey countryside until slain by the disease bacteria of this planet.

   B. That the radio had become an immense political force was being demonstrated in another way by the Axis dictators as well as by home-grown demagogues like Father Coughlin and Huey Long.

   C. Not only did it carry nuances and subtle emotion denied to print, but it tended to arrest in the listener those critical impulses that often led a reader to turn back to the dubious or imperfectly understood.

   D. Not pausing for that dénouement, at least a million auditors became upset or terror-stricken, many forsaking their homes afoot or by car in panic.

   E. Startling evidence of its hypnotic effect on the mass imagination was afforded by a broadcast of the young actor Orson Welles on the evening of October 30, 1938, a month after the Munich crisis.

3. A. While newspaper advertising never regained its 1929 peak of eight hundred million dollars, radio salesmanship mounted year by year until in 1941 it was doing a two-hundred-million-dollar business—over a third of that vouchsafed its competitor—with magazines occupying third place.

   B. The [number] . . . of commercial [as compared] to noncommercial or "sustaining" programs appeared steadily on the [increase] . . . , advertisers' demands relegating some of the best public-service features to unpopular listening hours.

   C. The potency of the air waves was not overlooked by the advertiser.

   D. Growing constantly more blatant, radio advertising featured the singing commercial, the middle commercial flanked by those incidental opening and closing plugs called by the trade "cowcatchers" and "hitchhikers," and the "give-away" to reward a listener's correct answer to a telephone call from the studio.

4. A. Three big chains commanded the field: the National Broadcasting Company, whose Red and Blue networks in 1938 controlled a hundred and forty-eight stations by ownership or affiliation, the Columbia Broadcasting System with a hundred and fifteen, and Mutual (a newcomer dating from 1934) eighty-three.

   B. Concentration also characterized the national networks, whose slickly professional programs, originating chiefly in New York and Hollywood, were piped to local stations all over the land.

   C. Within the single year 1935 the number of stations so owned doubled, and by 1940 no less than a third of the nation's eight hundred licensed stations were tied in one way or another to newspapers.

   D. At the same time newspapers rapidly increased their ownership of stations, sometimes monopolizing all the news outlets in a given community.

   E. Helpless to throttle the radio as an advertising medium, the newspaper press for a time tried to prevent its access to a regular flow of the world's news.

   F. In 1934, however, the feud was composed by the so-called press-radio agreement and formation of the Transradio Press Service, which outlasted that pact.

▶ Exercise 5
Of the topic sentences below, select the one that you feel best fits the paragraph.

1. Several things happened in the late 1930's.
2. The success of radio can be traced to several factors.
3. Fashions in entertainment came and went.

     After the success in 1936 of "Professor Quiz," question-and-answer programs like "Information Please" and "The Quiz Kids" burgeoned mightily. Such unrehearsed contests reflected a vogue similar to that featuring sidewalk interviews, guessing games and amateur hours, with a large element of audience participation. The radio serial proved to be a universal favorite, illustrated early in the era by the vast popularity of "Amos 'n' Andy" . . . or the plenitude of "soap operas" which later in the decade came to rule the daytime hours, dedicated to the praise of soap flakes and washing powders between interstices of tears and laughter in their plots of homely romance. For juveniles the decade's hero was the "Lone Ranger," who made his début in 1933—a stalwart without fear or vices, whose cry "Hi-Yo, Silver!" heralded his arrival upon that trusty steed to redress wrong and succor the weak. By the close of the era radio's best-known personality had come to be an impudent puppet named Charlie McCarthy, creation of the ventriloquist Edgar Bergen.

▶ Exercise 6
Analyze the following paragraphs and be ready to discuss (1) topic sentences, (2) use of detail, (3) unity, (4) order or sequence, and (5) transitions.

1. Music occupied over half of radio's daily log, and more of it than ever before was of high quality. In 1930 Columbia began its Sunday broadcasting of New York Philharmonic concerts; the following year the National Broadcasting Company launched its Saturday-afternoon series of grand operas from the Metropolitan; and in 1937 it persuaded the world-famous conductor Arturo Toscanini to undertake a memorable series with its own symphony orchestra. Over ten million families, according to a 1939 estimate, listened to such music; a poll in this year indicated that, save on the farm and at the bottom of the economic scale, those who enjoyed "classical" music outnumbered those desiring exclusively "popular." When in 1940 the Metropolitan Opera Company in severe financial straits appealed to its invisible audience, they contributed a third of a million dollars to "save the Met."

2. Music appreciation in the home saw the performer's rôle steadily supplanted, however, by the auditor's. While the radio was outstripping even the phonograph in popularity, father's fiddle gathered dust, and in affluent homes the piano remained oftentimes as a piece of prestige furniture. In 1939 only sixteen million copies of sheet music were sold as compared with forty-five million records of popular melodies. The invasion of music by radio, whether "live" or "canned," was greater still though harder to measure, while the life expectancy of a popular song, under furious exploitation by the "Lucky Strike Hit Parade" and similar programs, grew vastly shorter.

▶ Exercise 7
Make two paragraphs out of the following. Sentences are in their original order.

Both radio and phonograph fostered the continued popularity of dancing, which had swept the twenties under the heady inspiration of jazz, that powerful if almost indefinable rhythmic style.

About 1931, when a popular song was urging the depressed to "wrap your troubles in dreams, and dream your troubles away," the plangent bravado of jazz temporarily faded from fashion before the soothing hypnotic strains of "sweet" bands like those of Guy Lombardo, Wayne King, and Eddy Duchin.

An advance-guardist of new modes in jazz who died in that year—the trumpeter Leon ("Bix") Beiderbecke—would later be recalled nostalgically by Dorothy Baker's fine novel of the artist as jazzman, *Young Man with a Horn* (1938).

Early in 1934, perhaps as a harbinger of recovery, the spirit of jazz was reborn, largely by the superb clarinet recordings and dance-band broadcasts of Benny Goodman, exponent of what European connoisseurs called *le jazz hot*.

It soon gained a new name, swing. A more dynamic form of syncopation and superimposed rhythm, an intense yet easy floating that "gets there on time"—and in expert hands capable of rich improvisation—swing retained the essence of its parent, jazz.

"'Swing' is to jazz what the poetic spirit is to poetry," wrote one lyric journalist in the winter of 1935–1936 when "jam sessions" and Hot Clubs were springing up over the nation.

An incidental term in high favor was "boogie-woogie," signifying piano music in which an insistent rolling left-hand pattern mingled with the fancy-free inventions of the right.

46 Writing good themes

Stages in the process of composition overlap, but they can be separated for discussion. These include choosing and limiting a subject; determining your purpose and planning the development of your paper, often through an outline; writing the first draft; and revising and preparing the final draft.

Except for impromptu class assignments, a paper should not be completed at a single sitting. Allow yourself enough time so that you can think about your subject and plan adequately.

46a Choose a subject that interests you.

To find significant and interesting subjects, draw on your experience, memory, imagination, knowledge, interests, and study. Good subjects can come to mind at unexpected moments. You may think of one while your thoughts are wandering in class or while you are taking your clothes to the laundry. Never let a possible subject escape you. Reserve a page or two in your notebook for all the topics and titles which occur to you. Even the less promising possibilities may evolve into good subjects. When a theme must be written, it is better to have an excess of ideas than a blank sheet of paper staring at you from your desk. You can avoid false starts and lost time by examining your list of possibilities and settling on one good topic at the outset. (For suggestions about subjects for themes, see pages 214–217.)

46b Limit your topic.

Tailor your subject to the length of the assignment. Do not skim the surface of a broad topic, but select a limited part of it and develop that part fully through discussion, analysis, illustration, and detail.

A 250-word paper calls for a more limited treatment than a 500-word or a 1000-word paper; it may demand a different subject altogether. Generalized treatments of large subjects can be successful if they are handled with intelligence, breadth of perspective, and insight; many good editorials are written on just such topics. But the best themes deal with topics limited enough to allow room for plenty of explanation and detail.

Suppose a student starts with the idea of writing a 500-word theme on humor. The evolution of this subject in the student's mind can be shown as follows:

> *Humor:* Too broad . . .
> *The Nature of Humor:* Still too broad . . .
> *A Specific Kind of Humor:* Might have something here . . . think of a kind . . .
> *Sick Humor:* Sounds unpleasant . . . unattractive topic equals unattractive theme?
> *Jokes and Jokers:* Getting close, but still too broad . . .
> *Practical Jokers:* Almost have it, but what about practical jokers?
> *The Serious Intent of Practical Jokers:* That's it. A subject I'm interested in and can say something about.

Through association of ideas, this student arrived at what looks like a workable subject.

Even after the topic is thus limited, however, you cannot *know* that it is the right size until you have (1) considered its subdivisions and (2) sometimes actually written the theme. A subject which at first seems limited may open up into greater complexity and promise to yield a paper far beyond the assigned length. If so, you must turn to another subject—perhaps a still more limited aspect of the first.

Or if the paper is already written, you may reduce the length of it, usually by cutting out whole sections. But a theme shortened in this way is often confused, jerky, or badly proportioned because of omissions and condensations. A fresh start with a new topic may cost a high price in lost time. It is much better to write a theme of the proper length in the first place.

46c Formulate a thesis statement.

The central idea of a paper can usually be expressed in a single sentence. Sometimes this statement can be phrased early in the planning process, sometimes not until you are near the actual writing. In any event, it should be expressed early in the written paper, often in the opening paragraph.

A good **thesis statement** is specific and concise. It brings the subject into focus for the reader, suggests the scope of the paper, and shows coherently the idea or ideas that the theme will develop.

VAGUE AND STEREOTYPED
It is the purpose of this theme to discuss the serious intent of practical jokers.
VAGUE
Practical jokers have similar motivations.
MORE PURPOSEFUL
Practical jokers have four basic motivations: to obtain applause, to feel reassurance, to experience power, and to vent hostility.

46d Select an appropriate tone and be consistent.

Tone is the quality which reveals the writer's attitude toward the subject matter. It may be serious or humorous, ironical or straightforward, zealous or casual, brisk or nostalgic. As a general rule, a moderately serious tone is the most effective for most subjects. Unless you are extremely skilled, you should not run the risk of alienating your readers by treating a serious subject humorously. Whatever tone you choose, be consistent. An inconsistent tone confuses a reader about the writer's intention. The tone, on the other hand, need not be held unvaryingly in one key. It may, for example, move reasonably from the serious to a touch of humor, but it should not run from one extreme to another in the same piece of writing.

NOTE Avoid flippancy and sarcasm.

$46e$ Organize carefully.

You should never set out to write a paper without some kind of outline, even if it is only in your mind. A **scratch outline** is the simplest kind. It is a list of the points you want to make in any form you wish. It is a quick way to order your thoughts and remind you of that order when you are writing the paper. For brief themes or those written during the class hour, a scratch outline will usually suffice. Below is a scratch outline for a paper on "The Serious Intent of Practical Jokers":

> practical jokes—variety of
> serious motivations
> to get attention
> to be reassured
> to experience power
> to vent hostility

A **topic outline** is a formal and detailed structure to help you organize your materials. In making a topic outline, observe the following rules:

1. Number the main topics with Roman numerals, the first subheadings with capital letters, the next with Arabic numerals. If further subheadings are necessary, use a, b, c, and (1), (2), (3).

I. ....
  A. ....
    1. ....
      a. ....
        (1) ....
        (2) ....
      b. ....
    2. ....
  B. ....
II. ....

    2. Use parallel grammatical structures.

    3. Use topics, not sentences. Do not place periods after the topics. Punctuate as in the example that follows.

    4. Check to see that your outline covers the subject completely.

    5. Use specific topics and subheadings arranged in a logical, meaningful order. Each indented level of the outline represents a division of the preceding level and has smaller scope.

    Avoid single subheadings. Roman numeral I calls for II; subheading A calls for B, and so forth.

NOT
  I. Nature of reasons for practical jokes
    A. Variety
  II. Applause

    The following is an example of a topic outline with a title, a thesis statement, and a series of orderly and carefully developed topics.

The Serious Intent of Practical Jokers

Thesis Statement: Practical jokers share four basic motivations: to obtain applause, to feel reassurance, to experience power, and to vent hostility.

I. Nature of and reasons for practical jokes
   A. Variety
   B. Motivations
II. Applause
   A. For acting
   B. For cleverness
III. Reassurance
   A. Victim ridiculous
   B. Joker superior
IV. Power
   A. Over joke
   B. Over victim
V. Hostility
   A. Harmless jokes, normal hostility
   B. Harmful jokes, abnormal hostility
VI. Practical jokes and human nature

The **sentence outline** represents a more advanced kind of preparation for writing a theme. More thinking has to go into a sentence outline than into a scratch or topic outline, but it is often worth the effort because it offers a tight control over your writing and makes it harder to wander from the subject. As a rule, the more time you spend on your outline, the less time you will need to do the actual writing of the theme. The sentence outline follows the same conventions as the topic outline except that the entries are all expressed in complete sentences. Place periods after sentences in a sentence outline.

The Serious Intent of Practical Jokers

Thesis Statement: Practical jokers share four basic motivations: to obtain applause, to feel reassurance, to experience power, and to vent hostility.

I. The nature of practical jokers differs widely, but the motivations of practical jokers are common to all.
   A. Practical jokes vary from the humorous and harmless to the cruel.
   B. Practical jokers share four basic motivations: to obtain applause, to feel reassurance, to experience power, and to vent hostility.

II. Practical jokers, like most people, crave applause.
   A. They are actors expecting approval of an audience for playing a part well.
   B. They also expect approval for their cleverness.
III. Closely related to the desire for applause is the human need for reassurance.
   A. The practical joker always makes the victim look more or less ridiculous.
   B. By making the victim look silly, the practical joker feels superior.
IV. Practical jokes enable the performer to feel a sense of power.
   A. The joker controls the length and pace of the joke.
   B. The joker controls the victim like a puppeteer.
V. The practical joker is venting feelings of hostility toward others.
   A. Even jokes which are harmless reflect some degree of hostility in all of us.
   B. Cruel jokes show an abnormal degree of hostility in the performer.
VI. To understand the motivations of practical jokers is to see basic aspects of human nature.

46f   Use examples to illustrate generalizations.

Meaningful generalizations frequently rest on illustrations. An abstract truth may become evident only after concrete examples have been given (see **45e**). A string of unillustrated generalizations can make a theme dull and unconvincing. Examples give your paper clarity and color.

GENERALIZATION
In varying degrees the victim of a practical joke is always made to look ridiculous.

EXAMPLES
He may be tricked into talking into a mailbox where there is a hidden microphone, or he may slip on a banana peel planted in his path, or he may find himself trying to open a door with grease stuck to the knob.

$46g$ Use the following checklist of essentials in writing themes.

Title

The title should accurately suggest the contents of the paper.

It should attract interest without being excessively novel or clever.

It should not be too long.

NOTE Do not underline the title of your own paper (to represent italics), and do not put quotation marks around it.

Introduction

The introduction should be independent of the title. No pronoun or noun in the opening sentence should depend for meaning on the title.

It should catch the reader's attention.

It should properly establish the tone of the paper as serious, humorous, ironic, or otherwise.

It should include a thesis statement which declares the subject and the purpose directly but at the same time avoids worn patterns like "It is the purpose of this paper to. . . ."

Body

The materials should develop the thesis statement.

The materials should be arranged in logical sequence.

Strong topic sentences (see **45a**) should clearly indicate the direction in which the paper is moving and the relevance of the paragraphs to the thesis statement.

Technical terms should be explained.

Paragraphs should not be choppy.

Enough space should be devoted to main ideas. Minor ideas should be subordinated.

Concrete details should be used appropriately. Insignificant details should be omitted.

Transitions

The connections between sentences and those between paragraphs should be shown by good linking words (see **45g**).

Conclusion

The conclusion should usually contain a final statement of the underlying idea, an overview of what the paper has demonstrated.

The conclusion may require a separate paragraph; but if the paper has reached significant conclusions all along, such a paragraph is not necessary for its own sake.

The conclusion should not merely restate the introduction.

Proofreading

Allow some time, if possible at least one day, between the last draft of the paper and the final finished copy. Then you can examine the paper objectively for wordiness, repetition, incorrect diction, misspellings, faulty punctuation, choppy sentences, vague sentences, lack of transitions, and careless errors.

Model theme

NOTE If your instructor requires the thesis statement labeled and written in after the title and before the beginning of the paper (as indicated in the following theme), provide it.

The Serious Intent of Practical Jokers

THESIS STATEMENT: Practical jokers share four basic motivations: to obtain applause, to feel reassurance, to experience power, and to vent hostility.

Practical jokes vary as much as the people who indulge in them. Everyone has probably witnessed numerous harmless and often funny pranks like those played on April Fool's Day. Other forms of practical joking, such as those that once characterized college hazing, are far from humorous. In fact, they can be sadistically cruel. Even though differences are evident in their tricks, practical jokers share four basic motivations: to obtain applause, to feel reassurance, to experience power, and to vent hostility. The intensity of these motivations determines whether the joke is pleasant to all (including the victim) or only to the practical joker.

In one way or another most people strive for applause. Practical jokers are in a sense actors. They desire approval for playing a part well. An executive who puts a big plastic spider in the chair of a typist and then with a straight face asks what that is beside her loses much of his fun if no one else is present in the office to see her reaction. If onlookers are present, they may laugh with him and thus show their mark of appreciation for his acting. He feels that they are also saying to him with their laughter that he is clever and intelligent for thinking up such a prank, pulling it off so well, and providing amusement and relief from routine.

Closely related to the desire for applause is the human need for reassurance. A practical joke is a reflection of this craving in all of us to make ourselves look better at someone else's expense. In varying degrees the victim of a practical joke is always made to look ridiculous. He may be tricked into talking into a mailbox where there is a hidden microphone, or he may slip on a banana peel planted in his path, or open a door with dirty grease on the knob. By making his victim look silly, the practical joker feels a momentary flash of superiority. He senses that he is better than his victim because he is rational and composed whereas the victim is off his guard.

Although one may not think of a practical joker as a person who wants power, he nevertheless performs his jokes partly because they enable him to experience the thrill of control. He feels power by controlling the length and pace of the joke itself. He can hurry it to its conclusion, or he can prolong it and add refinements as he chooses. In a small way, his is the power of creativity. He also experiences power over his victim because he is like a puppeteer pulling the strings. He is in command; the other person merely responds. He has the advantage because he knows what is going on; his victim is in the dark.

Psychologists say that we manifest hostility toward others in dozens of ways that we do not realize. The practical joke offers one of these ways to vent feelings of hostility and aggression in a fashion that is socially acceptable provided the joke is not destructive. The degree of hostility in the practical joker can often be measured by the nature of his prank. If he sends a novice mechanic out for a left-handed wrench, he is probably reflecting the mild hostility that most people feel toward the greenhorns of the world. If, on the other hand, he arranges for the novice to slip on a banana peel on the way and to be hit with a flower pot, his feelings of hostility are probably beyond those of normalcy.

To understand the motivations of practical jokers is to understand something fundamental about human nature. The reasons behind practical jokes may not appear attractive, but they are not in themselves abnormal. Whether we actually perform the jokes or not, we are all practical jokers because in varying degrees we all share the four basic motivations.

Subjects for papers

Keep a notebook of items which you think may be useful to you as possible subjects and materials for papers. Some suggested subjects follow.

Fewer Years for College	The Center City
Old Photographs	Bad Teaching
Fair Journalism	Abortion
Return to the Country	Television Commercials
Political Cartoons	An Ice Storm
The New Music	Women's Equal Rights
Divorce	The Average Man
The New Freedoms	Working in a Political Campaign
Blackness	Good Fences and Good Friends
Patterns of Humor	Educating the Parent
City Folklore	Camping Out
Walking	Parks
A Deserted House	Censorship
Crime	The Subway at Night
Exploring	Credit
The Scientific Attitude	Welfare
The Emergency Ward	Acting in a Play
Trip Down River	A Description of a Painting

The following quotations may help you to develop subjects for themes. Support, refute, exemplify, or use these quotations in any appropriate way. You may think of a subject only remotely related to what the author says.

> The older generation had certainly pretty well ruined this world before passing it on to us. They give us this Thing, knocked to pieces, leaky, red-hot, threatening to blow up; and then they are surprised that we don't accept it with the same attitude of pretty, decorous enthusiasm with which they received it. . . .
>
> JOHN F. CARTER, JR.,
> "The Overnight Realists"

> For the 15 per cent of adolescents who learn well in schools and are interested in subjects that are essentially academic, the present catch-all high schools are wasteful.
>
> PAUL GOODMAN, "Freedom and Learning:
> The Need for Choice"

For generations we have tried to make the world a better place by providing more and more schooling, but so far the endeavor has failed.

> IVAN ILLICH, "The Alternative to Schooling"

Uncle Sam has become bankrupt when it comes to a conscience. . . .
> MALCOLM X, "The Black Revolution"

The outstanding objection to the modern dance is that it is immodest and lacking in grace. It is not based on the natural and harmless instinct for rhythm, but on a craving for abnormal excitement.

> THE HOBART COLLEGE *Herald*

For there is a cloud on my horizon. A small dark cloud no bigger than my hand. Its name is Progress.

> EDWARD ABBEY, *Desert Solitaire*

The humor in *Peanuts,* then, has a dimension apart from the obvious gag level. This is because the characters in *Peanuts* are reflections of ourselves, and we are funnier than any make-believe character could possibly be.

> MARTIN JEZER, "Quo Peanuts?"

The American seems to be becoming more unable to demonstrate the individuality which democracy requires. Continuing hypnotism, emulsification, and homogenization of men by the media is the opposite of what our nation needs. . . .

> HARRY J. SKORNIA,
> "Ratings and Mass Values"

The arts objectify subjective reality, and subjectify outward experience of nature. Art education is the education of feeling, and a society that neglects it gives itself up to formless emotion. Bad art is corruption of feeling.

> SUSANNE K. LANGER,
> "The Cultural Importance of Art"

The bad dreams of our Utopians will not come true; even the most complex, advanced thinking machine will not replace or dominate this [human] spirit.

> JOHN H. TROLL,
> "The Thinking of Men and Machines"

We are not so weak and timorous as to need to be free of fear; we need only use our capacity to not be afraid of it and so relegate fear to its proper perspective.

WILLIAM FAULKNER, "Faith or Fear"

Religion will not regain its old power until it can face change in the same spirit as does science.

ALFRED NORTH WHITEHEAD,
"Religion and Science"

No great and enduring volume can ever be written on the flea, though many there be who have tried it.

HERMAN MELVILLE, *Moby-Dick*

Whoso would be a man, must be a nonconformist.

RALPH WALDO EMERSON, "Self-Reliance"

Stay, stay at home, my heart and rest; / Homekeeping hearts are happiest.

HENRY WADSWORTH LONGFELLOW

A prophet is not without honor, save in his own country, and in his own house.

MATTHEW 13:57

Home life as we understand it is no more natural to us than a cage is natural to a cockatoo.

GEORGE BERNARD SHAW, *Getting Married*

To some extent a citizen of any country will feel that the tourist's view of his homeland is a false one.

MARY MCCARTHY, "America the Beautiful"

Labor disgraces no man; unfortunately you occasionally find men disgrace labor.

ULYSSES S. GRANT,
Speech at Birmingham, England

The mass of men lead lives of quiet desperation. What is called resignation is confirmed desperation.

HENRY DAVID THOREAU, *Walden*

Our life is frittered away by detail.

THOREAU, *Walden*

Ah, one doesn't give up one's country any more than one gives up
one's grandmother.
HENRY JAMES, *The Portrait of a Lady*

Man's Unhappiness, as I construe, comes of his Greatness; it is because there is an Infinite in him, which with all his cunning he
cannot quite bury under the Finite.
THOMAS CARLYLE, *Sartor Resartus*

The mobs of great cities add just so much to the support of pure government, as sores do to the strength of the human body.
THOMAS JEFFERSON, *Notes on Virginia*

▶ Exercise

*For this exercise you must assume the role of teacher. Imagine
that the three themes that follow were written by your students. Mark the mistakes with numbers that correspond to sections in this book (see pages xvii–xx). Write any comments
you deem appropriate in the margins and a summary opinion
at the end of each paper. Then give each theme a grade. Be prepared to defend all corrections, the comments, and the grades.*

*A theme may be filled with diverse errors. Or perhaps
one contains mainly a single kind of major flaw. Do not mark
so many errors that discussion of the theme will be hopeless
and endless.*

The Roles of Woman and Man

In my opinion people are too caught up in their ways. Just be-

cause something has always been done a certain way people be-

lieve it has to keep on being done the same way. I think that attitude is wrong. I believe that the past should not be allowed to control what is going on at the present. I am no expert but in my opinion most people are still afraid to do things any different from the way there parents did it. Not necessarily most people but alot of them.

What can be done about this? One thing that can be done about this is to re-examine how people think either conscious or unconscious about their roles in life. Take the average woman. In my opinion she has been so brainwashed that she believes that she cant do anything but light jobs. She expects, it seems to me, to have like doors opened for her and she thinks she has to look after the kids and clean the house and wash the dirty dishes and not ever do things that would develope her muscles. A woman has things she is supposed to do. If she does like do other things she is put down for being a women's lib.

Men have their roles too. Like they do not feel, in my opinion, right in taking care of the little ones and cleaning house and stuff like that, you know. People have always thought that if the husband stays home and does the choers and the woman is the bacon winner, then he must be some kind of a nut or something. In my opinion that is definately a wrong attitude. Staying home and washing the dirty dishes, a contribution can be made by the man just as much as the woman. Communication is the important thing I think not roles.

A marriage is not made in heaven. It has to be worked for. I believe although I admit I have never been married that alot of romantic noncense has been written on marriage. This romantic noncense that has been written puts the woman on a pedastal she is made to look like a shrinking violent and the man is a harry chested he man who helps only here and there in the house. His job is at the factory or ofice. I don't by any of this. Do whatever you feel like, like if you want to stay home and wash the dirty dishes and change the babbies dirty dipers, do it and if the woman wants to be a policeman or a executive thats alright too.

If this goes against the grain and gives you problems ask who made the rules to begin with? To begin with the rules were made

by people who in my humble opinion were narow minded and igno-
rant. Why should modern people who are enlighted pay attention
to people from the dark ages who were puretanical. Do whatever
turns you on.

Reading

A wise man once said, "When one is too tired to read, he is too
tired to breathe." What he meant was that reading is as important
to mankind as life itself. His exaggeration is excusable, for reading
is, indeed, just about as fundamental to civilized beings as any
other single activity. It is to the mind what eating is to the
body—sustenance.

But not everyone is civilized. Among us today are barbarians
just as there were at the dawn of time. It is as difficult to explain
the advantages of reading to these heathens as it is to communicate the finer points of professional football to a woman. The
joy of silent conversation, the stimulation of insight, the delight of

heightened imagination—all these advantages are lost to the automobile mechanic or the plumber who spends his days in grimy manual labor and his evenings in the inane world of television or in that haze produced by beer. Such a person believes that anyone who reads is an impractical intellectual who is so far removed from the real world that he is laughable. There is no scorn like the scorn of a non-reader toward a reader.

A recent poll conducted by the Estege Corporation reveals that seventy-three percent of the people surveyed on the street could not identify William Faulkner, perhaps the greatest American novelist of the twentieth century. One woman seemed to remember that he was an actor; another believed him to be a governor of some state. The fate of this land, and the world besides, is in the hands of a few intelligent people who can read a book and enjoy it. The "great unwashed" mass, as it was once called, is a blight that threatens to spread and destroy civilization. How can one respect or even trust a person who thinks that existentialism is a rare disease?

The most discouraging aspect of this problem is that illiteracy, which was once restricted to those who had little formal schooling, now is creeping up the educational ladder like a second-story thief on his way to entering the upper floor of a stately mansion. Recent results of the College Board Examinations, administered by the Educational Testing Service, shows that prospective college students are making lower and lower scores. Most students who come to college now hate to read. They consider it a torture that they must endure in order to receive the reward of a degree. And the degree is needed so that they can then become doctors or businessmen, who are more and more resembling the automobile mechanics, the truck drivers, the carpenters, and the farmers. They are merely high-class illiterates. They make more money than the ditch diggers and dish washers, but they are not fundamentally different because they do not read any more than they have to. They never pick up Shakespeare or Dickens for the sheer joy of reading. The poetry of Milton or Chaucer is as foreign to them as Chinese food to a Frenchman.

If civilization is to continue, it will do so only because of those who like to read good books. These few must ban together in mutual appreciation of the finer things of life and refuse to lower themselves to the level represented by the news media, television, and motion pictures. The evangelists of reading will be scorned, but their cause is just.

A Doctor's Waiting Room

A busy doctor's office offers many various and sundry studies in the human race. A patient comes in, checks in at the receptionist's desk, and sits down in the crowded room. Everyone looks up to study him. He is watched minutely as if he was a rare bird being observed by devoted ornithologists. The other patience seem to wander what his particular medical problem is. They search his face as if they were looking for symptoms. Finally they seem to tire of gazing at him and go back to their magazines he merges into the picture like a pebble sinking into quicksand.

In a few moments, a nurse calls a name as she opens a door into the waiting room. All look up, then all look at the woman who has risen to take her tern with the "doc." She is obviously worried. Her face is drawn and ashen. She appears to be a little bit dizzie as she gets up out of her chair. But she makes it up and goes toward the nurse and gets to the door and when she goes thru the door the nurse, who is hard at work with some chewing gum, speaks to her with an insincere smile: 'How are you today, Miss Emsey.' Almost incongrously, Miss Emsey replies: "Fine".

Occasionally a nervous patient tried to make conversation. A beefy woman reiterates: "Everytime I come I have to wait longer. The woman sitting on her left waits a few seconds, size, and then replies with a sorta frown: "Yes, I know. My husband says that the worse part of going to see the doctor the money is another matter of course is the waiting." They both laugh nervously. While they are carrying on this conversation just mentioned, some of the other patients stare at them in such a way that would be considered rude anywhere else. But for some reason staring is an excepted part of doctor's office ediquite. Soon all go back to turning over the pages of McCall's and old issues of Time and Newsweek.

A middle aged man who is obviously deaf as a doornail comes in and has great difficulty with the receptionist. He is not the least timid at all. She says to him, "May I help you?" He begins to loudly give her his symptoms. They are not nice ones. She is embarrased and hurriedly says: "You will have to explain all that to the doctor." He looks at her for a minute and replies: "What is that you say?" "The doctor," she says, now so loudly that everyone is watching with somewhat of an alarmed look on their various visages, "you'll have to see the doctor." "Well," he shouts back with apparent irritation, "what do you think I'm here for, to apply for a job?" Her face is now scarlet she just points to a chair, and he sits down. She still does not have his name. No one smiles. The receptionist closes the glass partition and begins to talk to one of the nurses while she points to the hard of hearing gent. He sees this going on and thinks it is his time and gets up and starts into the doctor's office before the nurse stops him and says, "It will be just a minute, Mr. Seper." She obviously has dealt with him before. He goes back and sets down in his chair and grunts. He has now become the center for all eyes, but still no one has smiled.

Why does no one smile? There are many reasons. Some of these reasons might be as follows. Firstly, folks are not in a smiling mood when they are in a doctor's office. Secondly, they are not really themselves. They do smile sometimes, but it is at things that are not really funny. They smile then because it is a nervous smile. But when someone is really a scream like Mr. Seper, don't get me wrong I really don't mean to put him down or anything like that then they will not smile. If you have ever spent any time in a crowded doctor's office I know that you will agree with me—provided that you are not slanted—that people are funny!!!

47 Writing about literature

Literature in its many forms is a representation of life and sometimes a comment on its meanings. In casual readings of literature, readers may notice little more than what happens in the work. Careful students, however, seek to understand a work more thoroughly: they study to learn how an author presents things and what the events and images mean. Amateur or professional, those who attempt to explain literature should reveal their own interaction with the work in a way that indicates their understanding of the meanings which other readers might not automatically see during a first reading.

47a Choose a work and a precise subject which arouse your interest.

Choosing the work and the particular aspect about which you wish to write is likely to be an important measure of your success. Writing a paper about a work which fails to arouse a significant response in you may mean that you will fail to attract the attention of your reader.

The good subject should come from the aspect of the work which causes the most precise and intense interaction between you and it. You should find something that you wish to comment about. If the work does not cause that sort of reaction, you may need to choose another work if the assignment allows.

Select a subject appropriate to the length of the assignment. A narrow topic can be significant. Indeed, a short paper on the last paragraph in a novel could provide perspective on the entire novel and perhaps on the literary character of the author.

Between the first reading of the literary work and the writing of your paper, you should study in detail every item in the work which relates to your particular topic—the way each part (chapter, paragraph, or stanza) develops the subject, the way the images reveal character and meanings, the relationship between the language and the theme, and so on. As you study the work, you should write down in some form every particular idea—right or temporarily wrong—that might be useful later. After reaching a full understanding of some aspect of the work, you should make general notes that will serve as introductions and conclusions to paragraphs and to the entire paper. The very best interpretation of a work of literature may come when it is least expected and when the writer is not striving for an idea. When the study of the work is completed and all the notes have been taken, much or even most of the paper may be written; and then the main task which remains is to assemble the parts and provide transitions.

47b Give the paper a specific and exact title.

A vague title does not prepare the reader for the paper. A title like "A Criticism of Robert Frost's 'The Ax-Helve'" is virtually meaningless; it is too general because it does not give an indication of the paper's approach to the work. A more exact title might be "Opposing Cultures in Frost's 'The Ax-Helve.'"

Although a paper may discuss several topics as they relate to the central point, it should have only one subject, one overall argument to which every paragraph is related. Do not try to cover every aspect of a literary work. Provide focus.

47c Give the subject an appropriate kind of development.

A standard method of writing a literary paper is first to announce the topic and then to explain what your methods will be. If you use secondary sources, depending perhaps on the assignment, you should show how your topic or view is different from previous views (see **48c**). Describe the work or the situation in the work briefly and generally (see **47d, 48a**). Then support your interpretation by citing and quoting and analyzing in the body of the paper. Always make it clear to your reader what you are doing. That is, your reader should have no difficulty knowing when you are stating your thesis, summarizing, paraphrasing, offering proof, analyzing, or concluding. A good paper announces what it will prove, proves it, and then shows the significance of what has been done.

The subject you choose will largely determine the way you write about it. The many kinds of writings about literature fall into several categories. Explanations of a few of the more significant categories follow with some remarks on special problems.

An interpretation Most critical papers about literature result from a close study of the work. The writer of an interpretative paper is concerned with identifying literary methods and ideas. Through analyzing the techniques by which these are worked out, the writer presents specific evidence to support the interpretation. Be careful to distinguish between the thinking of a character and that of the author. Unless an author speaks in the first person, you can only deduce from the work as a whole what she or he thinks.

A review A good review should tell precisely what a work attempts to do and what methods it follows in carrying out its aim. If length permits, the review may include a brief outline of the contents. Such information should not be presented for its own sake, however, but as part of the attempt to give a fair and exact view of what the work accomplishes.

A character analysis Many students seize on the character sketch as an easy kind of critical paper to write. Actually it is a demanding assignment. The critic accomplishes little by merely summarizing a character's traits and recounting actions without considering motivations, development, and interrelationships with other characters. Alternatively, the critic may choose to describe the method of characterization—*how* the author develops the character. Learn to distinguish between *character* and *characterization*.

A study of setting   Often the time and place in which a work is set suggest something significant about the way places and things interact with people. If you choose to write about setting, you should be able to show how it is more than just a backdrop for the action.

A comparative study   Much can be learned from comparing various facets of two or more works of literature. The purpose of the comparison is the crucial point here. To develop a comparison you must do more than discuss each work in turn. Many good comparative studies use one work to assist in the interpretation of another. Some comparisons reach conclusions that are more general. Two poems may be compared, for example, in such a fashion that the critic can then explain two ways in which poets create images.

Technical analysis   The analysis of technical elements in literature—imagery, symbolism, structure, prosody, genre, and so on—requires special study of the technical term or concept as well as of the literary work itself. You might begin by consulting a good basic reference book like C. Hugh Holman's *A Handbook to Literature*. Never use technical or critical terms merely as labels to impress your reader.

Combined approaches   Many papers combine different kinds of approaches. A thoughtful paper on imagery, for example, does more than merely point out the images, or even the kinds of images, in the work under study. Rather, it uses the imagery to interpret or analyze or clarify something else also—theme, structure, characterization, mood, relationship, patterns, and so on.

47d   Do not summarize and paraphrase excessively.

Tell only as much of the story as is necessary to clarify your interpretations and prove your arguments. Summarizing a plot involves little or no thinking; your thoughts about literature are the crucial measure of your work. When you paraphrase, make it clear that it is the author's thinking which you are reporting, not your own.

$47e$ Think for yourself.

The excellence of your paper will depend finally on the significance of your thinking, your opinion. Do not merely report something you learned *from* the literature; write something you learned *about* it. Spend little or no time telling your reader that it is your belief; it is understood that opinions expressed are your own. Your readers will determine for themselves the importance of your paper according to your accuracy, your evidence, your methods, your thinking. Wild and unsupported thoughts are perhaps worse than pure summary or paraphrase, worse than no thinking at all.

$47f$ Write about the literature, not about yourself or your reading process.

You may be interested in the difference between what you saw in a work on a first reading as opposed to your insights after a second reading, but omit such irrelevant information in your paper. Only your final and considered views should be presented to the reader.

Generally avoid the first person pronouns *I* and *we*. Excessive concern with yourself detracts from what you say about literature and causes irrelevance and wordiness.

$47g$ Provide sufficient evidence to support your points.

A fundamental criterion in the evaluation of a paper is whether it strikes a proper balance between generalization and detailed support. Do not write too abstractly and generally. Make a point; develop its particularities and ramifications; quote the work; and show how your point appears in the quotation. Do not use long quotations that force the reader to find the proof without help if it is there. Papers, paragraphs, and series of paragraphs usually should not begin with a quotation. A writer who lets someone else start a paper may leave the impression of being lazy and unthoughtful.

Paragraphs which conclude with quotations that are not followed by commentary and analysis may also indicate that the writer is leaving much of the thinking to the reader rather than providing sufficient thought. Long quotations are usually not nearly so good as brief quotations followed by analysis and discussion.

47h   Organize and develop the paper according to significant ideas.

Organizing your paper by the sequence of the story or the poem often results in weaknesses—poor topic sentences, summary rather than thought, mechanical organization, and repetitive transitional phrases. As a rule it is better to go from point to point, idea to idea. Do not begin several paragraphs with such mechanical expressions as "In the first stanza . . ." and "In the second stanza. . . ."

NOTE   Early in your paper provide such necessary information as the name of the author or the title of the literary work you are discussing. Do not rely on your own title to provide such information.

$47i$ Do not moralize.

Good criticism of literature is not preachy. Avoid the temptation to use your paper as a platform from which to moralize on the rights and wrongs of the world. A literary paper that is otherwise excellent can be spoiled by an attempt to teach a moral lesson.

$47j$ Read what other writers say about the literature and acknowledge your sources.

In papers written after a study of other critics' writings, you need to state your contribution, the difference between what they have written and what you think. Avoid opening your papers and paragraphs, however, with the names of critics and with their views. Develop your own thesis and work in the opinions of others in subordinate positions in your paragraphs. You may use sources to show that other critics have interpreted incorrectly, to correct errors in some criticism that is otherwise excellent, to show that a critic is right but that something needs to be added, or to show that no one has previously written on your subject at all. If no critic has written about the work or the point you are making, that is no problem unless your instructor requires that you have a number of sources. On the other hand, it can be a serious error to state that nothing has been done on your subject when the point has been previously studied, made, or contradicted.

For bibliographies of writings about literature, see **48b**. For information about plagiarism and documentation, see **48f; 48g**.

Model Paper
Read the following poem by John Keats carefully, and then study the critical paper about it. Always use the most reliable text for a literary work. For a discussion of a situation in which this can be a problem, see page 280.

La Belle Dame sans Merci

O what can ail thee, Knight at arms,
    Alone and palely loitering?
The sedge has withered from the Lake
    And no birds sing!

O what can ail thee, Knight at arms,
    So haggard, and so woebegone?
The squirrel's granary is full
    And the harvest's done.

I see a lily on thy brow
    With anguish moist and fever dew,
And on thy cheeks a fading rose
    Fast withereth too.

I met a Lady in the Meads,
    Full beautiful, a faery's child,
Her hair was long, her foot was light
    And her eyes were wild.

I made a Garland for her head,
    And bracelets too, and fragrant Zone;
She looked at me as she did love
    And made sweet moan.

I set her on my pacing steed
    And nothing else saw all day long,
For sidelong would she bend and sing
    A faery's song.

She found me roots of relish sweet,
    And honey wild, and manna dew,
And sure in language strange she said
    "I love thee true."

She took me to her elfin grot
    And there she wept and sighed full sore,
And there I shut her wild wild eyes
    With kisses four.

And there she lulléd me asleep,
 And there I dreamed, Ah Woe betide!
The latest dream I ever dreamt
 On the cold hill side.

I saw pale Kings, and Princes too,
 Pale warriors, death-pale were they all;
They cried, "La belle dame sans merci
 Thee hath in thrall!"

I saw their starved lips in the gloam
 With horrid warning gapéd wide,
And I awoke, and found me here
 On the cold hill's side.

And this is why I sojourn here,
 Alone and palely loitering;
Though the sedge is withered from the Lake
 And no birds sing.

Study carefully the following interpretative paper and the explanatory points about it.

The first paragraph announces the name of the author and of the poem. A general description of the poem is given, as well as where it is set and what has happened. This introduction gives just enough background for someone who has not read the poem and yet not too much for someone who knows the poem well.

Then the student first tells particularly what the poem is about and in the last of the paragraph states the thesis: that the poem seems to be supernatural but is indeed about an aspect of life that occurs at some time to nearly everyone.

The body of the paper develops a contrast between the unnaturalness of the woman and her human qualities.

The Magic and Reality of Love in Keats's "La Belle Dame sans Merci"

John Keats's poem "La Belle Dame sans Merci" ("the beautiful woman without pity") is a sad but beautiful work about a lover in a world where nature is dry and weirdly quiet. In winter a warrior languishes mentally and physically sick by a lake. The speaker of the poem asks him about his troubles, and the knight tells him a story about a love affair which has made his life not worth living. Keats seems to be writing a fairy tale which might appeal to a child, a lover, or anyone; but he is really telling a story of the unhappiness that comes from thwarted love. The subject of the poem is the magical beauties of early love and the horrid consequences that result when love is gone and one of the lovers still has not been able to return to the more customary feelings of everyday life.

Whatever the nature of the creature the knight falls in love with, natural or supernatural, she is highly desirable in human terms. Yet she seems to be something more than merely human. The first strange note is that she was a "faery's child," but any lovely woman may seem to be magical to an ardent man. The wildness of her eyes too could be attributed to her being a normal and beautiful woman. However, her supernatural qualities are emphasized in the poem, and she grows in mystery--a development that could occur either in an ordinary love relationship or in one belonging to a supernatural world. Natural as well as supernatural lovers make "sweet moan," but she sings also a "faery's song" (recalling the strangeness of her mother).

Notice how the writer uses brief quotations to analyze and also to prove points.

In this paragraph what seems to be much storytelling and summary at first glance really leads in each instance to a conclusion stated by the interpreter but only hinted at or implied in the poem.

What she discovers for her lover, gives to him, and shows him also suggests the supernatural. The "roots of relish," the "honey wild," and the "manna dew" are delicious foods uncultivated by man, supernatural gifts and narcotic drugs. The wild man in Coleridge's "Kubla Khan" has fed on "honey-dew." The "manna dew" recalls the manna supernaturally provided by God for the children of Israel in the wilderness. Her very language is strange; it might be merely a dialect foreign to the ears of the knight or some kind of supernatural tongue.

The fairy woman takes the knight to her "elfin grot," that is, a place where dwell other weird or supernatural creatures like her. Her home is not a place of this world: it is a cave, underground, away from the everyday surface of things. She weeps from her "wild wild eyes," but Keats gives no cause for the crying. She may be a different kind of creature from the knight, and she may regret that their relationship cannot be normal or permanent. She lulls the knight asleep, and he awakes from this unearthly dream to find himself on a "cold hill side" with others who have been enthralled and heartbroken by this beautiful lady without pity or others of her kind. So the knight sojourns by himself on a hillside where there are no living plants and no singing birds. The poet makes no statement about the length of the spell of suffering or indeed about whether the knight will ever recover.

"La Belle Dame sans Merci" may be a poem about a man who falls in love with an unearthly creature who refuses to establish a normal or permanent relationship because she is superhuman. On

Here near the end of the paper the writer describes how Keats uses imagery to show the mind of the knight.

The conclusion sums up the two skillfully combined but also seemingly contradictory realms of the knight's experience with love.

the other hand, the magic may be merely a figure of speech, a vehicle rather than the subject of the poem, an embodiment of the disappointments of any love affair that starts with all the promise of glory and ends with nothing left but the ashes of a burned-out love.

The disappointed lover is the knight. In the end he must face harsh reality. He is pale (a lily is on his brow), but he is sweating with anguish and has a fever. Keats reveals the knight's disappointed love and his mental state by showing how he looks and feels. The knight tells his own story about the magic of his love, and finally he tells of his horrid memories—both dream and reality—and of his pining sick and by himself. These are the external images of his physical condition which has resulted from his psychological state. Thus at the beginning and the end of the poem the poet presents a picture of a disappointed lover. In between, all the magic of the woman—her beauties, enticements, and general charm—reflect the joys of what starts out as a requited love.

"La Belle Dame sans Merci" is a poem metaphorically about a magical world, but it is about the real world as well. The great accomplishment of the poem is that it is both a poetic story of a magical relationship told with beautiful figures of speech and at the same time a treatment of the harsh truth of actuality.

48 Writing the research paper

The research paper is based on a systematic investigation of materials found in a library. This section provides instructions about the way to assemble materials from sources and to document them with footnotes.

48a Choose a subject which interests you. Limit it to manageable size.

Your subject should allow you to use the library extensively, think for yourself, and come to a significant conclusion which will be of interest to your reader. Above all, it should engage your attention so that you enjoy reading and thinking about it and writing it up for others.

Begin by choosing a general subject area. If you have long had a particular interest, it may be your starting point: photography, perhaps; or literature; or painting; or architecture. If nothing comes to mind, start with a list of broad areas, such as the following, decide on one you like, and then focus on a limited aspect of it.

the arts	government	industry
literature	sociology	science
philosophy	anthropology	archaeology
history	economics	medicine
religion	geography	agriculture

At this stage you are trying to relate your investigation to an active interest.

Limit your subject adequately. Suppose you have chosen photography as your general area. After a little thought and reading and a look at the card catalog of the library, you will see that this is too broad a topic for one paper. So you may begin by narrowing it to color photography, or aerial photography, or the history of photography. Any of these topics could be further restricted: for example, "The Effect of Color Photography on Advertising," or "Aerial Photography in World War II," or "Matthew Brady: Photographer of the Civil War." Still further limitation may be desirable, depending on the length of your paper and the resources of your library.

If you are starting with a broad area, such as anthropology, history, science, or literature, you may move gradually toward your final subject in a process like the following:

> Anthropology—tribal societies—a tribal people still surviving—American Indians—the Navajo—the lore of the Navajo—Navajo songs.
>
> Science—a study of science in some historical period—biology—evolution—evolution before Darwin—reactions to evolution in popular periodicals before Darwin.
>
> Literature—the supernatural in literature—science fiction—tales of horror—famous monsters—*Frankenstein*.

In practice, narrowing down from a general to a specific subject is seldom smooth and orderly. Glean ideas for limiting a broad area by skimming an article in an encyclopedia or the subject headings in the card catalog. You may even be well into your preliminary research (see **48b**) before you arrive at the final topic.

As you read and work, consider whether you are trying to cover too much ground or whether, at the other extreme, you are too narrowly confined. If you are not satisfied with your subject after you get into your preliminary reading, try with your instructor's help to work out an acceptable modification of it instead of changing your topic completely.

Avoid inappropriate subjects. Beware of subjects highly technical, learned, or specialized. Only a specialist can handle modern techniques in genetic research or experimental psychology. Avoid topics that do not lead to a wide range of source materials. If you find that you are using one or two sources exclusively, the fault may be with your method—or with your topic. For example, a process topic (how to do something) does not lend itself to library investigation. Instead of writing on "How to Ski," a student might harness an interest in skiing to a study of the effect of skiing on some industry or region in the United States.

48b Become acquainted with the reference tools of the library, and use them to compile a working bibliography.

Certain guides to knowledge are indispensable to library investigation. From them you can compile a **working bibliography,** a list of publications which contain material on your subject and which you plan to read. The items on this list should have only the author's name, the title, and the information you need in order to find the source in the library.

The basic tool for finding books in the library is the **card catalog.** Books are listed alphabetically by author and title with helpful subject headings, subheadings, and cross-references which will lead you to new aspects of your topics. Reproduced on pages 245–246 are three typical catalog cards—actually three copies of the same Library of Congress card filed for three different uses. Notice the typed title and subject headings.

The card catalog leads you to the books in your library. The periodicals are indexed in special reference books, which list articles by author, title, and subject. The following periodical indexes are the most useful.

Periodical indexes
Social Sciences and Humanities Index, 1965–1974. Formerly *International Index,* 1907–1965.
   Author and subject index to a selection of scholarly journals.
Humanities Index, 1974– .
Social Sciences Index, 1974– .

Subject Card
Subject (usually in red)

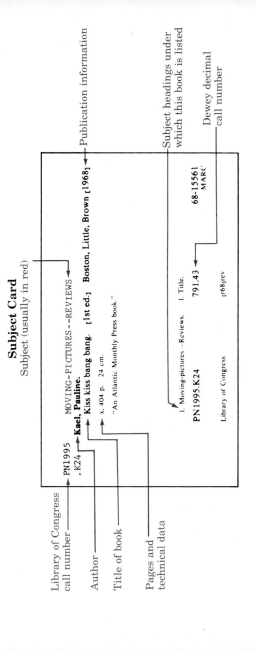

Library of Congress call number → PN1995 .K24

MOVING-PICTURES--REVIEWS ← Subject (usually in red)

Author → **Kael, Pauline.**

Title of book → Kiss kiss bang bang. [1st ed.] Boston, Little, Brown [1968] ← Publication information

Pages and technical data → x, 404 p. 24 cm.

"An Atlantic Monthly Press book."

1. Moving-pictures — Reviews.   1. Title. ← Subject headings under which this book is listed

PN1995.K24   791.43 ← Dewey decimal call number

68-15561
MARC

[r68]rev

Library of Congress

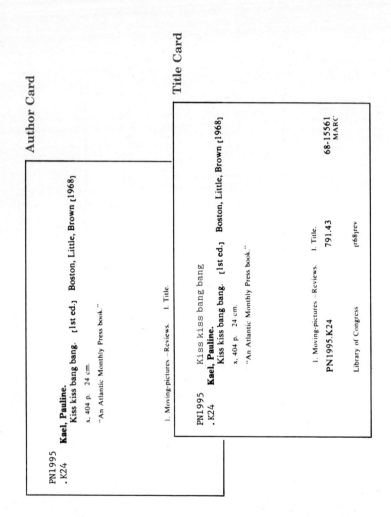

Author Card

PN1995
.K24

Kael, Pauline.
Kiss kiss bang bang. [1st ed.]   Boston, Little, Brown [1968]

x. 404 p.   24 cm.

"An Atlantic Monthly Press book."

1. Moving-pictures — Reviews.   I. Title.

Title Card

PN1995   Kiss kiss bang bang
.K24
Kael, Pauline.
Kiss kiss bang bang. [1st ed.]   Boston, Little, Brown [1968]

x. 404 p.   24 cm.

"An Atlantic Monthly Press book."

1. Moving-pictures — Reviews.   I. Title.

PN1995.K24   791.43   68-15561
                                                                MARC

Library of Congress   [r68]rev

Readers' Guide to Periodical Literature, 1900– .

An index to the most widely circulated American periodicals.

The Book Review Digest, 1905– .

Biography Index, 1946– .

"A Cumulative Index to Biographical Material in Books and Magazines."

Poole's Index to Periodical Literature, 1802–1906.

An index by subject to the leading British and American periodicals of the nineteenth century.

Nineteenth Century Readers' Guide to Periodical Literature, 1890–1899.

Author and subject index to some fifty English language general periodicals of the last decade of the nineteenth century.

The Art Index, 1929– .

"A Cumulative Author and Subject Index to a Selected List of Fine Arts Periodicals."

The Music Index, 1949– .

An index by author and subject to a comprehensive list of music periodicals published throughout the world.

The New York Times Index, 1851– .

"The Master-Key to the News since 1851."

Subject Index to Periodicals, 1915–1922, 1926–1961.

Superseded in part by *British Humanities Index,* 1962– . A subject index to a comprehensive list of British periodicals.

Public Affairs Information Service. 1915– .

Subject index to periodicals and government publications chiefly in the social sciences.

Current Index to Journals in Education, 1969– .

Covers "the core periodical literature in the field of education" and "peripheral literature relating to the field of education."

Education Index, 1929– .

"A Cumulative Subject Index to a Selected List of Educational Periodicals, Proceedings, and Yearbooks."

Agricultural Index, 1919–1964. Continued as *Biological and Agricultural Index,* 1964– .

"A Cumulative Subject Index to Periodicals in the Fields of Biology, Agriculture, and Related Sciences."

The Industrial Arts Index, 1913–1957.

In 1958 divided into the *Applied Science and Technology Index* and the *Business Periodicals Index.*

"Subject Index to a Selected List of Engineering, Trade and Business Periodicals."

Business Periodicals Index, 1958–.

A cumulative subject index to periodicals in all fields of business and industry.

Applied Science and Technology Index, 1958–.

A cumulative subject index to a selection of English and American periodicals in such fields as aeronautics, automation, chemistry, electricity, engineering, physics.

Suppose you are writing on Mary Shelley's novel *Franken-stein.* Looking under *Shelley, Mary Wollstonecraft (Godwin)* in the *Social Sciences & Humanities Index,* volume nineteen, April 1965 to March 1966, you find the following entry:

SHELLEY, Mary Wollstonecraft (Godwin)
Frankenstein, or the new Prometheus. H.
Bloom. Partisan R 32:611–18 Fall '65

Subject heading
Title of article
Author of article
Abbreviation of the name of the
        periodical in which the article
        appears. Learn the complete
        name by checking inside the
        front cover of the periodical
        index.
Volume number
Pages
Date

With this information, you should be able to find the article if the periodical is in your library. Of course, you will be unable to read through all the articles written about a broad subject. But you will be able to exclude some merely by studying their titles in the periodical indexes.

Besides using the card catalog and the periodical indexes, you will need to know about several **general reference aids.** Many of these will give you bibliographical listings as well as surveys of your subject.

General reference aids

Articles on American Literature, 1900–1950; and 1950–1967.

Cambridge Histories: Ancient, 12 vols.; Medieval, 8 vols.; Modern, 13 vols.

The Cambridge Bibliography of English Literature, 1941–1957. 5 vols.

New Cambridge Bibliography of English Literature, 1969–.

Contemporary Authors, 1962–.

Current Biography, 1940–. "Who's News and Why."

Dictionary of American Biography 1928–1937. 20 vols; 4 supplementary vols., 1944–1974.

Dictionary of National Biography, 1885–1901. 63 vols. Main work and 1st supplement; supplements 2–7, 1912–1971. British.

Encyclopaedia Britannica. Supplemented by *Britannica Book of the Year,* 1938–.

Encyclopaedia of Religion and Ethics, 1908–1927. 13 vols.

The Encyclopedia Americana. Supplemented by *Americana Annual,* 1923–.

Encyclopedia of Education, 1971. 10 vols.

The Encyclopedia of Philosophy, 1967. 8 vols.

Encyclopedia of World Art, 1959–1968. 15 vols.

Essay and General Literature Index, 1900–. "An Index to . . . Vollumes of Collections of Essays and Miscellaneous Works."

Grove's Dictionary of Music and Musicians, 5th ed., 1954. 9 vols. Supplementary volume, 1961.

International Encyclopedia of the Social Sciences, 1968. 16 vols.
*Literary History of the United States: History, 1974. Bibliography
    and Bibliography Supplement I,* 1963; *Bibliography Supple-
    ment II,* 1972.
*MLA International Bibliography of Books and Articles on the Mod-
    ern Languages and Literatures,* 1919–.
McGraw-Hill Encyclopedia of Science and Technology, 3rd ed.,
    1971. 15 vols. Supplemented by *McGraw-Hill Yearbook of
    Science and Technology.*
McGraw-Hill Encyclopedia of World Drama, 1972. 4 vols.
The Mythology of All Races, 1916–1932. 13 vols.
The New Century Cyclopedia of Names, 1954. 3 vols.
Oxford Classical Dictionary, 2nd ed., 1970.
Oxford History of English Literature, 1945–.
Princeton Encyclopedia of Poetry and Poetics, 1974.

Check your card catalog for special reference works in the area of
your subject.

   Your working bibliography should grow as you proceed. Be
sure to include all the information that will help you find each item
listed: along with the author and title, you will need the library
call number for books and the date, volume, and page numbers for
articles.

48c Distinguish between primary and secondary mate-
rials.

   Primary materials are such things as a painting, a poem, a
short story, a motor, a stock exchange, an animal, a fossil, a virus,
or a public opinion poll. In a paper on gasolines, for example, the
gasolines tested are primary materials; the writings of engineers
about them are secondary. Primary materials for a study of
tourists abroad would consist of published and unpublished diaries,
journals, and letters by tourists; interviews of tourists; and any-

thing that is part of the tourist's life. Select a topic which allows use of primary materials so that you can reach independent conclusions and not rely entirely on the thinking of others.

Secondary materials are those written *about* your topic. In a study of tourists abroad, for example, the writings of journalists and historians about them are called secondary sources. The significance and accuracy of such materials should be evaluated (see page 173). It is important to consider when a work was written; what information was available to its author at that time; the general scholarly reputation of the author; the extent of the author's knowledge and reliability as indicated in the preface, footnotes, or bibliography; the logic the author has demonstrated in proving points; and even the medium of publication. A general article in a popular magazine, for example, is likely to be less reliable than a scholarly article in a learned journal.

48d Locate source materials, read, evaluate, and take notes.

Before you begin to take notes, it is a good idea to do some broad **preliminary reading** in an encyclopedia or in other general introductory works. Try to get a general view, a kind of map of the territory within which you will be working.

After you have compiled a working bibliography (**48b**), located some of the sources you wish to use, and done some preliminary reading, you are ready to begin collecting specific material for your paper. If you are writing a formally documented paper, make a **bibliography card** for each item as you examine it. This will be a full and exact record of bibliographical information, preferably on a 3 × 5 inch filing card. From these cards you will later compile a final bibliography for your paper. A sample card is shown on page 252. The essential information includes the name of the author, the title of the work, the place and date of publication, and the name of the publisher. If the work has an editor or a translator, is in more

Bibliography Card
(reduced facsimile—actual size 3 × 5 inches)

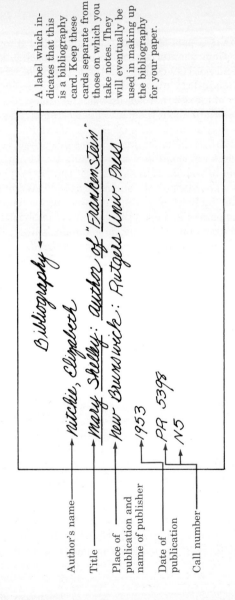

A label which in-
dicates that this
is a bibliography
card. Keep these
cards separate from
those on which you
take notes. They
will eventually be
used in making up
the bibliography
for your paper.

Bibliography

Author's name ——→ Nitchie, Elizabeth

Title ——→ Mary Shelley: Author of "Frankenstein"

Place of
publication and ——→ New Brunswick : Rutgers Univ. Press
name of publisher

Date of
publication ——→ 1953

Call number ——→ PR 5398
N5

than one volume, or is part of a series, these facts should be included. For later checking, record the library call number.

For **note-taking,** your next step, use cards or slips of paper uniform in size. Cards are easier to use than slips because they withstand more handling. Develop the knack of skimming so that you can move quickly over irrelevant material and concentrate on pertinent information. Use the table of contents, the section headings, and the index to find chapters or pages of particular use to you. As you read and take notes, consider what subtopics you will use. The two processes work together: your reading will give you ideas for subtopics, and the subtopics will give direction to your note-taking. At this point you are already in the process of organizing and outlining the paper. Suppose you wish to make a study of Mary Shelley's novel *Frankenstein*. You might work up the following list of tentative topics:

> Mary Shelley's background
> Stage and film versions of *Frankenstein*
> Modern concept of the term "Frankenstein"
> Mary Shelley's social philosophy
> Frankenstein's tragic flaw
> The quality of horror in *Frankenstein*

These headings may not be final. You should always be ready to delete, add, and change headings as you read and take notes. At this stage, the final order of headings—the outline—may be neither possible nor necessary.

To illustrate the methods of note-taking, suppose you have found the following paragraph about Mary Shelley.

> Mary had been well trained in liberal thought. She had been brought up in the household of the author of *Political Justice;* she had elected at seventeen to become the "affectionate companion" of Shelley. She had early imbibed ideas of the superfluousness, in a reasonable and benevolent society, of positive institutions. When the many were great and good, there would result an ideal world whose foundations would be political freedom and a social order based on equality and justice.
>
> ELIZABETH NITCHIE, *Mary Shelley:*
> *Author of "Frankenstein"*

Paraphrased Notes

(reduced facsimile—actual size 3 × 5 inches)

Subject heading ————→ Mary Shelley's social thought

Identification of source. ————→ Ritchie, *Mary Shelley*
Full bibliographical
information has been
taken down on the
bibliography card.

Page number ————→ 35   Mary Shelley, largely because of her family
background, believed that social institutions
would be unnecessary when people accepted
each other benevolently and equally.

You may make a note on this passage by paraphrasing, by quoting, or by combining short quotations with paraphrasing.

To **paraphrase** is to express the sense of a passage entirely in your own words, selecting and summarizing only information and ideas that will be useful. The card on page 254 identifies the source, gives a subject heading, indicates the page number, and then records relevant information in the student's own words. It *extracts* items of information instead of merely recasting the entire passage and line of thought in different words. Notice the careful selection of details and the fact that the paraphrase is considerably shorter than the original.

If at the time of taking notes you cannot yet determine just what information you wish to extract, you may copy an entire passage. For later reference you must then be careful to show by quotation marks that it is copied verbatim.

A photoduplication machine can guarantee accuracy and save you time. At an early stage in research it is not always possible to know exactly what information is needed. Photocopy some of the longest passages, and then you can study them and digest them during the writing of the first draft of the paper. Do not copy so many passages that you leave too much of the thinking until the last moment, but make enough duplicates to prevent constant returns to the same books in the library.

When writing your paper, you may either quote directly or paraphrase. Except for the ellipsis, the note at the top of page 256 went directly from book to card (see **28c**). Short quotations and paraphrasing may be combined on a single note card, as in the card at the bottom of page 256. It is most important to use quotation marks accurately when writing the note, to use your own words when not quoting, and to transfer quotations and quotation marks from card to paper with scrupulous care.

Any single card should contain notes from only one source, and all the notes on any single card should be about one single subject, such as Mary Shelley's social thought on the cards above. This will give you maximum flexibility in organizing materials as the plan of the paper takes shape. Arrange the cards by topic before you write the paper.

Quotation

Mary Shelley's social thought

Nitchie

35 "Mary had been well trained in liberal thought. She had been brought up in the household of the author of _Political Justice_.... She had early imbibed ideas of the superfluous-ness, in a reasonable and benevolent society, of positive institutions."

Quotation and Paraphrase

Mary Shelley's social thought

Nitchie

35 Mary Shelley was born into a family of liberal thinkers. Even when young she developed the idea of the "superfluousness, in a reasonable and benevolent society, of positive institutions."

The accuracy of your paper depends to a great extent on the accuracy of your notes. Indicate on each card the source, the page numbers, and an appropriate subject heading.

Note-taking is not a mere mechanical process; it involves interpretation and evaluation. Two persons writing on the same subject and using the same sources would not be likely to take quite the same notes, and their papers would differ accordingly in content and organization.

Study the following passage, which deals with the 1931 film about Frankenstein. Assume that you are writing a paper on that subject, and decide what kind of notes you would take.

> Florey was responsible for the plot twist whereby the Monster is given a madman's brain, hence betraying the author's original intention. Mary Shelley's tale tells of a scientist who creates a monster, a hideously misshapen creature, harmless at first but soon driven to commit murder and perform other acts of terror through the fear and revulsion his appearance provokes in others. The movie Monster is a murderous fiend, devoid (at least in this first appearance) of reason and barely glimpsed as human during the episode of the child who befriends him and whom he gratuitously drowns in a lake. This scene with the little girl, incidentally, was the only one to be deleted after audience reaction proved too violently adverse.
> CARLOS CLARENS, *An Illustrated History of the Horror Films*

From a passage as full of information as this one, it is possible to take several kinds of notes under different subject headings. Most of this material might eventually be used in a paper, but to a certain extent the material is adapted to the purposes of the paper by the way it is selected and classified under the student's subject headings. By the very process of reading and note-taking, the student is thinking about the subject and organizing thoughts. This is the supreme importance of taking notes, of quoting and paraphrasing. Now study the notes on pages 258–259, all from the preceding paragraph by Clarens. Observe the variety in subject headings and treatment.

Quotation

The novel and the film

Clarens, <u>Horror Films</u>
63 "Florey was responsible for the plot twist
whereby the monster is given a madman's
brain, hence betraying the author's original
intention.... the movie monster is a
murderous fiend, devoid...of reason and
barely glimpsed as human...."

Audience response to film

Clarens, <u>Horror Films</u>
63 "... the child who befriends him... he
[the monster] gratuitously drowns in a lake.
This scene..., incidentally, was the only one
to be deleted after audience reaction proved
too violently adverse."

Paraphrase

> Mary Shelley's Monster
>
> Clarens, Horror Films
> 63 Unlike the film monster, the
> creature in Mary Shelley's novel is
> made to commit his violent acts
> because he is rejected by others.

Quotation and Paraphrase

> Mary Shelley's Monster
>
> Clarens, Horror Films
> 63 In the film " the Monster is given a
> madman's brain, hence betraying the author's
> original intention." In the novel the monster
> is "driven to commit murder" because others
> react to him with " fear and revulsion."

48e Construct an outline.

As you read and take notes, think constantly about the organization of your paper. Revise subject headings; experiment with different ways of arranging your topics and your notes in order; study your notes to detect gaps in evidence or weaknesses in interpretation.

Your note cards should now be grouped by subject headings. Try to put the groups in the order in which you will present your material in your paper. You may shuffle the cards many times before you arrive at an order that satisfies you, and you may yet rearrange some topics during the process of writing. See the model outline on page 273.

48f Acknowledge your sources. Avoid plagiarism.

Acknowledge your indebtedness to others by giving full details of sources in footnotes and bibliography. Using others' words and ideas as if they were your own is a form of stealing called **plagiarism.**

Some of the principles of quoting and paraphrasing have already been discussed under the topic of taking notes (**48d**). They must be kept in mind during the writing and revision of the paper. Finally, quotations and paraphrases should be carefully checked for accuracy after the paper is written.

All direct quotations must be placed in quotation marks and acknowledged in your text. If you are writing a documented paper, specific details of the citation must be completed in a footnote (see pages 262–266). Even when you take only a phrase or a single unusual word from a passage, you should enclose it in quotation marks. You may quote words, phrases, clauses, sentences, or even whole paragraphs. Generally you should quote a sentence or a paragraph only when a writer has phrased something especially well and when you need to supply all the information given. Do not quote too much. A sequence of quotations strung together with a few words of your own is not satisfactory. Excessive quoting indicates that you have not properly digested your sources, thought about the ideas, and learned to express them in your own words and to relate them to your own ideas.

All paraphrases and citations must be acknowledged. Credit a source when you cite ideas or information from it even when you do not quote directly. Altering the wording does not make the substance yours. An acknowledgment not only gives proper credit but also lends authority to your statement. Whenever you consult a source or a note card as you write, you are probably paraphrasing, and you probably need an acknowledgment.

In paraphrasing you are expressing the ideas of another writer in your own words. A good paraphrase preserves the sense of the original, but not the form. It does not retain the sentence patterns and merely substitute synonyms for the original words, nor does it retain the original words and merely alter the sentence patterns. It is a genuine restatement. Invariably it should be briefer than the source. In the example below, notice the difference between a satisfactory and an unsatisfactory paraphrase:

ORIGINAL

Hemingway's debt to journalism was a large one, and he always acknowledged it. Unlike many ex-newspapermen, however, he neither sentimentalized the profession nor misunderstood its essential threat to creative writing.

CHARLES A. FENTON, *The Apprenticeship of Ernest Hemingway*

BADLY PARAPHRASED

Hemingway's indebtedness to journalism was very great, and he himself said so. Unlike so many writers who have been newspaper men, however, he did not sentimentalize journalism or misunderstand that it is a danger to creative talent.

BETTER
Hemingway admitted that he learned from newspaper work. But he also recognized that journalism can hurt a writer as well as help him.

If the source has stated the idea more concisely than you can, you should quote, not paraphrase.

Do not make use of extended paraphrases. If a good many of your paragraphs are simply long paraphrases, your reader will assume that even your organization is taken from someone else, concluding that you have not assimilated your materials and thought independently about them—in short, that you have not done an acceptable piece of original work.

48g Follow accepted practices of documentation.

Although there is common agreement on the *principles* of documentation, the *forms* vary with almost every field, periodical, and publisher, and indeed every instructor. There are several good guides to documentation, but the most widely adopted style in language and literature is that recommended by the Modern Language Association of America in the *MLA Handbook for Writers of Research Papers, Theses, and Dissertations* (1977). With a few exceptions, the sample footnote and bibliographical entries listed below, as well as those in the model paper on pages 275–295, are based on the *MLA Handbook*. The entries below may serve you as models, though your instructor may require modifications.

Sample footnotes

Standard reference to a book
[1] Henry Nash Smith, *Mark Twain: The Development of a Writer* (Cambridge: Harvard Univ. Press, 1962), p. 83.

Subsequent reference to a book
[2] Smith, p. 81.

NOTE Some instructors prefer "Ibid., p. 81." in footnotes of this kind.

Standard reference to a book (same kind as footnote 1)
> ³ Henry Nash Smith, *Virgin Land: The American West as Symbol and Myth* (Cambridge: Harvard Univ. Press, 1950), p. 143.
> ⁴ Smith, *Mark Twain,* p. 79.

NOTE When two or more works by the same author, like Smith above, have been cited previously, a new footnote should give the title or an abbreviated version of it.

Standard reference to an article
> ⁵ George Watson, "Quest for a Frenchman," *Sewanee Review,* 84 (1976), 474.

NOTE The abbreviation "p." is not used when the volume number is given. Inclusive page numbers for the article should be given in the bibliographical entry.

Standard reference to an article in a weekly or monthly magazine
> ⁶ Alan Brien. "Take Me to Your Union Leader," *Punch,* 3 May 1972, p. 610.

NOTE Page numbers in most weeklies and monthlies begin anew with each issue.

Subsequent reference to an article
> ⁷ Watson, p. 475.

NOTE See note for footnote 2 above.

Reference to a book by more than one author
> ⁸ Walter R. Cuskey, Arnold William Klein, and William Krasner, *Drug-Trip Abroad: American Drug-Refugees in Amsterdam and London* (Philadelphia: Univ. of Pennsylvania Press, 1972), p. 90.

Reference to a book by more than three authors or editors
> ⁹ Harvey A. Hornstein et al., eds., *Social Intervention: A Behavioral Science Approach* (New York: Free Press, 1971), p. 181.

NOTE The Latin abbreviation "et al." (from *et alii*) means "and others."

References to volumes in works of more than one volume
[10] George A. Simcox, *A History of Latin Literature from Ennius to Boethius* (New York: Harper, 1883), II, 438.

NOTE The abbreviation "p." is not used when the volume number is given. In works where separate volumes have different publication dates, the volume number cited is given immediately after the title.

[11] Herbert M. Schueller and Robert L. Peters, eds., *The Letters of John Addington Symonds,* III (Detroit: Wayne State Univ. Press, 1969), 667. [Bibliographical entry gives inclusive dates of all volumes.]

Reference to an essay in volume of essays
[12] Dorothy Emmet, "Coleridge and Philosophy," in *S. T. Coleridge,* ed. R. L. Brett (London: G. Bell, 1971), p. 210.

NOTE Use the following form to refer to essays and articles reprinted in casebooks and other collections of essays.

[13] Alain Renoir, "Point of View and Design for Terror in *Beowulf,*" *Neuphilologische Mitteilungen,* 63 (1962), 154–67; rpt. in *The Beowulf Poet: A Collection of Critical Essays,* ed. Donald K. Fry, Twentieth Century Views (Englewood Cliffs, N.J.: Prentice-Hall, 1968), p. 156.

Reference to a book that is part of a series
[14] Edward Hubler, *The Sense of Shakespeare's Sonnets,* Princeton Studies in English, No. 33 (Princeton: Princeton Univ. Press, 1952), p. 117.

Reference to second or later editions of a book
[15] Desmond King-Hele, *Shelley: His Thought and Work,* 2nd ed. (Teaneck, N.J.: Fairleigh Dickinson Univ. Press, 1971), p. 311.

NOTE A modern reprinting of an older edition of a book is listed as follows.

[16] Edwin E. Slosson, *Major Prophets of To-Day* (1914; rpt. Freeport, N.Y.: Books for Libraries Press, 1968), p. 91.

Reference to a book with an editor
[17] Ann Radcliffe, *The Mysteries of Udolpho,* ed. Bonamy Dobrée (London: Oxford Univ. Press, 1966), p. 363.

Reference to an introduction to a book
[18] Bonamy Dobrée, Introd., *The Mysteries of Udolpho,* by Ann Radcliffe (London: Oxford Univ. Press, 1966), pp. xv–xvi.

Reference to a book with a translator
[19] Erich Maria Remarque, *Shadows in Paradise,* trans. Ralph Manheim (New York: Harcourt, 1972), p. 123.

Reference to a signed article in an encyclopedia
[20] Samson Lane Faison, Jr., "Landscape Painting," *Encyclopaedia Britannica,* 1972 ed.

NOTE Authors with initials at the end of articles in encyclopedias are usually identified in a section (usually in the first volume) which lists contributors. Articles arranged alphabetically in reference books do not need to be identified by volume and page.

Reference to an unsigned article in an encyclopedia
[21] "Midway Islands," *Encyclopedia Americana,* 1964 ed.

NOTE A subsequent reference to this anonymous article could be merely the title.

[22] "Midway Islands."

Reference to a newspaper article
[23] "Churchill's Account of His Early Wars Is Ridiculed in a Contemporary's Notes," *New York Times,* 23 July 1972, Sec. 1, p. 12, cols. 1–6.

NOTE When an article is signed, the author's name should be given at the beginning of the footnote. When a newspaper issue has only one section, the section number, as given above, is not necessary.

Reference to a dissertation
[24] James Thomas Jenkins, "A Theory of Magnetic Fluids," Diss. Johns Hopkins 1969, p. 72.

Biblical reference
[25] I Kings iv.3. [Books of the Bible are not italicized.]

Reference to a play (with act, scene, and line)
[26] *King Lear* v.iii.245.

Reference to one author quoted in a book by another author
    [27] Ian Watt, *The Rise of the Novel* (Berkeley: Univ. of California Press, 1957), p. 125, quoted by Wayne C. Booth, *The Rhetoric of Fiction* (Chicago: Univ. of Chicago Press, 1961), p. 321.

Reference to an unsigned bulletin or pamphlet
    [28] *Enforcement of the Selective Service Law,* Special Monograph No. 14, Selective Service System (Washington, D.C.: GPO, 1951), pp. 102–103.

Reference to a signed bulletin or pamphlet
    [29] Charles E. Whieldon, Jr., and William E. Eckard, *West Virginia Oilfields Discovered before 1940,* Bulletin 607, Bureau of Mines, U.S. Dept. of the Interior (Washington, D.C.: GPO, 1963), p. 5.

Sample bibliography Items are listed in alphabetical order. The most frequently used types of entries are found under *Smith* for a book and *Watson* for an article.

Article in weekly or monthly magazine
Brien, Alan. "Take Me to Your Union Leader." *Punch,* 3 May 1972, pp. 610, 612.

Newspaper article
"Churchill's Account of His Early Wars Is Ridiculed in a Contemporary's Notes." *New York Times,* 23 July 1972, Sec. 1, p. 12. cols. 1–6.

Book by more than one author
Cuskey, Walter R., Arnold William Klein, and William Krasner. *Drug-Trip Abroad: American Drug-Refugees in Amsterdam and London.* Philadelphia: Univ. of Pennsylvania Press, 1972.

Introduction to a book
Dobrée, Bonamy, introd. Ann Radcliffe, *The Mysteries of Udolpho.* By Ann Radcliffe. London: Oxford Univ. Press, 1966.

Essay in a volume of essays
Emmet, Dorothy. "Coleridge and Philosophy." In *S. T. Coleridge.* Ed. R. L. Brett. London: G. Bell, 1971, pp 195–220.

Unsigned bulletin or pamphlet
Enforcement of the Selective Service Law. Special Monograph No. 14,
Selective Service System. Washington, D. C.: GPO, 1951.

Signed article in an encyclopedia
Faison, Samson Lane, Jr. "Landscape Painting." *Encyclopaedia
Britannica.* 1972 ed.

Book by more than three authors or editors
Hornstein, Harvey A., et al., eds. *Social Intervention: A Behavioral
Science Approach.* New York: Free Press, 1971.

Book that is part of a series
Hubler, Edward. *The Sense of Shakespeare's Sonnets.* Princeton
Studies in English, No. 33. Princeton: Princeton Univ. Press,
1952.

A dissertation
Jenkins, James Thomas. "A Theory of Magnetic Fluids." Diss. Johns
Hopkins 1969.

Second or later edition of a book
King-Hele, Desmond. *Shelley: His Thought and Work.* 2nd ed.
Teaneck, N.J.: Fairleigh Dickinson Univ. Press, 1971.

Unsigned article in an encyclopedia
"Midway Islands." *Encyclopedia Americana.* 1964 ed.

Book with a translator
Remarque, Erich Maria. *Shadows in Paradise.* Trans. Ralph Manheim. New York: Harcourt, 1972.

Essay reprinted in a casebook or other collection
Renoir, Alain. "Point of View and Design for Terror in *Beowulf.*"
Neuphilologische Mitteilungen, 63 (1962), 154–67. Rpt. in
The Beowulf Poet: A Collection of Critical Essays. Ed.
Donald K. Fry. Twentieth Century Views. Englewood Cliffs,
N.J.: Prentice-Hall, 1968, pp. 154–66.

Volume in a work of more than one volume with different publication dates
Schueller, Herbert M., and Robert L. Peters, eds. *The Letters of John
Addington Symonds.* 3 vols. Detroit: Wayne State Univ. Press,
1967–1969.

Volume in a work of more than one volume with same publication date

Simcox, George A. *A History of Latin Literature from Ennius to Boethius.* 2 vols. New York: Harper, 1883.

Modern reprinting of an older edition

Slosson, Edwin E. *Major Prophets of To-Day.* 1914; rpt. Freeport, N.Y.: Books for Libraries Press, 1968.

Standard reference to a book

Smith, Henry Nash. *Mark Twain: The Development of a Writer.* Cambridge: Harvard Univ. Press, 1962.

Standard reference to an article

Watson, George. "Quest for a Frenchman." *Sewanee Review,* 84 (1976), 465–75.

Signed bulletin or pamphlet

Whieldon, Charles E., Jr., and William E. Eckard. *West Virginia Oil-fields Discovered before 1940.* Bulletin 607, Bureau of Mines, U.S. Dept. of the Interior. Washington, D.C.: GPO, 1963.

Model research paper

A model research paper, with an outline and accompanying explanations, is given on the following pages for study. Generally this paper follows the form outlined in the *MLA Handbook for Writers of Research Papers, Theses, and Dissertations* (1977), with the following variations: footnotes are placed at the bottom of pages on which the references occur. However, a sample of the way footnotes may be grouped at the end of the paper is also included. All blocked quotations are single-spaced; footnotes and bibliographical entries are single-spaced with double-spacing between them. The *MLA Handbook* specifies that in research papers, blocked quotations, footnotes, and bibliography be double-spaced. In these, as in other matters of form, follow the preference of your instructor.

GENERAL APPEARANCE

Allow ample and even margins.
Double-space the text.
Indent five spaces for paragraphs.
Leave two spaces after periods and other terminal punctuation.
Leave one space after other marks of punctuation.

The material on the title page should be spaced so that it appears balanced on the page. Center the title and place it about one-third from the top of the page. Include your name and the name and section number of the course as indicated on the opposite page.

Frankenstein's Lonely Monster

By

Anita Brooks

English 101
Section 1

If your instructor requests that you submit an outline with your paper, it should occupy a separate, unnumbered page following the title page and should follow the form for the outline illustrated on pages 206–208.

Frankenstein's Lonely Monster

THESIS STATEMENT: An examination of Mary Shelley's <u>Frankenstein</u>
reveals a novel with a strong moral and social theme, the need of
human brotherhood.

  I. Versions of the story of Frankenstein

      A. The novel

      B. Later plays and motion pictures

      C. Common meaning of term "Frankenstein"

          1. Derivation of popular concept

          2. Difference between popular concept and theme of novel

 II. Background of Mary Shelley's social thought

      A. Mary Wollstonecraft and women's rights

      B. William Godwin's social philosophy

III. Creation of monster and Frankenstein's response

      A. Monster's moral sense and early tendencies

      B. Frankenstein's revulsion

 IV. Horror of loneliness

      A. Importance of loneliness as theme

      B. Robert Walton's search for companionship

      C. Monster's loneliness

          1. His plea for acceptance

          2. Nature of relationship with Frankenstein

          3. His grief over Frankenstein's death

      D. Frankenstein's isolation

  V. Frankenstein's tragic flaw

      A. His failure to love

      B. Mary Shelley's indictment of society

Center the title on the page. Triple-space between the title and the first line of text.

The first paragraph here provides exposition, information that the reader must have to understand the thesis statement and direction of the paper. After identifying the novel and the author, the paper tells how the adaptations of the original have created their own meanings of the scientist and the monster. Then in the last sentence of the paragraph, the paper gets back to the novel itself and provides direction and purpose with a strong thesis statement.

Place footnote numbers slightly above the line of type and after marks of punctuation. Do not leave a space before the number; do not place a period after the number. Number footnotes consecutively throughout the paper. Never repeat a number in the text even if the references are exactly the same.

Separate footnotes from the text by a short ruled line starting at the left-hand margin and placed far enough below the last line of the text so that it will not be mistaken for underlining to indicate italics.

Indent the first line of every footnote five spaces; do not indent succeeding lines.

In footnotes (but not in the bibliography) the author's name is written in normal order, first name first.

Footnote 1 shows how to refer to an article in a periodical and to a book. Note that the abbreviation "p." or "pp." is not used with the volume number.

Footnote 2 refers the interested reader to further material on the most famous film version of *Frankenstein*. Footnotes of this kind include information not directly relevant to the main subject of the paper but closely enough related to warrant mention in a footnote. Note particularly the form of a reference to a periodical with each issue separately paginated.

The page number for the first page may be omitted or centered at the bottom.

Frankenstein's Lonely Monster

Frankenstein, or the Modern Prometheus (1818) was written by nineteen-year-old Mary Wollstonecraft Shelley, the daughter of brilliant parents and the wife of a major poet, Percy Bysshe Shelley. Almost from the time of the novel's publication, Victor Frankenstein and his horrible monster have been the subjects of dozens of plays and, in the twentieth century, scores of motion pictures.[1] Most of them have two ingredients in common. They tend to make Victor Frankenstein a cold, inhuman scientist, and they portray the monster as a conscienceless, uncontrollable killer (with the diseased brain of a criminal), who grunts his way from one murder to another.[2] Mainly because of these popular and highly sensational versions of Mary Shelley's novel, "Frankenstein" has become a household word, "a synonym for a man whose own works bring him to disaster or destruction. And as the monster . . . bears no name, the name of his creator has been often

---

[1] See Elizabeth Nitchie, "The Stage History of Frankenstein," South Atlantic Quarterly, 41 (1942), 384-98; and Ivan Butler, The Horror Film (New York: A. S. Barnes, 1967), pp. 40-45.

[2] The most famous and influential of all motion pictures about Frankenstein starred Boris Karloff as the monster. When it appeared in December, 1931, in New York, one reviewer commented that the monster communicated its anger and frustration by "squeaking and grunting" ("Frankenstein," Time, 14 Dec. 1931, p. 25). See Carlos Clarens, An Illustrated History of the Horror Films (New York: Putnam's, 1967), pp. 62-65; Raymond Durgnat, Films and Feelings (Cambridge: M.I.T. Press, 1967), p. 106; and Pauline Kael, Kiss Kiss Bang Bang (Boston: Little, Brown, 1968), p. 148.

Place the page number in the upper right-hand corner, two lines above the first line of text. Use Arabic numerals; do not put a period after the number.

To place special emphasis upon these words, which will be used again later in the paper, the writer has underlined them. When this is done, the writer must indicate that his own emphasis has been added.

When an ellipsis is used to indicate omitted words at the end of a sentence, the three periods are preceded by a fourth.

Footnote 3 illustrates the standard form for a signed article in an encyclopedia.

Footnotes are used not only to give readers further references to read and to lead them to the sources used in the paper but also to aid in developing the argument by giving evidence or examples as footnote 5 illustrates.

Footnote 6 illustrates a reference to the editor's introduction to a work by another writer.

transferred to him so that 'a Frankenstein' has come to signify, in popular usage, a being of the most appalling ugliness and brutality, having no trace of the moral sense whatever" (italics mine).[3] This modern concept of Frankenstein and his monster differs widely from the original. An examination of Mary Shelley's novel reveals a book with a strong moral and social theme, the need of human brotherhood.

It was no accident that Mary Shelley should stress this social ideal in her first novel. She was nurtured on the principles of equality. Her mother, Mary Wollstonecraft Godwin, was a vigorous campaigner for women's rights.[4] Mrs. Godwin's most notable book, A Vindication of the Rights of Woman (1792), is a bold and brilliant plea for equality.[5] In it she "points out that among 'unequals there can be no society.' She insists on this condition of equality for all mankind. . . ."[6]

With even greater effectiveness, Mary Shelley's father, William Godwin, wrote about the need for a benevolent society that would allow every man his individual and equal place. He was one

---

[3] Wilbur L. Cross, "Frankenstein," Encyclopedia Americana, 1964 ed.

[4] See Ralph M. Wardle, Mary Wollstonecraft: A Critical Biography (Lawrence: Univ. of Kansas Press, 1951); and Elizabeth Robins Pennell, Mary Wollstonecraft Godwin (London: Allen, 1885).

[5] Mary Shelley did not know her mother, who died when Mary was born. However, she was well acquainted with Mary Godwin's writings and shared many of her ideas.

[6] Charles W. Hagelman, Jr., Introd., A Vindication of the Rights of Woman, by Mary Wollstonecraft (New York: Norton, 1967), p. 16.

Notice that this paragraph contains information from four different sources. Basing an entire paragraph on one source is often a sign of inadequate research and thought.

Since "a trace of the moral sense" was quoted and documented on page 2, a new footnote is not necessary here.

Quotations of more than two lines of poetry are generally set off as shown here. The writer has indicated in parentheses the book number and lines of the quotation from *Paradise Lost*. The punctuation mark at the end of a blocked quotation comes before, not after, the parenthesis.

Footnote 7 illustrates a reference to a book (Brailsford) which carries no copyright date.

Footnote 10 illustrates a reference to one volume in a multivolumed work. The number of volumes in the collected work and the inclusive dates of publication are not given here but in the bibliographical entry. With the volume number, which is given in Roman numerals in a reference to a volume in a multivolumed work, the abbrevation "p." is not used with the page number. The abbreviation "et al." indicates that the work has more than three authors (or, in this case, editors).

of the most famous thinkers of his time and author of the cele-
brated An Inquiry Concerning the Principles of Political Justice
(1793).[7] In that and other works, including such novels as Caleb
Williams (1794), he showed "vast faith in the individual's ability
to develop his reason and natural benevolence so that he could
live peaceably and usefully with other men."[8] It is not surprising, then, that Frankenstein is among other things a book with a
definite social message, a theme that follows in the tradition
of Mary Shelley's famous mother and father.[9]

In the novel the monster does have "a trace of the moral
sense." Indeed, he is a creature of great sensitivity who suffers
intensely. The responsibility for this suffering lies squarely
on the man who created him. A creator always has an obligation to
the thing he creates. As an epigraph for Frankenstein, Mary
Shelley chose the following lines from Milton's Paradise Lost that
reflect the creature's point of view:

> Did I request thee, Maker, from my clay
> To mould me Man? Did I sollicite thee
> From darkness to promote me . . . ? (X. 743-45)[10]

---

[7] See H. N. Brailsford, Shelley, Godwin, and Their Circle (New
York: Holt, n.d.); and Elton Edward Smith and Esther Greenwell
Smith, William Godwin (New York: Twayne, 1965).

[8] David McCracken, Introd., Caleb Williams, by William
Godwin (London: Oxford Univ. Press, 1970), p. viii.

[9] For a discussion of her parents' influence on Mary Shelley's
Frankenstein, see Mary Graham Lund, "Mary Godwin Shelley and the
Monster," University of Kansas City Review, 28 (1962), 253-58.

[10] Paradise Lost, ed. Frank Allen Patterson et al., II, pt. 2
(New York: Columbia Univ. Press, 1931), 331.

Note the proper way to place a footnote number after ellipsis and quotation marks at the end of a sentence.

Footnote 12 is the only footnote needed for page references to *Frankenstein*. Once the writer has indicated which text of the novel is being used, he or she may then place page numbers in the text in parentheses immediately following the quotations. Frequently the writer has a choice of which text of a novel or poem to use and should therefore investigate fully to determine the most reliable text, for texts sometimes vary. In the case illustrated here, scholars say both texts are reliable, but one is somewhat better than the other because it retains the epigraph which Mary Shelley included originally.

4

At his creation the monster is "a plain page on which could be written good or evil."[11] His original tendencies are toward love and unselfishness. Across this blank page of his mind, his creator immediately writes his rejection. Young Victor Frankenstein eagerly studies chemistry and physiology, patches together an eight-foot ogre with yellow complexion and watery eyes from the remains of charnel houses, fuses life into the creature through some process left mysterious in the novel, and then turns away in total disgust. His initial horror is not the result of any awareness that he has presumed to equal God. That awareness comes later. He rejects the monster simply because it is unbearably ugly: "Now that I had finished, the beauty of the dream vanished, and breathless horror and disgust filled my heart. Unable to endure the aspect of the being I had created, I rushed out of the room. . . ."[12]

Time and again Frankenstein, who tells his story to a young explorer named Robert Walton, returns to the monster's ugliness as the reason for his rejection of it: "Oh! no mortal could support the horror of that countenance. A mummy again endued with animation could not be so hideous as that wretch. I had gazed on him

---

[11] Elizabeth Nitchie, *Mary Shelley: Author of "Frankenstein"* (New Brunswick: Rutgers Univ. Press, 1953), p. 34.

[12] Mary W. Shelley, *Frankenstein, or the Modern Prometheus*, ed. M. K. Joseph (London: Oxford Univ. Press, 1969), p. 57. All references are to this edition. This is a recent and reliable edition of the novel. The Everyman Edition (New York: Dutton, 1912) does not include the epigraph noted above.

Note the proper way to indicate a page number in parentheses at the end of a sentence when the quotation is not blocked. The period goes *outside* the parenthesis.

Prose quotations of merely a few lines should generally be written like the regular text. It is annoying and distracting to read a page where the writer has set off every quotation, no matter how brief.

Always be certain that no words are erroneously attributed to the source and that all words in the source are properly enclosed in quotation marks. Follow punctuation of the source.

When prose quotations are over one hundred words, they should be set off as indicated here. Single-space within the quotation. Paragraphing within the passage should follow the source. Indent for paragraphs when you quote more than one. *Do not enclose blocked quotations in quotation marks.*

while unfinished; he was ugly then; but when those muscles and
joints were rendered capable of motion, it became a thing such as
even Dante could not have conceived" (p. 58). In later encounters
Frankenstein understandably feels hatred as well as horror, for
the monster is engaged in killing Frankenstein's family and friends.

When the monster tells his side of the story, beginning about
the middle of the novel, he stresses two feelings: his desperate
need for love and his bitterness over his rejection by his creator
(and by other men). It becomes clear that Mary Shelley has written
a horror story in a deeper sense than the obvious, for Frankenstein
is centrally about the horror of loneliness. This theme comes to
the surface early in the novel when Robert Walton, on his way to
explore the North Pole, writes home to his sister: "I have one want
which I have never yet been able to satisfy; and the absence of the
object of which I now feel as a most severe evil. I have no friend,
Margaret: when I am glowing with the enthusiasm of success, there
will be none to participate my joy; if I am assailed by disappoint-
ment, no one will endeavour to sustain me in dejection" (p. 19).

Walton's complaint foreshadows the monster's pathetic and
moving outcry to Frankenstein, whom he has followed into the wilds
of the Alps, hoping for acceptance:

> How can I move thee? Will no entreaties cause thee to turn a
> favourable eye upon thy creature, who implores thy goodness
> and compassion? Believe me, Frankenstein: I was benevolent;
> my soul glowed with love and humanity: but am I not alone,
> miserably alone? You, my creator, abhor me; what hope can I
> gather from your fellow-creatures, who owe me nothing? they
> spurn and hate me. The desert mountains and dreary glaciers
> are my refuge. I have wandered here many days; the caves of
> ice, which I only do not fear, are a dwelling to me, and the

After a blocked quotation the page reference in parentheses comes *outside* the final period.

A new paragraph may or may not be necessary after a blocked quotation. Here the student continues her discussion of the monster's desire for acceptance and links it with the writing of Mary Shelley's mother.

Footnote 13 illustrates one form for referring to a work mentioned in a previous footnote (see footnote 6). The *MLA Handbook* gives the following advice about subsequent references: "Be brief. Be clear. Make sure that the reader can recognize what work is being cited. In most cases the author's last name alone, followed by relevant page numbers, will do. . . . If two or more authors with the identical surname or two or more works by the same author are cited . . . citations after the first full reference note should include a shortened form of the title after the author's last name."

Footnote 14 illustrates the standard form for referring to a work mentioned in a previous footnote.

only one which man does not grudge. These bleak skies I hail,
for they are kinder to me than your fellow-beings. If the
multitude of mankind knew of my existence, they would do as
you do, and arm themselves for my destruction. (p. 100)

In this passage and others like it where the monster begs for so-

cial acceptance, one can hear the echo of Mary Shelley's mother as

she pleaded for equality: "Would men but generously snap our chains,

and be content with rational fellowship instead of slavish obedience,

they would find us more observant daughters, more affectionate

sisters, more faithful wives, more reasonable mothers--in a word,

better citizens. We should then love them with true affection,

because we should learn to respect ourselves."[13] This section of

Frankenstein, where the monster recounts the agony he has suffered,

presents, as Mary Graham Lund has put it, "some of the most beauti-

ful and tender scenes in the novel. We see a good and innocent

being transformed into a brutal, vengeful monster because it is re-

jected by society, thrust out into utter loneliness."[14]

Although the bitterness that comes from loneliness drives the

monster to vengeful killings, he never gives up his love for Frank-

enstein.[15] At the end, when Frankenstein has died of exhaustion

in chasing the creature across the icy wilderness of the far North,

Walton finds the monster on his ship grieving over the body of his

---

[13] Wollstonecraft, Vindication, p. 224.

[14] Lund, p. 255.

[15] The monster kills Frankenstein's brother William in an
early rage, but he later murders others because Frankenstein broke
his promise and did not create a female companion for him.

As a rule place page references at the end of a sentence. When a single sentence contains quotations from different pages, however, these quotations should be immediately followed by the appropriate references.

As illustrated here, quotations need not always be set apart in separate sentences. Frequently the flow of the argument is more graceful if quotations can be made a part of the writer's own sentences.

creator. Walton, who knows for himself the terrors of loneliness, is moved by the monster's words. As he speaks, it is clear that the modern concept of Frankenstein's monster as a creature that possesses "no trace of the moral sense whatever" bears little resemblance to Mary Shelley's creation. In his "exclamations of grief and horror" (p. 218), the monster addresses his dead creator: "Blasted as thou wert, my agony was still superior to thine; for the bitter sting of remorse will not cease to rankle in my wounds until death shall close them for ever" (p. 223). Again the monster returns to the causes of his evil--rejection and loneliness: "I cannot believe that I am the same creature whose thoughts were once filled with sublime and transcendent visions of the beauty and the majesty of goodness. But it is even so; the fallen angel becomes a malignant devil. Yet even that enemy of God and man had friends and associates in his desolation; I am alone" (p. 221). He succeeded in ruining Frankenstein's life, but now he feels only emptiness and remorse, and through it all, he says, "still I desired love and fellowship, and I was still spurned" (p. 221). As the novel ends, the monster tears himself away from Frankenstein and strikes out alone, soon to set fire to himself and end his life.

Frankenstein's loneliness is also intense. After giving life to the creature, he feels alienated from all of humanity. He prefers to be by himself. He is a solitary figure, walking in the Alps, living amid the lonely Orkney Islands, or chasing the monster across the desolate ice. His guilt and later his obsession-- which is to kill the monster--make it impossible for him to be a

In the long quotation brackets have been used to indicate that the words *the monster* are not in the original text (see **26**). Brackets are also used to enclose the abbreviation "sic" when a word in a quotation has been misspelled. This assures your reader that the misspelling is not yours and that you are quoting accurately. Note the following example: "Her mother, Mary Wollstonecroft [sic], who was from Dublin, wrote a treatise on the rights of woman. . . ." Robert Sencourt, "Mary Wollstonecroft [sic] Shelley," *Contemporary Review,* Oct. 1957, p. 215.

Although the quotation referred to in footnote 17 comes from the same volume as the quotations from *Frankenstein,* which are included in the text, a separate footnote is necessary because this reference is not to the novel proper but to its introduction by M. K. Joseph.

part of society. All three major characters, therefore, feel the terrible emptiness that comes from being cut off from human fellowship. The novel makes it plain that the knowledge which both Victor Frankenstein and the explorer Robert Walton seek after is not "a higher good than love or sympathy."[16]

If Frankenstein's creature had been treated with kindness and accepted into the brotherhood of man, loneliness would not have twisted his original benevolence into malignancy. As one critic argues: "The monster is essentially benevolent; but rejection by his creator and by mankind at large has made him first a fallen Adam and then a fallen Lucifer."[17] Percy Bysshe Shelley wrote perceptively of the theme of his wife's book:

> Nor are the crimes and malevolence of the single Being [the monster], though indeed withering and tremendous, the offspring of any unaccountable propensity to evil, but flow irresistibly from certain causes fully adequate to their production. They are the children, as it were, of Necessity and Human Nature. In this the direct moral of the book consists; and it is perhaps the most important, and of the most universal application, of any moral that can be enforced by example. Treat a person ill, and he will become wicked. Requite affection with scorn; --let one being be selected, for whatever cause, as the refuse of his kind--divide him, a social being, from society, and you impose upon him the irresistible obligations--malevolence and selfishness.[18]

Frankenstein's error is, as Harold Bloom has stated, "his failure

---

[16] M. A. Goldberg, "Moral and Myth in Mrs. Shelley's _Franken-stein_," _Keats-Shelley Journal_, 8 (1959), 33.

[17] M. K. Joseph, Introd., _Frankenstein_, p. xi.

[18] "On Frankenstein," _Prose Work_, ed. Roger Ingpen and Walter E. Peck, VI (New York: Scribner's, 1929), 264.

Footnote numbers should generally be placed at the end of a sentence. In the case of footnote 20, part of the sentence quotes a critic; the other part reflects the thought of the writer. Therefore to place the number at the end of the sentence would give the erroneous impression that the entire thought was the critic's.

The concluding paragraph sums up the argument of the paper. It is largely the writer's own thinking. Secondary sources can be made use of in the conclusion in a minor way, as here, but it is more effective not to make extensive use of them. Especially avoid beginning your paper and ending it with a quotation.

Footnote 19 illustrates that the name of the author of a work is not generally used in the footnote when the name has been mentioned in the text before the quotation.

Footnote 20 includes the title *"Mary Shelley"* because the same author was referred to in footnote 1 as the author of another work. If footnote 20 had read simply "Nitchie," with a page number, the reader might not know whether the writer meant to refer to the article mentioned in footnote 1 or to the book mentioned in footnote 11.

to love."[19]   But it is not his shortcoming alone. Mary Shelley,

who "had been well trained in liberal thought,"[20] indicted mankind

for its lack of genuine benevolence, for its prejudice and selfish-

ness. Frankenstein failed not merely because he presumed to equal

God in the creation of another being, but because he could not

follow through with the love and concern that a creator must have

for his creature, that one man must have for another no matter how

different they are. Intellectually he came close to being godly,

but his heart remained that of an ordinary man, too small to take

in anything as different and as ugly as the monster. Consequently,

he created a thing far worse than his monster--the despair of

loneliness.

_____

[19] "Frankenstein, or the New Prometheus," Partisan Review, 32
(1965), 614.

[20] Nitchie, Mary Shelley, p. 35.

This sample shows how footnotes can be grouped at the end of the paper. Follow your instructor's preference as to where you place the footnotes.

10

Footnotes

[1] See Elizabeth Nitchie, "The Stage History of Frankenstein," South Atlantic Quarterly, 41 (1942), 384-98; and Ivan Butler, The Horror Film (New York: A. S. Barnes, 1967), pp. 40-45.

[2] The most famous and influential of all motion pictures about Frankenstein starred Boris Karloff as the monster. When it appeared in December, 1931, in New York, one reviewer commented that the monster communicated its anger and frustration by "squeaking and grunting" ("Frankenstein," Time, 14 Dec. 1931, p. 25). See Carlos Clarens, An Illustrated History of the Horror Films (New York: Putnam's, 1967), pp. 62-65; Raymond Durgnat, Films and Feelings (Cambridge: M.I.T. Press, 1967), p. 106; and Pauline Kael, Kiss Kiss Bang Bang (Boston: Little, Brown, 1968), p. 148.

[3] Wilbur L. Cross, "Frankenstein," Encyclopedia Americana, 1964 ed.

[4] See Ralph M. Wardle, Mary Wollstonecraft: A Critical Biography (Lawrence: Univ. of Kansas Press, 1951); and Elizabeth Robins Pennell, Mary Wollstonecraft Godwin (London: Allen, 1885).

[5] Mary Shelley did not know her mother, who died when Mary was born. However, she was well acquainted with Mary Godwin's writings and shared many of her ideas.

[6] Charles W. Hagelman, Jr., Introd., A Vindication of the Rights of Woman, by Mary Wollstonecraft (New York: Norton, 1967), p. 16.

[7] See H. N. Brailsford, Shelley, Godwin, and Their Circle (New York: Holt, n.d.); and Elton Edward Smith and Esther Greenwell Smith, William Godwin (New York: Twayne, 1965).

[8] David McCracken, Introd., Caleb Williams, by William Godwin (London: Oxford Univ. Press, 1970), p. viii.

[9] For a discussion of her parents' influence on Mary Shelley's Frankenstein, see Mary Graham Lund, "Mary Godwin Shelley and the Monster," University of Kansas City Review, 28 (1962), 253-58.

[10] Paradise Lost, ed. Frank Allen Patterson et al., II, pt. 2 (New York: Columbia Univ. Press, 1931), 331.

[11] Elizabeth Nitchie, Mary Shelley: Author of "Frankenstein" (New Brunswick: Rutgers Univ. Press, 1953), p. 34.

Start the bibliography on a new page as the last section of your paper. Head the page Bibliography, centered. Triple-space below the heading.

Do not indent the first line of an entry; indent succeeding lines five spaces.

Double-space between entries, single-space within an entry.

List only those sources actually used in your paper and referred to in footnotes.

Authors are listed with surnames first. If a book has more than one author, however, the names of authors after the first one are put in normal order.

List entries alphabetically. When more than one book by the same author is listed, use a long dash (about one inch) in place of the author's name in entries after the first. An entry without an author (for example, an unsigned magazine article) is listed alphabetically by the first word.

List the inclusive pages of articles.

Notice that the important divisions of entries are separated by periods.

A bibliographical entry should include all the information that will enable readers to find the source readily if they wish to do so.

11

Bibliography

Bloom, Harold. "Frankenstein, or the New Promentheus." Partisan Review, 32 (1965), 611-18.

Brailsford, H. N. Shelley, Godwin, and Their Circle. New York: Holt, n.d.

Butler, Ivan. The Horror Film. New York: A. S. Barnes, 1967.

Clarens, Carlos. An Illustrated History of the Horror Films. New York: Putnam's, 1967.

Cross, Wilbur L. "Frankenstein." Encyclopedia Americana. 1964 ed.

Durgnat, Raymond. Films and Feelings. Cambridge, Mass.: M.I.T. Press, 1967.

"Frankenstein." Time, 14 Dec. 1931, p. 25.

Godwin, William. Caleb Williams. Ed. David McCracken. London: Oxford Univ. Press, 1970.

Goldberg, M. A. "Moral and Myth in Mrs. Shelley's Frankenstein." Keats-Shelley Journal, 8 (1959), 27-38.

Kael, Pauline. Kiss Kiss Bang Bang. Boston: Little, Brown, 1968.

Lund, Mary Graham. "Mary Godwin Shelley and the Monster." University of Kansas City Review, 28 (1962), 253-58.

Milton, John. The Works of John Milton. 18 vols. Ed. Frank Allen Patterson et al. New York: Columbia Univ. Press, 1931-1938.

Nitchie, Elizabeth. Mary Shelley: Author of "Frankenstein." New Brunswick: Rutgers Univ. Press, 1953.

_____. "The Stage History of Frankenstein." South Atlantic Quarterly, 41 (1942), 384-98.

Pennell, Elizabeth Robins. Mary Wollstonecraft Godwin. London: Allen, 1885.

Shelley, Mary Wollstonecraft. Frankenstein, or the Modern Prometheus. Ed. M. K. Joseph. London: Oxford Univ. Press, 1969.

Shelley, Percy Bysshe. The Complete Works of Percy Bysshe Shelley. 10 vols. Ed. Roger Ingpen and Walter E. Peck. New York: Scribner's, 1926-1930.

Smith, Elton Edward, and Esther Greenwell Smith. William Godwin. Twayne's English Authors Series. New York: Twayne, 1965.

Wardle, Ralph M. Mary Wollstonecraft: A Critical Biography. Lawrence: Univ. of Kansas Press, 1951.

Wollstonecraft, Mary. A Vindication of the Rights of Woman. Ed. Charles W. Hagelman, Jr. New York: Norton, 1967.

Glossary of usage and terms

49 Glossary *g*

Many items not listed here are covered in other sections of this book and may be located through the index. For words and terms found neither in this glossary nor in the index, consult an up-to-date dictionary. The usage labels (*informal, dialectal,* and so on) affixed to words in this glossary reflect the opinions of two or more of the dictionaries listed on page 141.

A, an Use *a* as an article before consonant sounds; use *an* before vowel sounds.

> *a* nickname
> *a* house
>   (the *h* is sounded)
> *a* historical novel
>   (though the British say *an*)

> *an* office
> *an* hour
>   (the *h* is not sounded)

a union (long *u* has the consonant sound of *y*)	*an* uncle

Absolute phrase See **20L**.

Accept, except As a verb, *accept* means "to receive"; *except* means "to exclude." *Except* as a preposition also means "but."

> Every legislator *except* Mr. Whelling refused to *accept* the bribe.
> We will *except* (exclude) this novel from the list of those to be read.

Accidently A misspelling usually caused by mispronunciation. Use *accidentally*.

Ad Informal: a clipped form of *advertisement*.

Adjective A word which modifies a noun or a pronoun.

> *Her young* horse jumped over *that high* barrier for *the first* time.

Adjective clause See **Dependent clause**.

Adverb A word which modifies a verb, an adjective, or another adverb. See **10**.

> The surrendering general *very humbly* handed the captain his *rather rusty* sword.

Adverbial clause See **Dependent clause**.

Advice, advise Use *advice* as a noun, *advise* as a verb.

Affect, effect *Affect* is a verb meaning "to act upon" or "to influence." *Effect* may be a verb or a noun. *Effect* as a verb means "to cause" or "to bring about"; *effect* as a noun means "a result," "a consequence."

> The patent medicine did not *affect* (influence) the disease.
> The operation did not *effect* (bring about) an improvement in the patient's health.
> The drug had a drastic *effect* (consequence) on the speed of the patient's reactions.

Aggravate Informal in the sense of "annoy," "irritate," or "pester." Formally, it means "to make worse or more severe."

Agree to, agree with *Agree to* a thing (plan, proposal); *agree with* a person.

> He *agreed to* the insertion of the plank in the platform of the party.
> He *agreed with* the senator that the plank would not gain many votes.

Ain't Nonstandard or illiterate.

All ready, already *All ready* means "prepared, in a state of readiness"; *already* means "before some specified time" or "previously" and describes an action that is completed.

> The hunters were *all ready* to take horse. (fully prepared)
> Mr. Bowman had *already* bagged his limit of quail. (action completed at time of statement)

All together, altogether *All together* describes a group as acting or existing collectively; *altogether* means "wholly, entirely."

> The sprinters managed to start *all together.*
> I do not *altogether* approve the decision.

Allusion, illusion An *allusion* is a casual reference. An *illusion* is a false or misleading sight or impression.

A lot Always write as two words. See **Lot of, lots of**.

Alright Not standard spelling for *all right*.

A.M., P.M, or a.m., p.m. Used only with figures, as in "6:00 P.M." Not to be used for *morning* or *afternoon* as in "The wreck occurred this P.M."

Among, between *Among* is used with three or more persons or things; *between* is used with only two.

> It will be hard to choose *between* the two candidates.
> It will be hard to choose *among* so many candidates.

Amount, number *Amount* refers to mass or quantity; *number* refers to things which may be counted.

> That is a large *number* of turtles for a pond which has such a small *amount* of water.

An See **A**.
And etc. See **Etc**.
Antecedent A word to which a pronoun refers.

>   *antecedent*   *pronoun*
>   ↓   ↓
> When the ballet *dancers* appeared, *they* were dressed in pink.

Anyplace Prefer *anywhere*.
Anyways Prefer *anyway*.
Anywheres Prefer *anywhere*.
Appositive A word, phrase, or clause used as a noun and placed beside another word to explain it.

>   *appositive*
>   ↓
> The *poet John Milton* wrote *Paradise Lost* while he was blind.

Around Informal for *about*.
Article *A* and *an* are indefinite articles; *the* is the definite article.
As Weak or confusing in the sense of *because*.

> The client collected the full amount of insurance *as* her car ran off the cliff and was totally demolished.

Auxiliary verb A verb used to help another verb indicate tense, mood, or voice. Principal auxiliaries are forms of the verbs *to be* and *to do*.

> I *am* studying.
> I *was* told to be ready by noon.
> I *do* not think so.

I *shall* be there next week.
He *may* lose his job.

Awful A trite and feeble substitute for such words as *bad, shocking, ludicrous, ugly.*

Awhile, a while *Awhile* is an adverb; *a while* is an article and a noun.

Stay *awhile.*
Wait here for *a while.*

Bad, badly See page 43.

Because See **Reason is because**.

Being as, being that Use *because* or *since.*

Beside, besides *Beside* means "by the side of," "next to"; *besides* means "in addition to."

Mr. Potts was sitting *beside* the stove.
No one was in the room *besides* Mr. Potts.

Between See **Among**.

Between you and me Avoid the incorrect *between you and I.*

Bring, take *Bring* denotes motion toward the speaker. *Take* denotes motion away from the speaker.

Bring me the hammer, and *take* the saw to him.
NOT
Bring the saw to him.

Bust, busted Slang as forms of *burst. Bursted* is also unacceptable.

Can, may In formal English, *can* is still used to denote ability; *may,* to denote permission. Informally the two are interchangeable.

FORMAL
May (not *can*) I go?

Capital, capitol *Capitol* designates "a building which is a seat of government"; *capital* is used for all other meanings.

Case English has remnants of three cases: subjective, possessive, and objective. Nouns are inflected for case only in the possessive (*father, father's*). An alternative way to show possession is with the "*of* phrase" (*the house, of the house*). Some pronouns, notably the personal pronouns and the relative pronoun *who,* are still fully inflected for three cases:

SUBJECTIVE (acting)
I, he, she, we, they, who

POSSESSIVE (possessing)
my (mine), your (yours), his, her (hers), its, our (ours), their (theirs),
    whose

OBJECTIVE (acted upon)
me, him, her, us, them, whom

Center around Illogical: use *center in* (or *on*) or *cluster around*.

Clause A group of words containing a subject and a predicate. See **Independent clause**; **Dependent clause**.

Climactic, climatic *Climactic* pertains to a climax; *climatic* pertains to climate.

Collective noun A word identifying a class or a group of persons or things.

Compare to, compare with After *compare* in similes, use *to;* in analyses of similarities and differences, use *with*.

He *compared* the wrecked train *to* strewn and broken matches.
He *compared* this train wreck *with* the one that occurred a month
    ago.

Complected Dialectal or colloquial: use *complexioned*.

Complement A word or group of words used to complete a predicate. Predicate adjectives, predicate nominatives, direct objects, and indirect objects are complements.

Complement, compliment *To complement* means "to complete"; *to compliment* means "to praise."

Complex, compound sentences A *complex sentence* has one independent clause and at least one dependent clause. A *compound sentence* has at least two independent clauses. A *compound-complex sentence* has at least two independent clauses and one dependent clause.

Conjunction A word used to connect sentences or sentence parts. See also **Coordinating conjunctions; Subordinating conjunctions**.

Conjunctive adverbs Adverbs used to relate two independent clauses which are separated by a semicolon: *however, therefore, moreover, then, consequently, besides,* and so on (see **22a**).

Considerable Basically an adjective, though used informally as a noun.

> STANDARD
> He had a *considerable* influence on his students.
> INFORMAL
> He made *considerable* each week.

Contemptible, contemptuous *Contemptible* means "deserving of scorn"; *contemptuous* means "feeling scorn."

> The sophomore who was *contemptuous* toward freshmen was *contemptible.*

Continual, continuous *Continual* refers to a prolonged and rapid succession; *continuous* refers to an uninterrupted succession.

Contractions Avoid contractions (*don't, he's, they're*) in formal writing.

Coordinating conjunctions The simple conjunctions which join sentences and sentence parts of equal rank (*and, but, or, nor, for, yet, so*).

Correlative conjunctions Conjunctions used in pairs to join coordinate sentence parts. The most common are *either—or, neither—nor, not only—but also, both—and.*

Cute Informal and overused, many think, for such expressions as *pretty, dainty, attractive.*

Data See **7e**.

Deal Informal and overused for *bargain, transaction,* or *business arrangement.* In *big deal,* slang.

Demonstrative adjectives and pronouns Words used to point out (*this, that, these, those*).

Dependent (subordinate) clause A group of words which contains both a subject and a predicate but which does not stand alone as a sentence. A dependent clause is frequently signaled by a subordinator (*who, which, what, that, since, because,* and so on) and always functions as an adjective, adverb, or noun.

> ADJECTIVE
> The tenor *who sang the aria* had just arrived from Italy.

> NOUN
> The critics agreed *that the young tenor had a magnificent voice.*

> ADVERB
> *When he sang,* even the sophisticated audience was enraptured.

Differ from, differ with *Differ from* expresses unlikeness; *differ with* expresses disagreement.

> The twins *differ from* each other in personality.
> The twins *differ with* each other about politics.

Direct object A noun, pronoun, or other substantive receiving the action of the verb.

> The angler finally caught the old trout.

Done Past participle of *to do:* not to be used in place of *did,* as the past tense of *to do* (He *did* it *not* He *done* it).

Don't Contraction of *do not;* not to be used for *doesn't,* the contraction of *does not.*

Double negative Avoid such uneducated phrases as *can't help but, didn't have scarcely,* and so on.

Effect See **Affect**.

Elliptical clause A clause in which one or more words are understood.

$$\textit{understood}$$
$$\downarrow \qquad \searrow$$

    The director admired no one else as much as (*he admired* or *he did*)
        her.

Enthused Use *enthusiastic* in formal writing.

Etc. Do not use *and etc. Etc.* means "and so forth." It should be set off by commas.

Ever, every Use *every* in *every other, everybody, every now and then;* use *ever* in *ever and anon, ever so humble.*

Every day, everyday *Every day* is used as an adverb; *everyday,* as an adjective.

    He comes to look at the same picture in the gallery *every day.*
    His trip to the gallery is an *everyday* occurrence.

Exam Informal: use *examination* in formal writing.

Except See **Accept**.

Expect Informal for *believe, suspect, think, suppose,* and so forth.

Expletive See **7h**.

Fabulous Informal for *extremely pleasing.*

Fantastic Informal for *extraordinarily good.*

Farther, further Generally interchangeable, though many persons prefer *farther* in expressions of physical distance and *further* in expressions of time, quantity, and degree.

    My car used less gasoline and went *farther* than his.
    The second speaker went *further* into the issues than the first.

Fewer, less Use *fewer* to denote number; *less,* to denote amount or degree.

    With *fewer* advertisers, there will also be *less* income from advertising.

Fine Often a poor substitute for a more exact word of approval or commendation.

Fix Informal for the noun *predicament*.

Flunk Informal: prefer *fail* or *failure* in formal usage.

Folks Informal for *family* or *relatives*.

Funny Informal for *strange, remarkable,* or *peculiar*.

Further See **Farther**.

Gerund See **Verbal**.

Good Incorrect as an adverb. See page 42.

Grand Often vaguely used in place of more exact words like *majestic, magnificent, imposing*.

Great Informal for *first-rate*.

Hang, hanged, hung See page 10.

Hardly See **Not hardly**.

Has got, have got Use simply *has* or *have*.

Himself See **Myself**.

Illusion See **Allusion**.

Imply, infer *Imply* means "to hint" or "suggest"; *infer* means "to draw a conclusion."

> The speaker *implied* that Mr. Dixon was guilty.
> The audience *inferred* that Mr. Dixon was guilty.

In, into *Into* denotes motion from the outside to the inside; *in* denotes position (enclosure).

> The lion was *in* the cage when the trainer walked *into* the tent.

Indefinite pronouns Pronouns not pointing out a particular person or thing. Some of the most common are *some, any, each, every, everyone, everybody, anyone, anybody, one,* and *neither*.

Independent (main) clause A group of words which contains a subject and a predicate and which grammatically can stand alone as a sentence.

Indirect object A word which indirectly receives the action of the verb.

The actress wrote the *soldier* a letter.

Usually *to* or *for* is implied before the indirect object.

The actress wrote (to) the *soldier* a letter.

Infer See **Imply**.
Infinitive See **Verbal**.
In regards to Unidiomatic: use *in regard to* or *with regard to*.
Intensive pronouns Pronouns ending in *-self* and used for emphasis.

The director *himself* will act the part of Hamlet.

Interjection A word used to exclaim or to express a strong emotion. It has no grammatical connections within its sentence. Some common interjections are *oh, ah,* and *ouch.*
Interrogative pronouns See **9i**.
Into See **In**.
Intransitive verb See **Voice**.
Irregardless Nonstandard for *regardless.*
Is when, is where Ungrammatical use of adverbial clause after a linking verb. Often misused in definitions and explanations.

NONSTANDARD
Combustion *is when* (or *is where*) oxygen unites with other elements.
STANDARD
Combustion occurs when oxygen unites with other elements.
Combustion is a union of oxygen with other elements.

Its, it's *Its* is the possessive case of the pronoun *it; it's* is a contraction of *it is.*

It's exciting to parents when their baby cuts *its* first tooth.

Kind of, sort of Informal as adverbs: use *rather, somewhat,* and so forth.

INFORMAL
Mr. Josephson was *sort of* disgusted.
FORMAL
Mr. Josephson was *rather* disgusted.

FORMAL (not an adverb)
What *sort of* book is that?

Kind of a, sort of a Delete the *a*; use *kind of* and *sort of.*

What *kind of* (not *kind of a*) pipe do you smoke?

Lay, lie See pages 10–11.
Learn, teach *Learn* means "to acquire knowledge." *Teach* means "to impart knowledge."

She could not *learn* how to work the problem until Mrs. Smithers *taught* her the formula.

Less See **Fewer**.
Liable See **Likely**.
Lie See pages 10–11.
Like Instead of *like* as a conjunction, prefer *as, as if,* or *as though.*

CONJUNCTION
She acted *as if* she had never been on the stage before.

PREPOSITION
She acted *like* a novice.

CONJUNCTION
She acted *like* she had never had a date before. (informal)

Such popular expressions as "tell it like it is" derive part of their appeal from their lighthearted defiance of convention.
Likely, liable Use *likely* to express probability; use *liable,* which

may have legal connotations, to express responsibility or obligation.

> You are *likely* to have an accident if you drive recklessly.
> Since your father owns the car, he will be *liable* for damages.

Linking verb A verb which does not express action but links the subject to another word which names or describes it. See **10c**. Common linking verbs are *be, become,* and *seem.*
Loose A frequent misspelling of *lose. Loose* is an adjective; *lose* is a verb.

> She wore a *loose* and trailing gown.
> Speculators often *lose* their money.

Lot See **A lot**.
Lot of, lots of Informal in the sense of *much, many, a great deal.*
May See **Can**.
Modifier A word (or word group) which limits or describes another word. See **Adjective**; **Adverb**.
Mood The mood (or mode) of a verb indicates whether an action is to be thought of as fact, command, wish, or condition contrary to fact. Modern English has three moods: the indicative, for ordinary statements and questions; the imperative, for commands and entreaty; and the subjunctive, for certain idiomatic expressions of wish, command, or condition contrary to fact.

> INDICATIVE
> *Does* she play the guitar?
> She *does*.

> IMPERATIVE
> *Stay* with me.
> *Let* him stay.
> *Let* us pray.

The imperative is formed like the plural present indicative, without *-s*.

> SUBJUNCTIVE
> If I *were* you, I would go.
> I wish he *were* going with you.
> I move that the meeting *be* adjourned.
> It is necessary that he *stay* absolutely quiet.
> If this *be* true, no man ever loved.

The commonest subjunctive forms are *were* and *be*. All others are formed like the present-tense plural form without *-s*.

Most Informal for *almost* in such expressions as the following.

> He is late for class *almost* (not *most*) every day.

Myself, yourself, himself, herself, itself These words are reflexives or intensives, not strict equivalents of *I, me, you, he she, him, her, it*.

> INTENSIVE
> I *myself* helped Father cut the wheat.
> I helped Father cut the wheat *myself*.

> REFLEXIVE
> I cut *myself*.

> NOT
> The elopement was known only to Sherry and *myself*.
> BUT
> The elopement was known only to Sherry and *me*.

> NOT
> Only Kay and *myself* had access to the safe.
> BUT
> Only Kay and *I* had access to the safe.

Nice A weak substitute for more exact words like *attractive, modest, pleasant, kind,* and so forth.

Nominative case See **Case**.

Not hardly Double negative: avoid.

Noun A word which names and which has gender, number, and case. There are proper nouns, which name particular people, places, or things (*Thomas Jefferson, Paris,* the *Colosseum*); common nouns, which name one or more of a group (*alligator, high school, politician*); collective nouns (see **7d** and **8c**); abstract nouns, which name ideas, feelings, beliefs, and so on (*religion, justice, dislike, enthusiasm*); concrete nouns, which name things perceived through the senses (*lemon, hatchet, worm*).

Noun clause See **Dependent clause**.

Nowheres Dialectal: use *nowhere*.

Number See **Amount**.

Object of preposition See **Preposition**; **9b**.

Objective case See **Case**.

Obsolete words Not used in modern English, for example, *jump* for "exactly" and *shrewd* in the sense of "bad" or "evil."

Off of *Off* is sufficient.

> He fell *off* (not *off of*) the water tower.

O.K., OK, okay Informal.

On a whole Confusion of two constructions, *as a whole* and *on the whole*.

Participle See **Verbal**.

Parts of speech The parts of speech are **Noun, Pronoun, Adjective, Verb, Adverb, Conjunction, Interjection, Preposition**. See each of these in this glossary.

Party Informal when used to mean *person,* except in legal usage.

Per cent, percent Use after figures, as "three *per cent,*" "50 *per cent.*" Do not use for *percentage:*

> Only a small *percentage* (not *per cent*) of the people had degrees.

Personal pronouns Words like *I, you, he, she, it, we, they, mine, yours, his, hers, its, ours, theirs.*

Phenomena Plural: the singular is *phenomenon*.
Photo Informal.
Phrase A group of closely related words which do not contain both a subject and a predicate. There are subject phrases (*The new drill sergeant . . .*), verb phrases (*should have been*), verbal phrases (*climbing high mountains*), prepositional phrases (see **Preposition**), appositive phrases (my brother, *the black sheep of the family*), and so forth.
Plenty Informal when used as an adverb.

> INFORMAL
> He was *plenty* sick.
> FORMAL
> He was *very* sick.

P.M. See **A.M.**
Predicate The verb in a clause (simple predicate) or the verb and its modifiers, complements, and objects (complete predicate).
Predicate adjective An adjective following a linking verb and describing the subject (see **10c**).

> The rose is *artificial*.

Predicate complement See **Complement**.
Predicate nominative See **Subjective complement**.
Predominate, predominant Do not use the verb *predominate* for the adjective *predominant*.
Preposition A connective which joins a noun or a pronoun to the rest of a sentence. A prepositional phrase may be used as either an adjective or an adverb.

> ADJECTIVE
>   *preposition*   *object of preposition*
>   ↓   ↓
> Joseph wore a coat <u>*of many colors,*</u>
>   ↑
>   *prepositional phrase*

ADVERB

preposition   *object of preposition*

He leadeth me beside the still waters.

prepositional phrase

Principal, principle Use *principal* to mean "the chief" or "most important." Use *principle* to mean "a rule" or "a truth."

> The *principal* reason for her delinquency was never discussed.
> The *principal* of Brookwood High School resigned.
> To act without *principle* leads to delinquency.

Pronominal adjective An adjective which is the possessive form of a pronoun (*my* book, *their* enthusiasm).

Pronoun A word which stands for a noun. See **Personal pronouns; Demonstrative adjectives and pronouns; Reflexive pronouns; Intensive pronouns; Interrogative pronouns; Indefinite pronouns; Relative pronouns**.

Quote A verb: prefer *quotation* as a noun.

Raise, rise See page 11.

Real Informal or dialectal as an adverb meaning "really" or "very."

Reason is (was) because Especially in writing, do not use for *the reason is that. Because* should introduce an adverbial clause, not a noun clause used as a predicate nominative.

> NOT
> The *reason* Abernathy enlisted *was because* he failed in college.
> BUT
> The *reason* Abernathy enlisted *was that* he failed in college.
> OR
> Abernathy enlisted *because* he failed in college.

Reflexive pronouns Pronouns ending in *-self* and indicating that the subject acts upon itself. See **Myself**.

> The butcher cut *himself.*

Relative pronouns See **9i**.

Respectfully, respectively *Respectfully* means "with respect"; *respectively* means "each in the order given."

> He *respectfully* thanked the president for his diploma.
> Crossing the platform, he passed *respectively* by the speaker, the dean, and the registrar.

Revelant A misspelling and mispronunciation of **relevant**.

Said Not to be used in the sense of *previously mentioned,* except in a legal context. (The *said* object was found in the room of the accused.)

Same Rarely used as a pronoun unless it is preceded by *the*, except in legal style. (Drinking by minors is illegal, and *same* shall result in arrest.)

Sensual, sensuous *Sensual* connotes gross bodily pleasures; *sensuous* refers favorably to what is experienced through the senses.

Set, sit See pages 10–11.

Shall, will In strictly formal English, to indicate simple futurity, *shall* is conventional in the first person (I *shall,* we *shall*); *will,* in the second and third persons (you *will,* he *will,* they *will*). To indicate determination, duty, or necessity, *will* is formal in the first person (I *will,* we *will*); *shall,* in the second and third persons (you *shall,* he *shall,* they *shall*). These distinctions are weaker than they used to be, and *will* is increasingly used in all persons.

Shape up Informal for *to develop satisfactorily*.

Simple sentence A sentence consisting of only one independent clause and no dependent clauses.

So For the use of *so* in incomplete constructions, see page 51. The use of *so* for *so that* sometimes causes confusion.

Sometime, some time *Sometime* is used adverbially to designate an indefinite point of time. *Some time* refers to a period or duration of time.

> I will see you *sometime* next week.
> I have not seen him for *some time.*

Sort of See **Kind of**.

Sort of a See **Kind of a**.

Subject A word or group of words about which the sentence or clause makes a statement.

> SIMPLE SUBJECT
> *Whitman* left the lecture on astronomy.

> COMPOUND SUBJECT
> *Whitman* and *Emerson* were transcendentalists.

> CLAUSE AS SUBJECT
> *That Whitman left the lecture on astronomy* is well known.

Subjective case See **Case**.

Subjective complement A word or group of words which follows a linking verb and identifies the subject.

> This book is a best-selling historical *novel*.

> His excuse was *that he had been sick*.

Subordinate clause See **Dependent clause**.

Subordinating conjunctions Conjunctions which join sentence parts of unequal rank. Most frequently they begin dependent clauses. Some common subordinating conjunctions are *because, since, though, although, if, when, while, before, after, as, until, so that, as long as, as if, where, unless, as soon as, whereas, in order that.*

Sure Informal as an adverb for *surely, certainly*.

> INFORMAL
> The speaker *sure* criticized his opponent.
> FORMAL
> The speaker *certainly* criticized his opponent.

Sure and, try and Use *sure to, try to.*

> Be *sure to* (not *sure and*) notice the costumes of the Hungarian folk dancers.

Suspicion Avoid as a verb; use *suspect.*

Swell Slang or informal for *good;* often vaguely used for more exact words of approval.

Teach See **Learn.**

Terrible Often a poor substitute for a more exact word.

Than, then Do not misspell one of these words and use it for the other.

Their, there Not interchangeable: *their* is the possessive of *they; there* is either an adverb meaning "in that place" or an expletive.

> *Their* dachshund is sick.
> *There* is a veterinarian's office in this block. (expletive)
> *There* it is on the corner. (adverb of place)

These (those) kinds, these (those) sorts *These (those)* is plural; *kind (sort)* is singular. Therefore use *this (that) kind, this (that) sort; these (those) kinds, these (those) sorts.*

Thusly Prefer *thus.*

Transitive verb See **Voice.**

Try and See **Sure and.**

Unique Means "one of a kind"; hence it may not logically be compared. *Unique* should not be loosely used for *unusual* or *strange.*

Use Sometimes carelessly written for the past tense, *used.*

> Thomas Jefferson *used* (not *use*) to bathe in cold water almost every morning.

Verb A word or group of words expressing action, being, or state of being.

> Automobiles *burn* gas.
> What *is* life?
> I *shall have returned.*
> The fire *has been built.*

Verbal A word derived from a verb and used as a noun, an adjective, or an adverb. A verbal may be a gerund, a participle, or an infinitive.

GERUND
1. ends in *-ing*
2. is used as a noun

gerund   *object of gerund*
 ↓   ↓
<u>Shoeing horses</u> is almost a lost art.
        ↑
gerund phrase, used as subject

PARTICIPLE
1. ends in *-ing, -ed, -d, -t, -n,* and so on.
2. is used as an adjective

prepositional phrase, modifying participle

participle
 ↓
<u>Riding at top speed,</u> he snatched the child from danger.
        ↑
participial phrase, modifying subject

INFINITIVE
1. begins with *to,* which may be understood
2. is used as an adjective, an adverb, or a noun

infinitive   *object of infinitive*
 ↓   ↓
<u>To rescue the child</u> was difficult.
        ↑
infinitive phrase, used as subject

                    infinitive, used as adjective

Charlotte's Web is a good book *to read* to a child.

        infinitive, used as adverb

He was eager *to ride* his new horse.

Verb phrase See **Phrase**.

Voice Transitive verbs have two forms to show whether their subjects act (active voice) or are acted upon (passive voice). See pages 15–16.

Wait on Unidiomatic for *wait for. Wait on* correctly means "to serve."

Ways Prefer *way* when designating a distance.

> a long *way*
> NOT
> a long *ways*

When, where See **Is when, is where.**

Where Do not misuse for *that.*

> I read in the newspaper *that* (not *where*) you saved a child's life.

Where at The *at* is unnecessary.

> NOT
> *Where* is he *at?*
> BUT
> *Where* is he?

Whose, who's *Whose* is the possessive of *who; who's* is a contraction of *who is.*

-wise A suffix overused in combinations with nouns, such as *budget-wise, progress-wise,* and *business-wise.*

Without Dialectal for *unless,* as in "I cannot come *without* you pay for the ticket."

Index

A, an, 297–298
Abbreviations, 112, 137–138
    acceptable in formal writing, 137
    agencies and organizations, 138
    A.M., P.M. 138
    B.C., A.D., 138
    capitalization of, 137–138
    dates and time, 138
    exclamation point with, 112
    in footnotes and bibliographical entries, 137
    period with, 112
    question mark after, 112
    titles with proper names, 137
Absolute adjectives and adverbs, 42
Absolute phrases, commas with, 90
Abstractions, 163–164, 232
Accept, except, 298
Accidently, 298

Accurate data, 172–173
Active voice, 156
Ad, 298
A.D., B.C., capitalized, 136
Addresses, commas with, 89
Adjectives, 41–43, 298
    absolute, 42
    clauses, 59, 62, 304
    comma between, 80–81
    comparative and superlative degrees, 42–43
    coordinate, 80–81
    cumulative, 80–81
    demonstrative, 195, 304
    distinguished from adverbs, 41–42
    after linking verb, 43
    modifying object, 43
    no comma between adjective and noun, 97
    position, 59
    predicate, 43, 312
    pronominal, 313

Adverbs, 41–43, 298
    absolute, 42
    comparative and superlative degrees, 42–43
    conjunctive, 4, 87–88, 102, 303
    distinguished from adjectives, 41–42
    not with linking verbs, 43
    -ly ending, 41
    position of, 59
Advice, advise, 298
Affect, effect, 298
Agencies and organizations, abbreviations for, 138
Aggravate, 299
Agreement, pronoun and antecedent, 27–30
    ambiguous reference, 30
    antecedents such as each, either, 28–29
    collective noun antecedent, 28
    compound antecedent with and, 27
    compound antecedent with or, nor, etc., 18–19, 27
    definite antecedent, 29–30
    which, who, that, whose, 29
Agreement, subject and verb, 17–23
    collective noun subject, 19–20
    compound subject with and, 18
    compound subject with or, nor, etc., 18–19
    with here, there, it, 22
    indefinite pronoun subjects (each, either, etc.), 20-21
    intervening phrases or clauses, 19
    none, some, etc., 21
    noun subjects plural in

form, singular in meaning, 20
    number as subject, 22
    person and number, 23
    relative pronoun subject, 23
    not with subjective complement, 22–23
    title as subject, 23
Agree to, agree with, 299
Ain't, 299
All ready, already, 299
All together, altogether, 299
Allusion, illusion, 299
A lot, 299
Alright, 299
Alternatives (in reasoning), 177
A.M., P.M., or a.m., p.m., 299
Among, between, 299
Amount, number, 300
An, a, 297–298
And, but, or, nor, etc., see Coordinating conjunctions
Antecedent, 300
    ambiguous, 30
    collective noun, 28
    compound, 27
    definite, 29–30
    of relative pronoun, 23
    singular, 28–29
    see also Agreement, pronoun and antecedent
Anticlimax, 71
Anyplace, 300
Anyways, 300
Anywheres, 300
Apostrophe, 133–134
    contractions, 37, 133–134
    indefinite pronouns, 37, 133
    joint possession, 133–134
    omissions, 133–134
    not with personal pronouns, 37, 133
    plurals of numbers, letters, words, 134

Apostrophe *(cont.)*
    possessive of nouns, 133
Appeal to emotions, 176
Appositive, 300
    case, 35
    colon before, 106
    punctuation with, 84–85
    restrictive and nonrestric-
        tive, 84–85
Arabic numerals, 205
Archaisms, 143
Argument, 172–177
Argumentum ad hominem, see
    Name-calling
Around, 300
Articles *(a, an, the)*, 300
    capitalizing, 134
    underlining, 124
As, 300
    case after, 36
    in a comparison, 53–54
    misuse of, for *because,* 300
Authority, reliable, 173
Auxiliary verbs, 11n, 300-301
Awful, 300
Awhile, a while, 301

Bad, badly, 43
Balanced sentence, 69–70
B.C., A.D., capitalized, 136
Be, in subjunctive mood, 17
Begging the question, 175
Being as, being that, 301
Beside, besides, 301
Between, among, 299
Between he and I, 34-35
Between you and me, 301
Bible, 124, 137, 265
Bibliography
    entries, 106, 268
    sample, 266–268, 295
    working, 244–250
Blocked quotation, 268, 282–284
Body of theme, 209

Brackets, 108, 288–289
Bring, 301
Business letter, 106, 122–123
Bust, busted, 301
But, see Coordinating conjunctions

Can, may, 301
Capital, capitol, 301
Capitalization, 134–137
    articles *(a, an, the)* not
        capitalized, 134
    B.C., A.D., 136
    conjunctions, 134
    days of week, 136
    degrees, 135
    Deity, 136–137
    direct quotations, 134
    first word of sentence, 134
    holidays, 136
    I and *O,* 134
    months, 136
    movements, periods, events,
        136
    names of specific courses,
        137
    prepositions not capitalized,
        134
    proper nouns, 134, 136
    seasons and centuries not
        capitalized, 136
    sentence in parentheses,
        108
    titles, literary, 134
    titles, personal, 135
    words of family relation-
        ship, 135–136
Card catalog, 244–246
Case, 34–39, 302
    apostrophe with, 37
    appositive, 35
    interrogative pronoun, 37–39
    nouns, possessive, 34
    objective before a participle,
        36–37

Case *(cont.)*
    object of preposition, 34–35
    of phrase for possession, 29, 37
    possessive preceding
        gerund, 36–37
    pronouns, 34–39
    relative pronouns, 37–39
    subjective for subjects and
        subjective comple-
        ments, 34
    subject of infinitive, 35
    after *than* or *as,* 36
Cause and effect, 177
Center around, 302
Century, not capitalized, 136
Character analysis, in literary pa-
    per, 229–230
Characterization, 229–230
Checklist for themes, 209–210
Choosing a subject
    literary paper, 227–228
    research paper, 242–244
    theme, 202–204
Choppy paragraphs, 187–189, 203
Choppy sentences, 68
Circular reasoning, 175
Clarity, 51, 160
Clauses, 302
    adjective, 59, 62, 304
    adverb, 304
    dangling, 61
    dependent, 3–4, 47–49, 70,
        78–79, 82–84, 304
    elliptical, 36, 61, 305
    independent, 3–4, 45–46, 48,
        77–79, 102–103, 106,
        306
    intervening, 19
    introductory, punctuation
        of, 82–83
    nonrestrictive, punctuation
        of, 84–85
    noun, 304
    overlapping, 48–49

    relative, 39
Clear and logical thinking, 172–
    177
    accurate and verified data,
        172–173
    adequate alternatives, 177
    appeal to emotions, 176
    begging the question, 175
    cause and effect, 177
    conflicting evidence, 175
    false conclusion, 177
    flattery, 176
    labels, 176
    loaded words, 176
    mass appeal, 176
    moderation, 177
    name-calling, 176
    omission of steps in thought,
        175–176
    reasoning in a circle, 175
    relevance of content, 174–
        175
    reliable authority, 173
    snob appeal, 176
    specific evidence, 174
    sticking to the point, 174–
        175
    sweeping generalizations,
        173–174
    unwarranted conclusions,
        175–176
Clichés, 149
Climactic, climatic, 302
Climactic order, 71, 194
Coherence, *see* Modifiers; Paral-
    lelism; Transitions;
    Unity in paragraphs
Collective noun, 302, 311
    antecedent, 28
    as subject, 19–20
Colloquial English, 141
Colon, 105–107
    in bibliographical entries,
        106

Colon *(cont.)*
 before elements introduced
  formally, 105
 before formal appositives,
  106
 between hours and minutes,
  106
 between independent
  clauses, 106
 with quotation marks, 111
 after salutation of letter,
  106
 unnecessary, 106–107
Comma, 77–114
 after abbreviations, 112
 with absolute phrases, 90
 between adjectives, 80–81
 with conjunctive adverbs,
  87–88
 for contrast and emphasis,
  89
 with dates, places, ad-
  dresses, degrees,
  titles, 89
 with direct address and
  salutation, 90
 with elements out of normal
  word order, 87–88
 with *he said,* etc., 90
 with *however,* 88
 with independent clauses
  and coordinating con-
  junction, 77–78
 to indicate omission, 90–91
 after introductory phrases
  and clauses, 82–84
 with mild exclamation, 114
 with mild interjections, 89
 with nonrestrictive mod-
  ifiers, 84–85
 with other punctuation, 99,
  111
 to prevent misreading, 78,
  90

 with quotation marks, 110
 with sentence modifiers,
  87–88
 in a series, 78–79
 with short interrogative
  elements, 89
 two or none, 77
 unnecessary, 97–100
 with *yes* and *no,* etc., 89
Comma fault, 3–8, 102
Comma splice, 3–8, 102
Common nouns, 311
Comparative and superlative
  degrees, 42–43
Comparative study as literary
  paper, 230
Compare to, compare with, 302
Comparison and contrast, 194
Comparisons, 52–54
 with *as,* 53–54
 with *more,* 53
 with *most,* 53–54
 with *other,* 53
 with *than,* 53–54
Complected, 302
Complement
 of predicate, 302
 subjective, 22–23, 34, 43, 315
Complement, compliment, 302
Completeness, 51–54
Complex sentence, 68, 303
Composition, *see* Paragraph;
  Research paper;
  Theme; Literature,
  writing about
Compound antecedent, 27
Compound-complex sentence, 303
Compound numbers, 132
Compound sentence, 103, 303
Compound subject, 18–19, 22
Compound words, 131–132
Conciseness, 156–157
 active voice, 156
 sentence structure, 156–157

Conclusion of theme, 210
Conclusions, unwarranted, 175–176
Concreteness, 162–164, 208
Concrete nouns, 311
Conditional verbs, shifts in, 56
Conflicting evidence, 175
Conjunctions, 303
    capitalization of, in titles, 134
    coordinating, 3–4, 18, 19, 45–46, 65–66, 77–78, 102
    correlative, 65–66, 303
    subordinating, 315
Conjunctive adverbs, 4, 87–88, 102, 303
Connectives, 45, 195
Connotation, 165–166
Considerable, 303
Consistency, 13, 56–58
Contemptible, contemptuous, 303
Continual, continuous, 303
Contractions, 37, 133–134
Contrast
    commas for, 89
    in developing paragraphs, 194
Coordinate adjectives, 80–81
Coordinating conjunctions, 3–4, 18, 19, 45–46, 65–66, 77–78, 102, 303
Coordination, 47–49
    excessive, 45–46, 47
Correlative conjunctions, 65–66, 303
Course names, capitalization, 137
Critical paper, *see* Literature, writing about
Criticism of literature, 227–241
Cumulative adjectives, 80–81
Cute, 303

Dangling modifiers
    elliptical clauses, 61
    gerunds, 60

infinitives, 60
    loosely attached verbals, 61
    participles, 60
    prepositional phrases, 60–61
Dash, 107
    with breaks in construction, 107
    distinguished from hyphen, 107
    for emphasis, 107
    to introduce summaries, 107
    no comma with, 99
    for parenthetical remarks, 107
Data, accuracy, 172–173
Dates
    abbreviations with, 138
    commas with, 89
Days of the week, capitalized, 136
Deal, 304
Definition, 194–195
Degrees
    capitalization of, 135
    punctuation of, 89
Degrees of adjectives, 42–43
Deity, capitalization of, 136–137
Demonstratives, 195, 304
Denotation, 165–166
Dependent clause, 3–4, 47–49, 70, 78–79, 82–84, 304
Details
    in paragraph, 192–194
    in theme, 208, 209
Development
    in literary paper, 228–230
    in paragraph, 192, 194–195
    in theme, 205–208
Dialect, 142–143
Dialogue, quotation marks with, 108–109
Diction, 140–151
    archaic words, 143

Diction *(cont.)*
    clichés, 149
    colloquial English, 140–141
    dialect, 142–143
    exactness, 149–150
    gobbledygook, 148
    idioms, 145–146
    improprieties, 144–145
    informal English, 140–149
    nonstandard English, 140–149
    slang, 141–142
    specialized vocabulary,
       146–148
    Standard English, 140–149
    technical words, 146–148
    triteness, 149
    vocabulary, 151
    vocabulary tests, 151–153
    see also Style
Dictionaries
    idioms in, 145
    labels in, 140–141
Different, incomplete, 54
Differ from, differ with, 304
Digression, 174–175, 185
Direct address, comma with, 90
Direct object, 304
Direct quotation, 108–109
Discourse, direct and indirect, 58
Documentation, 262–268
Dogmatism, 177
Done, 304
Don't, 304
Double negative, 304

Each, either, neither, etc.
    as antecedents, 28
    as subjects, 20–21
Effect, affect, 298
Effect and cause, 177
Either . . . or, 18, 65
Ellipsis, 113, 276–277
Elliptical clause, 305
    case with, 36

    dangling, 61
Emotions, appeal to, 176
Emphasis
    active voice, 5
    climactic order, 71
    comma for, 89
    dash for, 107
    italics for, 125
    repetition for, 160
End punctuation, 111–114
Enthused, 305
Envelope, addressing, 123
Essential modifier, *see* Restrictive
    elements
Etc., 305
Ever, every, 305
Every day, everyday, 305
Evidence, 174, 175, 231–232
Exactness in diction, 149–150
Exam, 305
Examples, 208
Except, accept, 298
Excessive coordination, 45–46, 47
Exclamation point, 111, 113, 114
    after abbreviations, 112
    for heightened feeling, 114
    not for humor or sarcasm,
       114
    no comma with, 99, 111
    with quotation marks, 111
    in titles, 113
    used sparingly, 114
Expect, 305
Expletives, 22

Fabulous, 305
Facts, errors in, 172–173
Fallacy, logical, 175–176
False conclusions, 175–176
False dilemma, *see* Alternatives
    (in reasoning)
Fantastic, 305
Farther, further, 305
Fault, comma, 3–8

Fewer, less, 305
Figurative language, 167–168
Figures and letters
    apostrophe with plural, 134
    italicized, 125
Figures of speech, 167–168
Fine, 306
Fine writing, 169
First person, in literary paper, 231
Fix, 306
Flattery, 176
Flowery language, 169
Flunk, 306
Folks, 306
Footnotes, 262–266, 268, 274, 293
For, see Coordinating conjunctions
Foreign words, underlined, 125
Forms of verbs, 8–11
Fragment, sentence, 1-3
Funny, 306
Further, farther, 305
Furthermore, see Conjunctive adverbs
Fused sentence, 3–8, 102
Future tense, 11, 13

Generalizations, 173, 208, 232
Genitive, *see* Possessive case
Gerund, 317
    comma with, 83
    dangling, 60
    possessive pronouns before, 36–37
Glossary of usage and terms, 297–318
Gobbledygook, 148
Good, 306
Government agencies, abbreviations, 112
Grand, 306

Has got, have got, 306
Headings for notes, 253–254, 260
Here, 22

He said, etc., commas with, 90
His, his or her, 28
Historical present tense, 12, 56
Holidays, capitalized, 136
Hours of the day, figures for, 139
    and minutes, colon between, 106
However, comma with, 88 *see also* Conjunctive adverbs
Hyphen, 131–132
    with compound numbers, 132
    with compound words, 131–132
    distinguished from dash, 107
    at end of line, 132
    with two words used as single modifier, 132
    when not used, 132

I, capitalized, 134
Ibid., 263
Idioms, 17, 52, 145–146
Illiteracies, 142–143
Illusion, allusion, 299
Imperative mood, 309–310
Imply, infer, 306
Improprieties, 144–145
In, into, 306
Incomplete comparison, 53–54
Incomplete construction, 51
Incomplete sentence, 1–3
Indefinite pronouns, 20–21, 37, 133, 306
Independent clause, 3–4, 45–46, 48, 77–79, 102–103, 106, 306
Indexes, periodical, 244, 247–248
Indicative mood, 309
Indirect and direct discourse, 58
Indirect object, 306–307
Indirect question, 112
Infer, imply, 306

Infinitive, 317
    dangling, 60
    split, 65
    subject of, 35
    tense, 8–11, 13–14
Informal English, 140–149
In regards to, 307
Intensives, 307, 310
Interjections, 307
    commas with, 89
    exclamation point with, 114
Interpolations in quotations, 108
Interpretation, literary paper, 229
Interrogative elements, commas
        with, 89
Interrogative pronouns, 37–39
Intervening phrases or clauses, 19
Into, in, 306
Intransitive verbs, 10–11
Introduction of theme, 209
Introductory phrases, punctuation
        of, 82–83
Inversion, 70
Investigative paper, *see* Research
        paper
Irregardless, 307
Irregular verbs, 8–11
Irrelevance in paragraph, 184–185
Is when, is where, 307
It, as subject, 22
Italics, 124–126
    excessive, 125–126
    for emphasis, 125–126
    for foreign words, 125
    for names of ships and
        trains, 125
    for title of your own theme,
        126
    for titles, 124
    underlining to indicate,
        124–126
    for words, letters, figures re-
        ferred to as such, 125
It is . . ., avoiding, 157

Its, it's, 307
It's me, it's us, etc., 34

Joint possession, 133–134

Kind of, sort of, 307
Kind of a, sort of a, 308

Labels
    in dictionaries, 140–141
    false, 176
Lay, lie, 10
Learn, teach, 308
Length
    of literary paper, 227
    of paragraph, 187–190
    of sentence, 68
    of theme, 202-204
Less, fewer, 305
Letter, business, 106, 120, 122–123
Letters, words, and figures,
        italicized, 125
Liable, likely, 308–309
Library, use of, 244–250
Library paper, *see* Research paper
Lie, lay, 10
Like, 308
Likely, liable, 308
Limiting the subject
    of research paper, 242–244
    of theme, 202–204
Linking verbs, 43, 106–107, 309
Literature, reading, 227–228
Literature, writing about, 227–241
    character analysis, 229–230
    characterization, 230
    choosing a subject, 227–228
    comparative study, 230
    development, 228–230
    evidence, 231–232
    excessive use of first person,
        231
    imagery, 230
    interpretation, 229

Literature, writing about *(cont.)*
    kind of development, 228–230
    length, 227
    model paper, 233–241
    moralizing, 233
    organization, 232
    originality, 231
    paraphrasing, 230–231
    review, 229
    secondary sources, 233
    setting, 230
    subject, 227–228
    summary, 230–231
    technical analysis, 230
    title of paper, 228
    use of quotations, 232
Loaded words, 176
Localisms, 142–143
Logical fallacy, 175–176
Logical thinking, 172–177 *see also* Clear and logical thinking
Loose, 309
Loose sentences, 68
Lot of, lots of, 309

Magazine indexes, *see* Periodical indexes
Main clause, *see* Independent clause
Manuscript form, 120–122
    margins, 120
    paper and ink, 120
    revision and correction, 122
    spacing, 120
Margins, 120
Mass appeal, 176
May, can, 301
Mechanics, 120–139
    abbreviations, 137–138
    apostrophe, 133–134
    capitals, 134–137
    contractions, 134

    hyphen, 131–132
    italics, 124–126
    numbers, 138–139
    spelling, 126–131
    syllabication, 131–132
    underlining, 124–126
Metaphor, 168
Misleading parallelism, 66
Misplaced modifiers, 62
Misreading, commas to prevent, 90
Mixed figures, 168
MLA Handbook for Writers of Research Papers, Theses, and Dissertations, 262, 269, 284
Mode, *see* Mood
Model paper
    literary, 233–241
    research, 268–295
    theme, 210–213
Moderation, 177
Modifiers, 59–62, 309
    dangling, 60–61
    hyphenated, 132
    misplaced, 62
    position of, 59
    restrictive and nonrestrictive, 84–85
    sentence, 61, 87–88, 102
    squinting, 62
Monosyllables, not hyphenated, 132
Months, capitalized, 136
Mood, 309–310
    shifts in, 57
    subjunctive, 17
Moralizing, 233
More, in a comparison, 53
Moreover, see Conjunctive adverbs
Most in a comparison, 53–54
Movements in history, capitalized, 136
Myself, yourself, himself, etc., 310

Name-calling, 176
Namely, colon before, 106
Names, proper, 136
Natural or scientific law, tenses
        with, 12
Neither . . . nor, 18-19, 65
Nice, 310
No, comma with, 89
Nominative case, *see* Subjective
        case
None, some, etc., as subjects, 21
Nonrestrictive elements, 84-85
Non sequitur, 177
Nonstandard English, 140-149
Nonwords, 150
Nor, see Coordinating conjunctions
Note-taking, 251-259
Not hardly, 311
Nouns, 311
    abstract, 311
    capitalization of, 134-137
    case of, 34
    collective, 19-20, 302, 311
    collective antecedent, 28
    common, 311
    concrete, 311
    before gerund, 36-37
    plural in form, singular in
        meaning, 20
    possessive case of, 34, 36-37
    proper, 134, 136, 311
Nowheres, 311
Number
    of pronoun and antecedent,
        27-29
    shift in, 56
    of subject and verb, 17-23
Number versus amount, 300
    as subject, 21, 22
Numbers, 138-139
    apostrophe for plural of, 134
    beginning sentence with,
        138
    compound, 132

    figures for, 138-139
    page, 120, 276-277
    spelled out, 138

O, capitalized, 134
Object
    direct, 10-11, 304
    indirect, 306-307
    of preposition, 34-35
Objective case, 35
Obsolete words, 311
Off of, 311
Of phrase for possession, 37
O.K., OK, okay, 311
Omissions
    apostrophe to indicate, 134
    commas to indicate, 90-91
    of preposition or verb, 52
    of steps in thought, 175-176
    of *that,* 52
    see also Ellipsis
On a whole, 311
Or, see Coordinating conjunctions
Or, nor, etc.
    with pronoun, 27
    as subjects, 18-19
Order, climactic, 71, 194
Order in sentence, 70-71
Organization
    of literary paper, 232
    of research paper, 255, 257,
        260
    of theme, 205-208
Originality, 231, 242
Other in a comparison, 53
Outline
    scratch, 205
    sentence, 207-208
    topic, 205-207, 272-273
Overlapping subordination, 48-49
Overstatement, 177

Page citations in text, 276-277,
    286-287

Page numbers, 120
Paper, *see* Theme
Paragraph, 182–196
    beginning of, 182
    choppy, 187–189
    climactic order, 194
    comparison and contrast,
        194
    definition, 194–195
    details, 192–194
    development, 192–195
    dialogue, 108–109
    length, 187–190
    main idea, 182–184
    skimpy, 187–189
    topic sentences, 182–184,
        192–193, 196, 209
    transitions in and between,
        195–196, 210
    unity, 184–185
Parallelism, 65–66, 69–70
    in outlines, 206
Paraphrasing, 254–262
    excessive, 230–231
Parentheses, 107–108
    comma after, 99
    with figures numbering
        items in a series, 107
    for loosely related comment,
        107
    with page number in text,
        282–283
    with question mark, to show
        doubt, 114
Parenthetical sentence, capitals
        and periods with, 108
Participle, 317
    case before, 37
    dangling, 60
    past, 8–11
    perfect, 14
    present, 9
Parts of speech, 311
Party, 311

Passive voice, 15–16
Past participle, 8–11
Past tense, 11, 13, 8–11
Per cent, percent, 311
Perfect participle, 14
Perfect tenses, 11–14
Period, 111, 112–113
    after abbreviations, 112
    comma with, 112
    at end of sentence, 112
    no comma with, 99
    with parentheses, 108
    with quotation marks, 110
    not after titles, 113
Period fault, *see* Sentence frag-
        ment
Periodical indexes, 244, 247–249
Periodic sentence, 68–69
Person
    shifts in, 56–57
    of subject and verb, 18–19
Personal pronouns, 37, 133, 311
Personification, 168
Phenomena, 312
Photo, 312
Photoduplication, 255
Phrases, 312
    absolute, 90
    adverbial, 59
    dangling, 60–61
    intervening, 19
    introductory, punctuation
        of, 82–83
    prepositional, 59, 317
    restrictive and nonrestric-
        tive, punctuation of,
        84–85
    verbal, at end of sentence,
        61
Place names, commas with, 89
Plagiarism, 260–262
Plenty, 312
Plurals, of numerals, letters,
        words, 134

P.M., A.M., 299
Poetry, quoting, 109, 278–279
Polls, 174
Position of modifiers, 59–62
Possession, joint, 133–134
Possessive case
        apostrophe with, 133–134
        before gerund, 36–37
        of indefinite pronoun, 37
        of nouns, 34
        of phrase, when used, 37
        of personal pronouns, 37
        whose, for *of which,* 29
Predicate, 312
Predicate adjective, 43, 312
Predominate, predominant, 312
Prejudice, appeals to, 176
Prepositional phrases, 317
        dangling, 59–61
Prepositions, 19, 312–313
        capitalization of, in titles,
                134
        faulty omission of, 52
        idiomatic, 145–146
        no colon before, 106–107
        object of, 34–35
Present infinitive, 8–11
Present participle, 9
Present tense, 11–14
Primary and secondary materials,
                250–251
Principal, principle, 313
Principal parts of verbs, 8–11
Progressive tenses, 11–12
Pronominal adjective, 313
Pronouns, 313
        agreement and reference of,
                27–30
        antecedent of, 23, 300
        as appositives, 35
        case of, 34–39
        demonstrative, 195, 304
        before gerund, 36–37
        indefinite, 20–21, 37, 133, 306

        intensive, 307
        interrogative, 37–39
        one antecedent, not two, 30
        personal, 37, 133, 311
        reflexive, 313
        relative, 23, 29–30, 37–39,
                52, 57–58
        and sexism, 28
        after *than* or *as,* 36
        for transition, 195
        vague reference of, 29–30
Proofreading, 211
Proper nouns, 134, 136, 311
Punctuation, 77–114
        brackets, 108
        colon, 105–107
        comma, 77–91
        dash, 107
        end, 111–114
        exclamation point, 111, 114
        parentheses, 107–108
        period, 111, 112–113
        question mark, 111, 113–
                114
        quotation marks, 108–111
        semicolon, 102–103
        single quotation marks, 109
        unnecessary comma,
                97–100

Question, indirect, 112
Question mark, 111, 113–114
        after doubtful date or figure,
                114
        not for humor or sarcasm,
                114
        after interrogative sen-
                tence, 113–114
        within interrogative sen-
                tence, 114
        no comma with, 99, 111
        within parentheses, 114
        with quotation marks, 111
        after titles, 113

Quotation marks, 108–111
　　with direct quotations and
　　　　dialogue, 108–109
　　to enclose quotation within
　　　　a quotation, 109
　　other punctuation with, 111
　　single, 108, 109
　　with titles, 109–110
　　unnecessary, 110
Quotations
　　accuracy of, 260–261
　　blocked, 268, 282–284
　　brief, 282–283
　　capitals in, 134
　　colon before, 105
　　commas before, 90
　　ellipsis in, 113
　　excessive separation caused
　　　　by, 65
　　in literary paper, 232
　　long, 109
　　in notes, 255–260
　　of poetry, 109, 278–279
　　sources of, cited in text,
　　　　280–281
Quote, 313

Raise, rise, 11
Real, 313
Reasoning in a circle, 175
Reason is (was) because, 313
Redundancy, 159–160
Reference books, 249–250
Reference of pronouns, 27–30
　　ambiguous, 30
　　collective noun antecedent,
　　　　28
　　compound antecedent, 27
　　definite, not implied idea,
　　　　29–30
　　singular antecedents *(each,
　　　　either,* etc.), 28–29
Reflexive pronouns, 310, 313
Regular verbs, 8–11

Relative clause, 39
Relative pronouns
　　case of, 37–39
　　faulty omission of, 52
　　reference to animals or
　　　　things, 29
　　shift from one to another,
　　　　57–58
　　vague reference, 29–30
　　verb with, 23
Relevance, 174–175, 184–185
Reliability of sources, 173, 251
Repetition, 159–160
　　for emphasis or clarity, 160
　　ineffective, 159–160
　　pronouns to avoid, 159
　　of sound, 160
　　synonyms to avoid, 159
　　for transition, 195–196
Research paper, 242–295
　　bibliographical form, 260,
　　　　266–268, 294–295
　　bibliography, compiling,
　　　　244–253
　　card catalog, use of, 244
　　choosing a subject, 242–244
　　documentation, 262–268
　　footnoting and footnotes,
　　　　262–266, 268, 274–
　　　　275
　　general reference aids,
　　　　249–250
　　library, use of, 242, 244–250
　　limiting the subject, 242–
　　　　244
　　model paper, 268–295
　　note-taking, 251–259
　　organizing, 260
　　originality, 242
　　outlining, 260, 268, 272–273
　　paraphrasing and quoting,
　　　　254–262
　　periodical indexes, 244,
　　　　247–249

Research paper *(cont.)*
    photoduplication, 255
    plagiarism, 260–262
    primary materials, 250–251
    quotations, 255–259
    reference books, 244, 249–
        250
    secondary materials, 250–
        251
    subject headings, 260
    working bibliography,
        244–250
Respectfully, respectively, 314
Restrictive elements, 84–85
Revelant, 314
Review, 229
Revising of themes, xvii–xx, 122
Rise, raise, 11
Roman numerals, 205
Run-on sentence, 3–8

Said, 314
Salutation
    colon after, 106
    comma after, 90
    omission of, 123
Same, 314
Scientific law, tenses with, 12
Scratch outline, 205
Seasons, not capitalized, 136
Secondary materials, 250–251
Semicolon, 102–103
    improper use of, 103
    between independent
        clauses, 102–103
    to prevent comma fault or
        fused sentence, 3–4,
        102
    with quotation marks, 111
    in a series, 103
Sensual, sensuous, 314
Sentence
    balanced, 69–70
    choppy, 68
    completeness, 51–52
    complex, 68, 303
    compound, 103, 303
    fragmentary, 1–2
    fused, 3–8, 102
    incomplete, 1–3
    length, 68
    loose, 68
    order in, 70–71
    periodic, 68–69
    run-on, 3–8
    simple, 314
    stringy, 45–46, 48
    structure, 45–71
    symmetry, 69–70
    topic, 182–184, 192–193,
        196, 209
    unnecessary separation of
        parts, 64–65
    variety, 68–71
    wordy, 45–46
Sentence fragment, 1–3
Sentence modifiers, 61, 87–88, 102
Sentence outline, 207–208
Separation of elements, 64–65
Sequence of tenses, 11–14
Series
    colon to introduce, 105
    commas in, 78–79
    semicolons in, 103
Set, sit, 10
Setting, of literary work, 230
Sexism, and pronouns, 28
Shall, will, 314
Shape up, 314
Shift
    in conditional verb, 56
    from indirect to direct dis-
        course, 58
    in mood, 57
    in person, 56–57
    in relative pronoun, 57–58
    in tense, 11, 13, 56
    in voice, 57

Ships and trains, names italicized, 125
Sic, 288–289
Similes, 168
Simple sentence, 314
Simple tenses, 11–14
Single quotation marks, 108, 109
Sit, set, 10–11
Skimpy paragraphs, 187–190
Slang, 141–142
Slanted words, 173
Snob appeal, 176
So, 314
Sometime, some time, 314
So, such, too, 51
Sort of, kind of, 307
Sort of a, kind of a, 308
So that, 314
Sounds, repetition of, 160
Sources
    in literary paper, 233
    in research paper, 243–262
Specialized vocabulary, 146–148
Spelling, 126–131
    adding *s* or *es,* 128–129
    changing syllables, 126
    changing *y* to *i,* 127
    dropping final *e,* 127
    doubling final consonant, 128
    ie or *ei,* 126–127
    list of commonly misspelled words, 129–131
    mispronunciation and misspelling, 126
    omission of syllables, 126
    plurals of proper names, 129
Splice, comma, 3–8, 102
Split infinitive, 65
Squinting modifier, 62
Standard English, 140–149
Statement, thesis, 204, 209
Statistics, 174
Sticking to the point, 174–175

Stringy sentences, 45–46, 48
Structure, sentence, 45–71
Style, 140–141, 156–169
    balanced sentence, 69–70
    conciseness, 156–157
    concreteness, 162–164
    connotation, 165–166
    denotation, 165–166
    figurative language, 167–168
    fine writing, 169
    flowery language, 169
    loose sentence, 68
    periodic sentence, 68–69
    redundancy, 159–160
    repetition, 159–160
    sentence variety, 68–71
    specific and concrete words, 162–164
    vagueness, 162–164
    wordiness, 156–157
    see also Diction
Subheadings in outlines, 206
Subject and verb, agreement, *see* Agreement, subject and verb
Subjective case, 34
Subjective complement, 22–23, 34, 43, 315
Subject of infinitive, 35
Subject of literary paper, 227–228
Subject of sentence, 315
    agreement of verb with, 17–23
    compound, 18–19, 22
    literary titles as, 23
Subject of theme
    choosing, 202–204, 214–217
    limiting, 202–204
Subjunctive mood, 17, 309–310
Subordinate clause, 38
    see also Dependent clause
Subordinating conjunctions, 315
Subordination, 47–49
    faulty, 48

Subordination *(cont.)*
    main idea in independent
      clause, 48
    overlapping, 48–49
    subordinate idea in subor-
      dinate clause, 48
    upside-down, 48
Such, so, too, 51
Summary, in literary paper, 230–
    231
Superlative degree, 42–43
Sure, 315
Sure and, try and, 316
Suspicion, 316
Sweeping generalizations, 173–174
Swell, 316
Syllabication, 131–132
Symmetry of sentence, 69–70
Synonyms
    excessive, 159–160
    for transition, 195

Tabulations, numbers in, 139
Take, 301
Taking notes, 251–259
Tautology, 157
Teach, learn, 308
Technical analysis of literature, 230
Technical words, 146–147, 209
Tense, 8–14
    future, 11, 13
    historical present, 12, 56
    for natural truth or scien-
      tific law, 12
    past, 11, 13
    perfect, 11–14
    present, 11–14
    progressive, 11–12
    sequence, 11–14
    shifts in, 11, 13, 56
    simple, 11–14
    of verbals, 13–14
Term paper *see* Research paper
Terms, glossary of, 297–318

Terrible, 316
Than
    case after, 36
    in a comparison, 53
Than, then, 316
That
    not at beginning of nonre-
      strictive clause, 84
    omission of, 52
    person and number of verb
      with, 23
    as reference to persons,
      animals, things, 29
That is, colon before, 106
Their, there, 316
Theme, 202–217
    body, 209
    checklist of essentials,
      209–210
    choosing a subject, 202–204
    conclusion, 210
    detail, 209
    generalizations, 208
    introduction, 209
    length, 202–204
    limiting subject, 202–204
    list of subjects, 214–217
    manuscript form, 120–122
    model theme, 210–213
    organization, 205–208
    outlining, 205–208
    proofreading, 210
    revising, xvii–xx, 122
    scratch outline, 205
    sentence outline, 207–208
    subject, 202–204, 214–217
    thesis statement, 204, 209
    title, 209
    tone, 204–205, 209
    topic outline, 205–207
    transitions, 210
Theme title
    not quoted, 110
    not underlined, 126

There, 22
There, their, 316
There are ..., avoiding, 157
Therefore, see Conjunctive adverbs
These kinds, these sorts, 316
Thesis, in literary paper, 233
Thesis statement, 204, 209
They, vague, 29–30
This, vague, 29–30
Thusly, 316
Times, abbreviations with, 138
Title
    appropriate, 209
    capitalization of, 134–135
    commas with, 89
    of literary paper, 228
    not quoted, 110
    not underlined, 209
    punctuation of, 112, 113
    quotation marks with, 109
    as subject of sentence, 23
    underlining of, 124
Title page, 270–271
Tone of theme, 204–205, 209
Too, so, such, 51
Topic outline, 205–207
Topic sentence, 182–184, 192–193, 196, 209
Transitions
    between paragraphs, 195–196
    between sentences, 195–196
    in theme, 210
Transitive verbs, 10–11, 15, 318
Triteness, 149, 168
Troublesome verbs, 9–11
Typescript
    example of, 121
    model research paper, 270–295

Underlining for italics, 124–126
Unique, 316
Unity in paragraphs, 184–185

Unnecessary commas, 97–100
Unwarranted conclusions, 175–176
Upside-down subordination, 48
Usage
    glossary of, 297–318
    labels, in dictionary, 140–141
    see also Diction
Use, 316

Vagueness, 162–164
Variety, 68–71
Verbals, 317
    case used with, 36–37
    dangling, 60
    gerund, 36, 60, 83, 317
    infinitive, 8–11, 13–14, 35, 60, 65, 317
    introductory, comma after, 83
    participle, 8–11, 14, 37, 60, 317
    phrases at end of sentence, 61
Verbs, 316
    agreement, 17–23
    auxiliary, 11n, 300–301
    conditional, 56
    consistency, 13
    faulty omission of, 52
    forms, 8–11
    idioms, 145
    intransitive, 10–11
    irregular, 8–11
    linking, 43, 106–107, 309
    number, 18–19
    objects of, 10–11
    principal parts, 8–11
    progressive forms, 11–12
    regular, 8–11
    tenses, 8–14
    transitive, 10–11, 15, 318
    troublesome, 9–11
    voice, 10–11, 15–16

Vocabulary, 146–148, 151
Vocabulary tests, 151–153
Voice, 10–11, 318
    active, 15–16, 156
    passive, 15–16
    shifts in, 57

Wait for, 318
Wait on, 318
Ways, 318
What, 37–39
Where, 318
Where at, 318
Which, 23, 29, 37–39
Who, 23, 29, 37–39
Whom, 37–39
Whose, 29, 37–39
Whose, who's, 318
Will, shall, 314
-wise, 318
Without, 318

Wordiness, 45–46, 156–157
Words
    abstract, 163–164
    apostrophe with plural of,
      134
    compound, 131–132
    concrete, 162–164
    connotations and denota-
      tions, 165–166
    italicized, 125
    specific, 162–164
Working bibliography, 244-260
Writing
    about literature, 227–241
    paragraphs, 182–196
    research papers, 242–297
    themes, 202–217

Yes, and *no,* commas with, 89
You, vague, 29–30
You and me, you and I, 34

Abbreviations Often Used in Marking Student Papers

numerals refer to page numbers

ab abbreviations, 137

adj/adv adjectives and adverbs, 41

agr agreement:
    pronouns, 27
    subject and verb, 17

archaic archaic, 143

c case, 34

cap/no cap capital letters, 134

co coordination, 45

coh coherence, 59

comp comparison, 52

con connotation, 165

cons consistency, 56

cs comma splice, 3

d diction, 140

dial dialect, 142

dg dangling, 60

exact exactness, 149

fig figurative language, 167

fl flowery language, 169

frag sentence fragment, 1

fus fused sentence, 3

g see Glossary, 297

id idiom, 145

imp impropriety, 144

inc incomplete, 51

ital/no ital use of italics, 124

k awkward, 47, 64, 159

log logic, 172

mo mood, 17

ms manuscript form, 120

num use of numerals, 138

○ omission

obs obsolete word, 143

pct punctuation, 77

po position of modifiers, 59

pv point of view, 56

ref vague or faulty reference, 30

rep repetition, 159

sep separation, 64

seq sequence of tenses, 11

sl slang, 141

sp spelling, 126

sub subordination, 47

t tense, 11

tech technical diction, 146

tr transition, 195

trite triteness, 149

ts topic sentence, 182

vag vague, 162

var sentence variety, 68

vf verb form, 8

vo voice, 15

vocab vocabulary, 146

w wordy, 156

✕ obvious error

∧ insert

¶/no ¶ paragraphing, 182

// parallelism, 65

⊓⌐ transpose